CW00543382

THE AMERICAN REED ORGAN

and the Harmonium

A Treatise on its
History, Restoration and Tuning,
with descriptions of some
Outstanding Collections,
including a Stop Dictionary
and a Directory of Reed Organs

by Robert F. Gellerman

The Vestal Press, Ltd.
Vestal, New York 13850

The Vestal Press, Ltd.
P.O. Box 97
Vestal, NY 13851-0097

Copyright © 1996 by Robert F. Gellerman.
All rights reserved.
First Printing — 1996
This book has been printed on acid-free paper.

Printed in the United States of America

Permission is hereby granted to copy the material included in Appendices A, B and C for
    personal use only.

Library of Congress Cataloging-in-Publication Data

Gellerman, Robert F. 1928–
    The American reed organ and the harmonium : a treatise on its history, restoration and
tuning, with descriptions of some outstanding collections, including a stop dictionary and
a directory of reed organs / by Robert F. Gellerman.
        p.   cm.
    Completely rev. and updated ed. of: The American reed organ.
    Includes bibliographical references (p.) and index.
    ISBN 1-879511-07-X (hardcover), – ISBN 1-879511-12-6 (softcover)
    1. Reed-organ--United States.   I. Gellerman, Robert F.,   1928–
American reed organ.   II. Title.
ML597.G44   1996
786.5 ' 51973--dc20
                                                                    96-8805
                                                                      CIP
                                                                      MN

ii

To my wife
Donna Gillette Gellerman, 1930-1992
and to my daughter
Susan Gellerman Nilsen, 1957-1993

Figure 1: A two-manual and pedal Burdett organ.

Contents

Introduction

It is over twenty years since *The American Reed Organ* was published. Harvey Roehl, the founder of The Vestal Press, told me then that the book, if successful, had a probable life of ten years. In fact it remained in print for seventeen. Admittedly, that was a few years too long, as research meanwhile had revealed much previously unknown information and corrected many errors and misconceptions. Many readers have written over the years expressing the pleasure they have gotten from the book, and this is the real reward for the hours of effort.

In the early 1970s reed organs were little more than almost-forgotten curiosities. A handful of pioneers, among them Arthur Sanders of the Musical Museum at Deansboro, New York; Bob Whiting in Schwenksville, Pennsylvania; L. B. Green in Birmingham, Alabama; the Culps in New London, North Carolina; Dr. Jules J. Duga in Columbus, Ohio; Lee Conklin in Michigan, and Floyd C. Miles at the Miles Mountain Museum in Eureka Springs, Arkansas, had put together collections enjoyed by themselves and all too few visitors. A few professional restorers were laboring away in near anonymity, such as Charles Gunzinger in Williamsville, Vermont; Bill Keiser in Toronto; Coleman Kimbrell in Florence, Alabama; and the Mulls in York, Pennsylvania. Small numbers of new reed organs were still being built in Germany, Japan, China, and India. Durrell Armstrong's Player Piano Company in Wichita, Kansas, was busily selling components and materials for restoration of

mechanical musical instruments, and did a small but steady business in reed organ materials, as did several major piano supply houses.

Printed material on the reed organ was scarce at that time. *Michel's Organ Atlas*, published in 1969, was the only book then in print on the subject of reed organs. That book contained information valuable to researchers that N. E. Michel had collected over a lifetime in the music business. Arthur Sanders and Dr. Jules Duga had published magazine articles, and a few articles had appeared in *The Tracker,* the bulletin of The Organ Historical Society, and in *The Diapason.* In 1977 Horton Presley's book, *Restoring & Collecting Antique Reed Organs,* was published by TAB Books. It contained detailed instructions on repairing and restoring reed organs. Also in 1977, I published a reprint of portions of several reed organ method and music books under the name *Playing the American Reed Organ.* Since Michel's *Organ Atlas* had been long out of print I planned to include a directory of all known reed organ manufacturers throughout the world as an appendix to a new edition of *The American Reed Organ.* By 1985 this list had grown to book size by itself and was published separately by The Vestal Press as *Gellerman's International Reed Organ Atlas.* Arthur W. J. G. Ord-Hume, a noted authority on antique musical instruments and author of several books on the subject, turned his attention to the reed organ. In 1986 his beautifully illustrated book, *Harmonium,* published in England by David

& Charles, provided insights into many aspects of the instrument.

This book follows the general outline of the original but is completely new in content, with a few minor exceptions. Many people have contributed to making it better. *The Reed Organ Society Bulletin* has become an invaluable resource, and I have borrowed extensively from the information it contains. Dr. Edward Peterson, its editor, has been generous with his time and advice. To mention each author individually would require a listing of the authors of all the articles published over the years, so a collective thank you will have to suffice. After he retired from his successful career as a reed organ and piano manufacturer, George P. Bent collected stories from his many friends in the industry and published them in his book, *Four Score and More* in 1929. Portions of many of these stories make up most of Chapter 2. Many drawings in Chapter 3 are redrawn from those appearing in H. F. Milne's *The Reed Organ*, published by *The Musical Opinion*, London, in 1930. Thomas Schaettle has helped make the Stop Dictionary more appropriate for the reed organ. Prof. E. Lee Chaney located a mine of information in the National Archives on organs in the military and wrote "When Reed Organs Went to War," published in *The Reed Organ Society Bulletin*, November 1990. I am indebted to him for sharing this information with me, some of which appears in Chapter 5. Finally, literally hundreds of people have sent information and photographs, only a portion of which were used. All are greatly appreciated.

Robert F. Gellerman
DeLand, Florida
April, 1996

Figure2: George Woods & Co., Boston, Massachusetts.

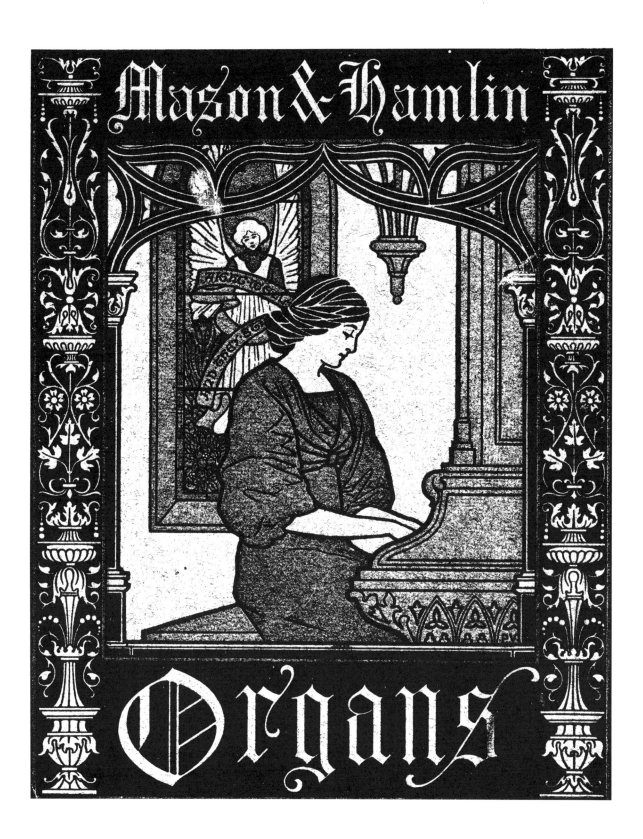

The Estey Church Phonorium

Chapter One

History of the Reed Organ

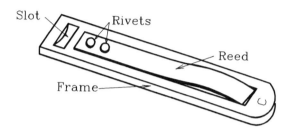

Figure 3: A typical free reed used in American organs. The end of the reed is slightly curved to improve the tone. A slot at one end is used in removing the reed for cleaning. The pitch is often stamped into the frame at the other end.

The reed organ is essentially a creation of the nineteenth century. The first simple instruments appeared shortly after 1800, and by 1890 the reed organ reached the peak of its popularity. After 1900 the piano, the player piano, and the phonograph began to replace reed organs as the musical instrument in the home. By the time of World War I, reed organ production in the United States for home use had dropped almost to nothing while a few were still being made for use in small churches, and by the 1930s electronic organs began to displace reed instruments as inexpensive substitutes for church pipe organs. In Europe and Japan, reed organs were still being made after World War II, although in small quantities.

To generate its tones the reed organ uses *free* reeds, as opposed to the *beating* reed commonly found in pipe organ reed stops.

The free reed consists of a long, narrow, thin strip of brass set into a slot in a brass plate or frame. One end of the reed is fastened, usually with rivets, to the frame and the other end is free to move in the slot. The slot is made just slightly larger so that the reed can vibrate freely through the slot without touching the sides or end. The reed will vibrate at a particular rate, or pitch, determined by its dimensions, weight, and stiffness. A separate reed is used for each note, and the reeds are carefully adjusted so that each one vibrates at the pitch of the

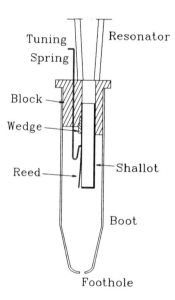

Figure 4: A typical beating reed is shown here in a sectional view. The reed is held in place with a small wedge. The tuning spring can be moved up or down to tune the reed.

Figure 5: The Chinese Sheng.

on the previous page. The reed itself is larger than the slot and curved away from it. Air pressure causes the reed to close the slot, abruptly interrupting the air flow. Since the reed is made of springy brass, it immediately returns to its original open position, allowing air to flow through the shallot into the resonator or pipe placed above it, and the process is repeated. The abrupt closing and opening of the slot creates a great many overtones, the sound of which is a braying, unmusical noise. To be useful, the beating reed is set into the base of a pipe, the shape and dimensions of which are chosen to enhance certain of the overtones. By careful design of the pipe and proper curvature of the reed, the pipe can be made to produce a wide variety of pleasing tones.[1]

The first use of the free reed in a musical instrument was in an ancient Chinese instrument, the Sheng, attributed variously to the Chinese female sovereign Nü-Wa in 2852 B.C. or to the Emperor Huang Tei about 2500 B.C. The first written mention of this instrument dates from 1100 B.C, and the earliest picture, on a votive stela now in the University Museum, Philadelphia, dates from A.D. 551. The Sheng, shown at left, uses a free vibrating metallic reed placed in a pipe made of bamboo. The bamboo pipes, usually 13, 17, 19, or 24 in number, are placed upright in a bowl, originally made from a gourd, which serves as a wind chest.

corresponding note on the keyboard. Air pressure or vacuum is applied to one side of the reed through a valve, mechanically connected to the key, causing the reed to vibrate. Vibration will continue as long as the pressure differential is present—that is, as long as the key is depressed. The sound is produced by two means: the vibration of the reed coupled through its mounting plate to the body of the organ, and the air flow through the slot interrupted by the moving reed. A more detailed discussion of the reed sound will be found in Chapter 3.

The beating reed is also made of brass, and is placed over a slot cut lengthwise in a tube with a closed end, called a shallot, as shown in Figure 4

Figure 6: A single pipe from the Sheng, showing the reed at the left and the tuning slot at the right.

Figure 7: Closeup of a Sheng pipe showing the reed, tuned with sealing wax, set into the end of the pipe. Stopping the hole causes the reed to sound.

The pipes are arranged in two groups, with the largest pipe in the middle and successively smaller ones on each side. They are shaved along each side so that they fit tightly together. This arrangement is supposed to symbolize the folded wings of the phoenix. The instrument shown here has seventeen pipes of five different lengths.

The pipes are slightly inclined toward each other at the top and held in place by a circular retainer. By sliding off the retainer the pipes can be loosened and removed from the bowl for cleaning or repair. The pitch is determined both by the reed and the pipe. The reed is made of a single piece of thin brass set into a hollow dowel at the base of the pipe. The reed, held in place and coated with beeswax, is given its final tuning by placing a drop of sealing wax on the tip. A slot cut into the back of the pipe near the top tunes the pipe to the same pitch as the reed. A hole drilled through the pipe above the reed prevents the reed from sounding unless the hole is closed. The pipe thus acts both as a valve and as a qualifying chamber.

Wind is provided by blowing either in or out through a mouthpiece connected to the bowl, and the sounds are produced by fingering the openings in the pipes. Air flows through all the pipes continuously, whether the reed is sounding or not, so that it takes strong lungs to play the instrument. The Sheng is held in the right hand, and the left is used to finger the notes. When the openings are covered with the fingers the reeds sound, and when the fingers are lifted the reeds are silent. By closing several holes simultaneously, a chord can be played. The Chinese play melodies with occasional fourth or fifth harmonies. In Japan, where the same instrument is called the Sho, the traditional style of play produces complex chords.

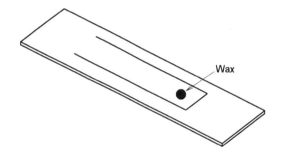

Figure 8: The Sheng reed is formed by making three cuts in a thin piece of brass. A small drop of sealing wax tunes the reed to the exact pitch.

A Sheng is said to have been used at the funeral of Confucius in 479 B.C. By the fourteenth century the Sheng had acquired a keyboard and in appearance was similar to the Regal. According to a traditional account, Kublai Khan presented a Sheng to the Moslem Kingdom, and it was brought to Europe by Jesuit missionaries shortly afterward, serving as the inspiration for the application of free reeds to pipe organs. The Sheng is still used in China and Japan to perform folkloric music. In China in recent years modern versions of the Sheng have been produced with conventional keyboards, foot pedals, metal pipes and multiple stops.

Figure 9: Replica of a late 16th-century German Regal.

The Regal, a small instrument using force-operated beating reeds, was used in Europe from the latter part of the fifteenth through the eighteenth century. A Regal appeared in an engraving dated 1519, and George Voll of Nuremburg made the first book Regal or bible Regal about 1550. This was a small portable instrument made to look like a large book when closed. The name Regal was applied to a variety of instruments ranging from a chamber pipe organ to a portable keyboard reed instrument without pipes, the latter being the most common modern usage. Since the bellows were located behind the keyboard, an assistant was required to operate them, although with weighted bellows it is possible for the organist to reach back and lift the bellows.

The name is said to derive from "royal," since it was often given as a gift to kings, from "regale," meaning gift, or from "regolare," meaning to regulate. This latter meaning refers to its use to regulate, or accompany, singing of the plain chant. An account of the coronation of Mary Tudor of England on September 25, 1553, mentions the sound of the Regal, and the instrument was used in Monteverde's opera *Orpheus* in 1607. This instrument used beating reeds and thus is not strictly speaking a direct predecessor of the free-reed organs, but it differs only in the type of reed used and undoubtedly influenced later reed organ developments. In 1700 an Italian instrument maker named Filippo Testa built the Organino, a free-reed version of the Regal, which would appear to be the first free reed organ.

Authorities differ on who was responsible for first using free reeds in a pipe organ; some credit George Voll of Nuremburg in 1540. A Danish physicist, Professor Christian Gottlieb Kratzenstein, is said to have heard a musician named Johann Wilde play the Sheng in St. Petersburg and to have built, between 1782 and 1789, a small pneumatic organ using free reeds. Kirschnik, an organ builder in St. Petersburg, built pipe organs, which he called Organochordiums, using Kratzenstein's ideas. An assistant to Kirschnik, Rachwitz, built an organ in Rotterdam for Abbé Georg Joseph Vogler, who in turn used the free reed in pipe organs built under his supervision throughout Europe. These organs most likely served as inspirations for the variety of reed organs which began to appear after 1800. In particular, Vogler is said to have contributed his ideas on free reeds to J. N. Maelzel of Vienna, who used them in his Pan Harmonicon about 1805.

Reed organs were also being built in the United States in the early 1800s. Ebenezer

Goodrich, a Boston pipe organ builder, built free-reed stops into some of his organs during this period. Ebenezer's older brother and partner William was employed from September 1811 to June 1812 to travel from city to city exhibiting the Pan Harmonicon. According to Henry A. Goodrich, writing in 1906[2], at the suggestion of Dr. Lowell Mason, Ebenezer Goodrich built a complete reed organ and gave it to the painter Gilbert Stuart in 1809. This organ was said to be still in existence a few years prior to 1906. It seems to have since disappeared and no other details as to its design have survived. While this story is for the most part probably true, it has a weak point: in 1809 Lowell Mason would have been only seventeen

years old. Thus it seems possible that the organ was made later than 1809 if indeed Lowell Mason had a part in it. Mason was employed from 1820 to 1827 as organist for the Goodrich three-manual organ built for the Independent Presbyterian Church in Savannah, Georgia, so he was certainly acquainted with the Goodrich brothers. Henry Goodrich also reported that Ebenezer Goodrich had a Sheng hanging in his shop.

The first half of the nineteenth century was a period of intense activity in the creation of the reed organ. Especially in Germany and France, a variety of different instruments began to appear. Gabriel-Joseph Grenié (1757-1837) of Bordeaux, France, made an instrument which he called the "Orgue Expressif" and exhibited it in Paris on June 23, 1810. The diagram of the instrument clearly shows it to be a pipe organ, although it used free reeds in the pipes and was foot-pumped. The presence of reeds in the pipes, or qualifying tubes, permitted a pipe to speak the same note over a wide range of wind pressures, producing loud or soft notes at the will of the artist. Placing the bellows pedals in front of the instrument allowed the artist to vary the expression by varying the vigor of his pumping. About his invention, Grenié wrote:

Figure 10: Grenié's Orgue Expressif, 1810.

> For it is seen in the work of D. Bedos, which I have read, that the reed pipe has a tongue which should move freely and must be entirely enclosed in the mouth to be made to speak. I thought therefore, that a tongue not striking against the reed (one metal against the other) should produce softer and pleasanter sounds. I had a free reed made as best I could, and was fairly well satisfied with it and thought I could make a scale of several octaves. Fortunately, chance came to my aid, as I found in the house of one of my

friends an old organ which had lain in an out-of-the-way corner of the house for 30 years, which contained two octaves of a free reed stop. By means of this organ, in which I had all the necessary tones remade, I was enabled to create an instrument which, beginning with a sound as soft as that of a Harmonica, could be increased in power to that of a full military band.[3]

John Green of Soho Square, London, built an instrument which he called a "Royal Seraphine" in 1833. His advertisements described it as follows:

This truly extraordinary instrument is brought after some years of exertion and experience, to the greatest perfection. The beauties of which are not to be equalled for sweetness of Harmony and Melody, coupled with an extraordinary power of tone, which astonishes every hearer; although in size not larger than a Chiffonnier. Being highly finished at the back and portable, may readily be removed to the centre of the room or from one to the other, without the least inconvenience, or danger of being out of tune . . . the sound of the Seraphine, proceeding from the vibration of a metal bar, acted upon by wind, produces, within the space of a few inches, the same tone which would require a pipe sixteen feet long.

Green's Seraphine had a five octave compass, crescendo, and diminuendo. It was two feet ten inches high by three feet five inches wide by two feet eight inches

Figure 11: The Physharmonica, made by Anton Haeckel of Vienna in 1821, became the standard for many years, and later instruments were largely modifications of its basic design.

Figure 12: Kirkman & White's improved Seraphine.

deep. This instrument was used in the performance of *Quasimodo, or the Gipsy Girl of Notre Dame* when it opened at the Covent Garden Theatre, London in 1836. Green obtained British Patent No. 7154 on July 27, 1836.

The Musical Courier, a trade journal, in its October 15, 1884, issue said:

> The Mason & Hamlin Company have in their possession the original patent issued by the United States Government to Aaron Merrill Peaseley . . . for what he styles 'an improvement in organs', which was, so far as we know, the first large keyed instrument in which the tones were produced by reeds. In the description of his invention Mr. Peaseley explicitly states that either a force bellows, or a suction bellows may be employed.

A check of the early patent records shows this patent was issued on November 11, 1818, to A. M. Peaseley of Massachusetts. The improvement as claimed in the patent consisted in ". . . substituting in place of the pipes usually called reed pipes a plate of metal or any other fit substance in which a number of holes of proper form, in each of which is fitted a piece of brass or any other elastic substance capable of vibrating so as to produce a tone."

This patent is of special interest because it predates many of the early European reed organs and it contains the explicit mention of both pressure and vacuum bellows. The Patent Office fire of 1836 destroyed all the official patent files up to that date, and details of Peaseley's patent were lost until the copy mentioned above appeared. In the reforms to the U.S. patent system after the fire all new patents were issued numbers. Numbers ending with X were assigned to earlier unnumbered patents, and every effort was made to

reconstruct the original files which had been destroyed. Mason & Hamlin sent their copy of the Peaseley patent to Levi K. Fuller, vice-president of the Estey Organ Co., who in turn forwarded it to the Patent Office. Presumably it was filed under Patent No. 3019X, but apparently was subsequently removed and disappeared again. Some early Patent Office correspondence has been preserved in the U.S. Archives, but unfortunately not for the years around 1884 when the Fuller correspondence probably took place.

Not much is known of Peaseley himself. An Aaron Peeseley was included in the first U.S. census in 1790 for Boxford Town, Essex Co., Massachusetts. He does not appear in 1800, but in 1810 and 1820 an Aaron M. Peaseley is shown in the Boston census. The list of Boston taxpayers in 1821 shows Aaron Merrill Peaseley owned real estate on Middle Street valued at $700 and a shop, also on Middle Street, valued at $300. The *Boston Directory* for 1826 lists Bradford & Peaslee, booksellers, at 53 Washington St., Joseph N. Bradford and Jonathan P. Peaslee, proprietors, but Aaron Merrill Peaseley had dropped out of sight.

On May 5, 1832, Lewis Zwahlen, a musical instrument maker in New York, was issued a patent for a "Seraphina or harmonicon organ." Unfortunately, details on this instrument are lacking, although the date is significant since it precedes the patent date of John Green's Royal Seraphine by four years.

Probably the most influential of the very early American reed organ makers was James A. Bazin of Canton, Massachusetts. He is one of the few to leave any significant record of his work. At the age of 82 he wrote the following article for the Feb. 14, 1880 , issue of *The Musical and Sewing Machine Gazette* of New York.

Figure 13: James Amireaux Bazin.

First Reed Organs in America
by James A. Bazin

Late in the year 1821 there was brought to me to be repaired a small round pipe, with the letter A marked on it, and a piece of thin brass screwed on one side, which had the appearance of having been made to vibrate through an opening about half the length of the pipe, but had been broken off near the screw. Having ascertained how the sound was produced, I made several of the same kind, and soon afterwards made an improvement in the pipe by making it so as to vary the length of the vibrating part of the tongue or reed. This was effected in various ways, one of which is the well-known brass sliding pitch-pipe with which I supplied the dealers in Boston for many years.

During the same winter I made a small instrument, by making the pipe large enough to allow of nine openings for reeds, which were made of different lengths. Inside of this there was a smaller pipe, with one opening, which, by turning the pipe round, could be brought opposite to each of the outer ones in succession. Over the whole was a case which fitted tight round the butt ends of the reeds, giving it the appearance of a small pocket inkstand. Any tunes which came within the compass of nine notes could be played upon it, and by placing a bell, like a trumpet, on the end of the inner or revolving pipe, the tone was nearly as powerful as that of a bugle. The next instrument that I made was finished in the course of the succeeding summer. This was composed of a set of 22 small square pipes, producing the natural scale of three octaves. These pipes were placed in a series of boxes, forming a cap over each reed, the whole being put in a wooden case about $4^1/_2$ inches long by 2 inches wide and $^1/_4$ inch thick, in such a manner as to allow of a free passage for the wind through the pipes and for a mouthpiece to slide on the ends of the boxes. As this could only be played in the natural scale, or in that which it was tuned, I made another, with twelve pipes to the octave, and so contrived that the keynote could be instantly changed to any one of the twelve semi-tones. This was called a revolving reed trumpet, the pipes, 36 in all, being arranged in a circle and radiating from the centre. Thus, by turning the circle, each pipe could be brought in succession between the mouthpiece and the bell.

This instrument was finished in the summer of 1824, and for many years used as an accompaniment to the choir in the Unitarian Church in Canton, Mass. The small instrument having been shown to the music dealers in

Boston, and none of them thinking that they could sell them if they were manufactured, nothing further was done in the matter, except to supply the small demand for tuning and pitch pipes, until the year 1827, when I contrived a double-acting bellows for the reed trumpet. This consisted of a centre block, with two inward and two outward valves, and two heads connected together by wires, so that when the chamber on one side was full the other would be exhausted. This was operated by a handle on one of the heads, the motion being similar to that of the bow of a bass viol.

Some time in the following year 1828, having disposed of my two smaller instruments for less than half their cost, and another being wanted, I contrived a cheaper way of making them, by dispensing with the boxes and using but fifteen pipes. Instead of the ends of the reeds being set outward, so as to be blown in to produce the sound, they were set as much into the pipes so as to be blown outward. In this way the pipes could be all soldered together and the mouthpiece made to slide on their open ends, thus greatly reducing the cost. Having made two of this kind and not finding a purchaser for more than one of them, I laid the other by till February or March, 1830, when having read in the papers a notice of a wonderful instrument called a harmonica, which had been got up somewhere in Germany, and which by the description appeared to bear a strong resemblance to mine, I offered mine to a dealer in Boston, who not only took it, but engaged as many more as I could furnish. I now found that though I could not dispose of the article at any price as an original invention, I could scarcely supply the demand for it at three times the cost when it appeared to be only an improvement on a foreign one, the fact of its having come by way of Paris and

New York to Boston establishing its claim to be received in good society.

The demand for harmonicas increasing and finding it necessary to have some kind of bellows for tuning them, I contrived the double bellows with swinging treadles, such as I afterward used in my small reed organs. These bellows were at first made with cloth and made air-tight by means of indiarubber. But as the art of making that kind of cloth was yet in its infancy, it was not found to answer so well as leather. The framework of the bellows was made like a small table, on which the reed trumpet of one or more harmonicas could be played. In the summer of 1831 I made a small instrument with pipes like the harmonica, but instead of playing by sliding the set of pipes, the wind was let into them by means of valves and knobs arranged in two lines, thus: There being twelve pipes to the octave and only seven valves, there was a contrivance for changing the key, as well as for sounding the accidental flats and sharps when required. Within two years after this I made two other instruments with knobs arranged in the same manner, but the valves and pipes differently, and with tilting bellows like those which were afterwards called melodeons. I also, about this time, made an instrument which was called a reed organ, with swinging bellows and with square knobs for keys, the regular scale arranged the same as the others, but the semi-tones placed in another row back of the regular notes. There was a shifting movement in this organ, consisting of a bar behind the keys, with unequal projections, and a plain bar in front. The knobs being all of equal size and the keys of equal length, they could be all pushed back into one line. When in this position the bars could be moved lengthwise so as to bring the mark on the front one opposite to the knob which was to sound the keynote, when by drawing the bars forward the knob would be thrown into the position required.

In this organ the player was not obliged to use the shifting movement, as there was a knob for every semi-tone. Several more of this kind were made before the introduction of the kind which were first called seraphims. These were first brought from Germany, I believe, in the early part of 1832 as I find that in September and the following months of that year I made several sets of reeds, riveted in brass plates, for individuals in Boston, the instruments in which they were to be used having piano keys, and made on the pattern of one which had been imported a short time previous.

The accordion was first introduced about the same time, or a very short time before, as the first one sent to me to be repaired was in June, 1834, at which time they were but little known. The first accordion I ever saw was a German one with eight reeds to each key, sounding a chord of four notes each way. They were afterwards imported from France with single notes. Those of my make, which were first sold in Boston in January, 1835, were made in a different manner from either of the foreign kinds, resembling them only in the form of the bellows. The reed plates in my accordion were made of thin sheet brass, the edges of the plates being turned so as to be let into the wood, leaving a channel for the two reeds to vibrate in, the point of one reed being turned upwards and the other downwards to answer the drawing and pushing motion of the bellows.

The name melodeon was first applied to a reed instrument in March, 1836. This was a kind that I made with the tilting bellows before mentioned, but instead of the reeds being in pipes they were in separate plates, which were let into the wood in the same manner as my accordion plates. As the current of air in the melodeon was all one way there was but one reed in each plate, the point of the reed being bent downward through the plate. In the first six that I made I tried a new arrangement of the knobs or keys, but this being objected to they were afterwards placed in the same order as those of the pianoforte, the front knobs being made of ivory and the back ones of ebony.

After these instruments had been for some time on sale in Boston, a music-dealer in Concord, N. H. bought one or two of them for a young man who worked for him to copy from, and soon afterward sent some to Boston for sale. Others soon took up the business in different parts of the country and the name melodium, now generally spelled melodeon, has been since indiscriminately applied to reed instruments of whatever size or shape they may be made.

As the melodeon was originally intended for a light and portable instrument, some pains was taken so to arrange the reeds and keys as to bring the greatest number into the smallest compass. Of course the application of piano keys was only a retrograde movement, and about as wise a one as to attempt to apply the same kind of keys to a flute. Having always thought that there were better ways of arranging keys than the one always practiced in the organ in which the order of the notes and the fingering for the common chord is changed with every change of key, I so contrived my keyboard that it was only necessary to learn to play in the natural scale in order to play with equal ease in any of the twelve changes.

That some method of this kind, if it could be generally adopted, would be of real advantage to learners, no one not interested in the continuance of the old method could fail to perceive. As it appears evident that where at least seven changes of fingering are required for ordinary playing, if any method can be devised by which the learning of one scale would answer for the whole, the end would be accomplished in a proportionately shorter space of time with this additional advantage that no further trouble will be required in making use of the remaining five changes which none but experienced players can ever do in the ordinary way.

The attempt to introduce a new method of playing having been first made with reeds has given occasion to some who have refused to adopt it to claim as an invention of their own what was merely the continued use of the old method. But any one who will examine into the construction of the first reed instruments of my make will find that nothing further was required to adapt them to piano keys than to increase the distance between the valves. In all the instruments which I have mentioned the valves were placed between the reeds and the reservoir but the reverse of this has been thought to allow of a quicker action, and has been claimed as a late improvement. This is altogether a mistake, as the action can be made as quick in one case as in the other. And in nearly all the German seraphims which were first imported the back ends of the keys were used as valves and of course the reeds must have been between them and the reservoir.

There are several other so called improvements which can be shown to be only re-inventions of what has been long in use. In the bellows, with swinging treadles before described, I found that the reservoir might be dispensed with by making the windchest, or space between the top of the table and the bellows of some flexible material forced inwards by springs so as to allow of its expansion when too much wind was forced in. One of this kind I have had in use since the year 1832. It will also be found that the upper division of the tilting bellows of the melodeon is in reality an expanding windchest. And in addition to this I have frequently applied the same contrivance to remedy defects in instruments which have been brought to me to be repaired. And still further, the sounding box made of thin boards, like that in use in stringed instruments, as well as the double sounding board over the reeds, which has lately been claimed as new may be found in some of my oldest instruments and the adjustable reeds, which some manufacturers have lately advertised as a new invention, and for which a great number of patents have been granted, will be found to be only slight variations from the sliding pitch pipes which have been publicly sold in Boston for over half a century, though the contrivance had not been used in instruments, as it has been found to occasion not only a useless expense, but decided injury to the tone.

The Musical and Sewing Machine Gazette, having changed its name to *The Courier,* (later the *Musical Courier*), published a follow-up story on Bazin in its March 13, 1880, issue.

Boston Notes
[From our regular correspondent]
Boston, March 12, 1880

Having seen in a recent number of your paper an interesting account of the 'First Reed Organs in America,' by James A. Bazin, of Ponkapog, Mass., John and I agreed to spend an afternoon in exploring that almost unknown locality, for the sake of personal investigation, knowing that your readers would have an equal interest in the subject.

Taking the cars for Readville, we

obtained a conveyance, which took us four miles into the country, around the south of Blue Hill, an eminence of 635 feet elevation, to a small village midway between Readville and South Canton, deriving its name from the Indian tribe which formerly inhabited the shores of Ponkapog Pond, and whose descendants still inhabit the vicinity in an amalgamated condition.

We found Mr. Bazin awaiting us on the portico of a goodly-sized residence, inhabited by himself and sister, near the post-office. His father was a French Huguenot, living in the Isle of Jersey, both parents emigrating to this country at the close of the Revolutionary war, for the sake of bringing up a family with independent religious and political thought. The miniature portraits of the father and mother, executed by the court painter to George III, over a century since, evince both intellect, refinement and rare beauty. The father settled in Boston and opened a hardware store on the corner of what was Brattle street and Dock Square, but, meeting with misfortune and being wronged out of his property, he moved from the city into this quiet district, and carried on the manufacture of hardware implements, living to the old age of 92.

James A. Bazin is now 82 years of age, but has the mental and physical freshness of a young man. Entering the house, we found a number of different styles of incipient reed-organs, made 40 or 50 years ago—among them a reed-organ in the form of a piano-case, with a transposing keyboard, giving the player an opportunity to play in twelve different keys, with the keyboard in the key of C. This instrument was tuned in the unequal temperament then prevailing at the time of its manufacture, and to provide for an equal flattening of the thirds in all the keys when transposed an ingenious device, automatic in connection with the transposing mecha-

nism, was inserted—an amount of brain-work expended worthier a better cause.

Rooms upstairs exhibited relics of an inventor's mind, which formed a curiosity-shop in themselves. Mechanical devices for proving astronomical problems, models of improvements in the development of the reed-organ, which afterwards were made practical and remunerative by others. Mr. Bazin has also been interested in optical science, and was the first manufacturer of folding stereoscopes in this country. He has a revolving camera-obscura projecting through the roof of his house, giving a view of the scenery in every direction from a room below.

Descending to his workshop in the southern end of his house, we found many samples of his rare inventive genius. Here stood the first stocking-loom manufactured in this country, invented in 1812, by his brother, who died in 1860.

Mr. Bazin was the first inventor of a machine for spinning flax, the principle of which was soon after brought into general adoption by ropemakers. Added to his inventive talent, his artistic genius is manifest by the many family portraits he executed more than sixty years ago in india ink with a fine camel's-hair brush, done with the perfection of modern lithographs. Added to this a poetic faculty which easily turns given subjects into rhyme and of symmetrical measure. He was baptized in Old King's Chapel, Boston, in 1798, and is a regular attendant at the Unitarian Church at Canton Corner. Such a modest, cheerful, unreproachful old gentleman is rarely met with, possessing a spirit full of wit and humor, wondering what ails him that he lives so long and well!

Concerning the introduction of the reed-organ trade in the United States, the following statements may interest your readers:

'From the Report of the Judges of the Second Exhibition of the Mechanic Association, Sept., 1839.

'C. Austin, Concord, N.H.—One Seraphine. This instrument not being in proper order—the lower octave hardly producing anything like musical sounds—the committee were unable to pronounce upon its merits.

'Third Exhibition, Sept. 1841.

'Organ Pianoforte. An instrument with this title, constructed upon the principle of the Seraphine or Melodeon, was placed in the exhibition by the maker, James A. Bazin, of Canton, Mass., which, in the opinion of the committee, deserves much praise. Its tones are more prompt and better in quality than is common in instruments of this kind. The committee think that this instrument (if it will stand in tune, of which they cannot judge) may be used as a very convenient and agreeable substitute for an organ, to accompany the voices in church music, where it is not practicable to have an organ.—SILVER MEDAL.'

The following comments are given in Mr. Bazin's own language:

'In an article published in *Appleton's Annual Cyclopedia for 1868*, it is stated that Mr. Prescott, of Concord, N.H., began the manufacture of Melodiums and Seraphines about the year 1832 or 1833, and also that Charles Austin, who worked for him in 1833, made at that time the first Seraphine he ever saw. This is a mistake, as it was not till 1836 that Mr. Prescott bought two Melodiums of my make, of Jos. L. Bates, of Boston, with whom I had left some for sale. And Charles Austin, who undertook to copy them, did not, for some time, succeed in making the joints of the tilting bellows properly, and never succeeded in making the springs to throw properly, and never succeeded in making the springs to throw the bellows open, like the ones he attempted to copy from. And he could not have known anything about the Seraphine till long afterwards, as one was sent, in his name, to the Mechanics' Fair in Boston, in 1839, in which all the bass notes failed to respond to the touch.

'It is also a mistake to say that Mr. Peloubet was the first to tune reeds in equal temperament, as he did not begin the business until 1852; and I find, by my books, that I sold, in 1844, to T. Gilbert & Co., who were proprietors of the 'Coleman Attachment,' reeds which were required to be tuned in equal temperament, a method of tuning which had been introduced about four or five years before, by an Englishman who pretended that he could tune instruments so as to be perfect in every key. Well knowing that this was impossible, I only tuned instruments in this way for those whose ears had become accustomed to discordant thirds. But as this method soon became the general practice I contrived a way of flatting the third, sixth and seventh of the scale, for which I obtained a patent (No. 9,892, August 2, 1853). The reason why a contrivance of this kind has never been brought into use appears to be that very few persons can distinguish the difference between a true third and one which must invariably result from the tempered scale. But any one who will take the pains to tune all the thirds and fifths of one scale perfect cannot fail to perceive the difference in the effect.

'In an article in the *Useful Cabinet* (Boston, 1808), it is recommended, in tuning instruments, to begin with the C and tune by fifths, tuning each fifth as flat as it will bear. This amounts to what is now called equal temperament. But it seems that this was not the general practice, as there is appended to this article a note by P. A. Von Hagen, who was at that time the organist at King's Chapel, advising the tuner to go back over the same keys and leave between

G sharp and D sharp any imperfection that may occur; thus leaving what used to be called the wolf where it would be least likely to make a disturbance.

'It is also a mistake to suppose that it was any improvement in the instrument that caused an increase in the demand for them, as it was only the fear of what Mrs. Grundy might say that prevented all but the very few who depend upon their own judgment from buying them, there having been as good-toned instruments made before Carhart's invention as afterward. Exhaustion bellows have had nothing whatever to do with the tone of the reeds, that depending altogether upon the form of the passage-way for the wind, the current of air having the same effect whether drawn through or forced through this passage.'

I hope, at some future time, to present your readers with a sketch of the life of this remarkable genius, who has spent so many years of mental activity in the unappreciative quietude of country life.

Winthrop

Three of Bazin's melodeons as well as a trumpet and a harp of novel design are in the Canton Historical Society's collection. While he had an inventive mind and was an excellent craftsman, Bazin apparently lacked commercial ability, as most of his innovations were exploited by others. He spent most of his later years as City Clerk of Canton, Massachusetts.

The number of reed organs built in the United States before 1846 was exceedingly small. Elias P. Needham and Emmons Hamlin, in a patent hearing in 1860, both estimated that the total number of reed organs of all kinds built in the United States before 1846 was less than three hundred.[4] The organs were handmade in small shops by individual craftsmen who usually built different kinds of instruments. Abraham Prescott, for example, was a self-taught maker of bass viols in Deerfield, New Hampshire, starting in 1809. The bass viols were used to accompany church choirs, and Prescott established a reputation for excellent craftsmanship as he traveled throughout the surrounding area selling his instruments. In 1831 he established a shop and store in Concord, New Hampshire with two of his employees, David and Andrew Dearborn and in 1833 moved the rest of his Deerfield business to Concord.

On a visit to Boston in 1836, Prescott bought a three-octave Bazin elbow melodeon or lap organ with round buttons and shortly thereafter began manufacturing his own version. In 1837 his display of musical instruments won a silver medal at the New Hampshire State Fair, and in October of the same year he exhibited at the annual fair of the American Institute in New York. In 1845 he took his son Abraham J. into the business, changing the firm name to Abraham Prescott and Son. When his father retired in 1850, Abraham J. brought his brothers Josiah B. and Joseph W.

Figure 14: A Prescott lap organ, 1847.

16

Prescott into the business, changing the name to Prescott and Brothers. In 1850 the name changed to Prescott Brothers. Joseph withdrew from the firm in 1853 and went into business for himself. Abraham senior died on May 1, 1856, and Josiah the following year. In 1859 Abraham J. took his youngest brother George D. B. into the firm, which by 1869 had fifty employees. In 1871 they changed the firm name to Prescott Organ Company, and incorporated it in 1881. They began manufacturing pianos in 1886 and eventually changed the name to Prescott Piano and Organ Company. Abraham J. died on July 8, 1891, and in the same year the firm name was changed to Prescott Piano Company. The corporation went out of business in 1912, ending one of the first successful reed organ manufacturing enterprises in the United States.

Concord became one of the early centers of reed organ manufacturing as a result of Prescott's activities. Some of the other firms located in that city were Dearborn and Bartlett; Austin and Dearborn; Liscom, Dearborn & Co.; Andrew Dearborn; Dearborn, Severance & Co.; Charles Austin; Charles E. Austin, (son of the former); D. B. Bartlett; Ingalls & Crockett; Parker & Secomb; Parker & Tracy; J. B. Rand; and Ballou & Curtis. John A. Farley, who became a partner in the firm of Taylor & Farley in Worcester, Massachusetts, was born in Concord and lived there until the age of 27, undoubtedly gaining his experience in one of the Concord firms.

George A. Prince was born in Boston on February 17, 1818, the son of a sea captain. He showed an early interest in music and, as a boy worked in the music store operated by his cousin in Boston. When his family moved to Buffalo, New York in 1833, young Prince opened a branch of the store in partnership with his cousin. Shortly afterward, the cousin withdrew, selling out to George. Prince began manufacturing melodeons in 1846 in some rooms over his music store at 200 Main Street. He built a factory at the corner of Niagara and Maryland streets in 1851, and later another on Pearl Street. The George A. Prince Company was the leading manufacturer of organs in the United States in the 1850s and 1860s. Many of the pioneers in the reed organ industry worked for Prince in the early days. Jeremiah Carhart built his first melodeon at Prince's, and Emmons Hamlin was superintendent of the tuning department there when he made his experiments in reed voicing. The business declined in later years, and Prince finally closed the factory and retired about 1879. He died in Buffalo on March 3, 1890. His brother, Samuel N. Prince, and his former partner, Charles E. Bacon, formed a new company, Prince & Bacon, to carry on the business in 1880.

FRONT VIEW OF MANUFACTORY—CORNER OF MARYLAND AND SEVENTH STREETS.

Figure 15: George A. Prince & Co., Buffalo, New York.

In 1842 Gustavus W. Ingalls and Cyrus W. Eaton of Bristol, New Hampshire began manufacturing seraphines. Ingalls later was employed by Prescott's and by Charles Austin, and then formed a partnership with David M. Dearborn. Ingalls began manufacturing reeds for the trade in 1866 in Worcester, Massachusetts as G. W. Ingalls & Co.

Riley Burditt, born in Vermont in 1819, joined with J. L. Jones and H. Woodbury to form Jones, Woodbury & Burditt in Brattleboro, Vermont in 1846 for the purpose of manufacturing reed organs. Woodbury left the following year and the firm became Jones & Burditt. E. B. Carpenter bought out Jones on October 1, 1850, changing the name to Burditt & Carpenter. At that time there were thirty-five employees in the firm, many of whom went on to become well known in the industry. At a reunion held in Brattleboro forty years later, eight of these men were present: E. B. Carpenter, J. L. Jones, A. Cathan, L. H. Dearborn, A. S. Field, A. Sherwin, H. R. Rose and P. S. White. Burditt sold his interest to Jacob Estey in 1852, and the firm name changed to E. B. Carpenter and Company. Burditt remained as an employee, however, until 1865 when he became a partner with Estey and Silas M. Waite in Estey's branch factory, established that year in Chicago. When he went to Chicago, Burditt legally changed the spelling of his name to Burdett. In 1866 he dissolved his partnership with Estey, sold the rights to his many patents, and went into business for himself. In 1870 he brought a law suit against Estey for infringement of his patent on a reed board with three sets of reeds. The suit was bitterly fought through the courts for fourteen years and finally decided by the Supreme Court in favor of Estey. Burdett's factory was destroyed in the Chicago fire of 1871, and he moved to Erie, Pennsylvania, establishing the Burdett Organ Company there with C. C. Converse. Riley Burdett died in Chicago on January 26, 1890.

Amos L. Swan, of Cherry Valley, New York began manufacturing melodeons in 1849, continuing until his business was broken up at the time of the Civil War. O. H. Eldridge & Company also made melodeons in Cherry Valley. In later years the firm name changed to Alex Fea and Sons, and it was finally abandoned in 1874.

Clearly one of the most ingenious and prolific contributors to reed organ development in the United States was Jeremiah Carhart. He began experimenting with the accordion in 1836 and with the lap organ in 1839. While Carhart has many innovations to his credit, the two most important generally attributed to him were probably originated by others. The concept of the suction bellows was developed by Peaseley at least as early as 1818, and Friedrich Buschmann made a Physharmonica with a suction bellows in Hamburg, Germany in 1836. Carhart, however, was granted United States Patent number 4912 on December 28, 1846 for the suction bellows. Carhart licensed the use of his patent to other organ builders such as George A. Prince, who was his employer at the time. From then on the suction operated instruments gained rapidly in popularity until they completely dominated the American reed organ industry. Carhart surrendered his original patent for the purpose of changing the claim, and it was reissued on June 24, 1856; it was again surrendered and reissued on August 18, 1857 with three additional claims. Carhart then sued Charles C. Austin in the U.S. District Court of New Hampshire for patent infringement. During the trial there were rumors of the existence of an earlier patent on the exhaust bellows, but because of the

18

Patent Office fire in 1836 the records had been destroyed. It was not until many years later that a copy of the Peaseley patent appeared. Carhart lost the case and the patent was declared void as a result. An appeal to the Supreme Court was dismissed. Carhart's widow, Lydia E. Carhart, later appealed to Congress for relief but was turned down by recommendation of the House Committee on Patents in the second session of the 41st Congress on March 3, 1870. Col. Levi Knight Fuller, a son-in-law of Jacob Estey and superintendent of the Estey factory in Brattleboro, Vermont for many years said, ". . . Carhart was not the first inventor of either the exhaust bellows or the reed or tube board. . . Charles Austin made them before Carhart and a man by the name of [Peaseley] made one or more in 1818. . . but Carhart appeared to be the first to take out a patent for what proved to be an old device." Jeremiah Carhart invented and patented a machine for making reed boards. The firm he formed with Elias Parkman Needham manufactured and supplied reeds to the trade, as well as complete reed organs. The Carhart & Needham factory was located near 172 Fulton Street in New York in 1849 and later moved to a new six story building at 99 East 23rd Street. By 1866 they had produced a total of 15,000 instruments and were turning them out at a rate of forty per week. The largest model produced, called a Hall Organ, had fourteen sets of reeds, the lowest reed being a pedal bass of 32 foot pitch. When a full chord was sounded on this organ using both hands and feet, 138 reeds spoke simultaneously!

By the middle of the nineteenth century the stage was set for the explosive growth of the industry. During the period from 1840 to 1860 the reed organ evolved into its now-familiar form. Alexandre-François Debain

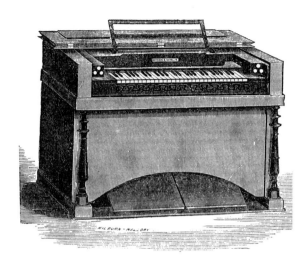

Figure 16: The "4¹/₂ Octave Harmonium," a wood block engraving from Mason & Hamlin's 1856 catalog.

(1809-1877) patented his Harmonium in Paris on August 9, 1840. In this instrument he adopted the pressure bellows with the expression technique used previously in many European organs and added a stop knob to permit turning the expression on and off. Debain also introduced hinged sub-assemblies; resonating chambers for the reeds; multiple stops designated by number, name, and range on the stop face; and the division of the reeds into bass and treble parts with separate stop knobs. Other European makers were quick to copy this instrument and even the patented name became the generic name for the typical European reed organ.

In the United States, Mason & Hamlin introduced their new style of instrument in July of 1855. It was first called the Harmonium or Organ-Harmonium and later the Cabinet Organ, a type now usually referred to as a flat-topped organ. They retained the suction bellows, by then almost universal in American-made organs, and tilted it from the usual horizontal position used in melodeons to a vertical position, placing it in the lower rear of the cabinet. Two exhausters were used, connected to two foot pedals, as opposed to the single exhauster and single pedal of the melodeons. Most of these instruments had multiple stops, divided into treble and bass sections. While the melodeon style continued to be built for many years, the new cabinet style was destined to set the standard for the American reed organ.

THE GOLDEN YEARS

During the first part of the nineteenth century, great changes in society and in manufacturing and distribution were taking place.

• Precision machines to cut and shape metal and wood were being developed as were steam engines to provide power for large factories.

• In the United States, the first railroad line, the Baltimore and Ohio, opened in 1830 with 13 miles (21 km) of track between Baltimore and Ellicott's Mills, Maryland. By 1840 there were 2,800 miles (4,500 km) of track in operation, and by 1860 the total had reached 30,000 miles (50,000 km).

• Though the settlement of the mid- and far west had begun earlier, the coming of the railroads opened vast new areas for settlement and created a huge demand for people to occupy and exploit the land. Large numbers of Europeans, attracted by low cost land and freedom from the almost constant wars, came to establish farms, build houses, work in the factories and build the railroads.

• With the great increase in economic activity, the number of people with good incomes rose sharply, bringing increased demand for new products.

By mid-century all of these elements were in place. The combination of factors created an atmosphere of confidence, optimism, and enthusiasm, almost a national euphoria. The landless European peasant could realistically dream of becoming the owner of a large, fertile farm. The small New England mechanic could become a factory owner. New products could be produced in quantity and, even more importantly, could be sold throughout a country as large as all of Europe, with no language, customs, currency problems or import duties at the borders. It was at this point in American history when, among other products, the reed organ had reached an advanced state of development and was ready to be tested in the new national marketplace.

One of the classical stories in the American reed organ business is that of Jacob Estey of Brattleboro, Vermont. Estey, born in Hinsdale, New Hampshire on September 30, 1814, started a plumbing business in Brattleboro in 1835 and operated it successfully until 1855. He also sold tombstones. In 1852, seeing the possibilities in the reed organ business, he bought Riley Burditt's interest in the melodeon manufacturing firm of Burditt & Carpenter, which was then renamed E. B. Carpenter & Co., and moved the factory into his plumbing shop.

Burditt & Carpenter had its beginnings with a pipe organ builder, Joseph Foster, of Winchester, New Hampshire. Foster built his first reed organ in 1831, and finding success in this venture, took Albert Thayer into partnership in 1842 to make lap organs. They hired the twenty-year-old Samuel H. Jones to help out in the shop. When Foster & Thayer was dissolved two years later, Jones had learned enough to go into business for himself in Winchester, where he remained until 1846. Clearly the reed organ business was beginning to prosper. In that year he

Figure 17: Jacob Estey's plumbing shop, about 1855. The Estey & Green factory was in this building and its ware-rooms were in the building to the left.

moved to Brattleboro, Vermont, occupying the former Smith & Woodcock grist mill in the nearby village of Centerville. He took into partnership John Woodbury and Riley Burditt, calling the firm S. H. Jones & Co. The eventual Estey Organ Company dated its beginnings from this point in 1846, although Jacob Estey's involvement didn't begin until 1853. Woodbury left in 1847 and the business was renamed Jones & Burditt. In 1850 Jones sold his interest to Edwin B.

Figure 18: The former Smith & Woodcock grist mill, location of S. H. Jones & Co.'s factory in Brattleboro, Vermont, 1846.

Carpenter, who had come to Brattleboro from Guilford, Maine, the firm name then becoming Burditt & Carpenter. In the four years from 1846 to 1850 a total of about 400 organs had been built by the company.

The name E. B. Carpenter & Co. lasted only one year until 1853 when Carpenter left, selling his interest to Isaac Hines. A new firm, named Isaac Hines & Co. was established with Hines, Estey and H. P. Green as partners. Carpenter then associated with Samuel H. Jones and George Woods in a new reed organ venture called Jones, Carpenter & Woods, located in Brattleboro. From 1850 to 1855 some two thousand organs had been built, or an average of four hundred per year, an increase no doubt due in large part to the firm hand of Jacob Estey. In 1855 Estey sold his plumbing and tombstone businesses, bought out Isaac Hines' interest and began to devote his full attention to the successor firm of Estey & Green. The next year, 1856, Estey & Green bought out S. H. Jones and George Woods and absorbed the Jones, Carpenter & Woods business into the Estey & Green firm. Estey also eventually bought out E. B. Carpenter's interest.

The original factory in the plumbing shop, which was located on Main Street in Brattleboro, burned in 1857. But business was booming, and a new factory was completed in February of 1858. Two months later the factory had 20 employees and produced ten organs per week. During the 1855-1860 period production averaged 640 instruments per year in spite of the loss of production after the 1857 fire. In January of 1863 Jacob Estey bought H. P. Green's interest in the firm,

Figure 19: Estey factory building about 1858.

Figure 20: Estey factory building about 1866.

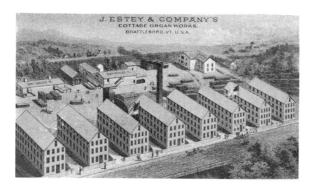

Figure 21: The final Estey factory location on the Dickinson farm property in Brattleboro, Vermont.

which was renamed J. Estey & Co., with Estey becoming the sole owner. The new factory burned in 1864 but another larger building was soon completed.

In 1865 the company was reorganized with Jacob Estey, Riley Burdett (formerly Burditt), Joel Bullard and Silas M. Waite, a Brattleboro banker, as partners. Burdett was by then the head of Estey and Burdett, Estey's Chicago sales branch. During 1866 in excess of two hundred organs were completed per month. In that year J. Estey & Co. was again reorganized, with Burdett and Waite forming the Burdett Organ Co. Ltd. to manufacture organs in Chicago for the booming midwest market. In the 1866 reorganization, Jacob's son Julius J. and son-in-law Levi K. Fuller became partners, an arrangement which remained in effect until Jacob's death in 1890. Also in 1866 a larger factory was built on Flat Street.

In 1869 Estey bought the Dickinson farm near Brattleboro and built some shops there, which eventually grew into a large factory complex. This location eventually came to be known as Esteyville. The company was incorporated in 1872 as Estey Organ Company, and it operated under that name until the company discontinued operations in 1959. The name was then sold and is still used for a line of electronic organs and pianos. By 1890 there were about seven hundred employees with a payroll of $30,000 per month.

J. ESTEY & CO.'S
Cottage Organ Manufactory

Is situated on BIRGE STREET, in the beautiful Village of BRATTLEBORO, VERMONT. They consist of EIGHT MAIN FACTORIES, forty feet apart, one hundred feet long, and three stories high, and varying from thirty to thirty-eight feet in width, according to the work to be done in them.

The DRY HOUSES are in the rear, and are two in number, divided into various apartments, and of sufficient capacity to hold several hundred thousand feet of lumber, enough to ensure an ample supply of well-seasoned material at all times.

In the rear of Factory No. 4, is a FIRE-PROOF ENGINE AND BOILER HOUSE, containing six large boilers, of three hundred horse power, furnishing steam for the engine and heat for the buildings. The ENGINE is of the celebrated CORLISS patent, and of one hundred horse-power.

The PACKING, STORE and GAS HOUSES, and several other buildings for the use of and connected with the establishment, are situated about the works at convenient distances and form altogether the most complete system yet devised.

Everything within the reach of skill and capital has been done to secure the comfort, convenience and health of the workmen, and the safety, perfection, and economical working of the establishment.

Other improvements are being made, and buildings erected, to carry out the grand scheme projected by Messrs. ESTEY & Co., in order that they may be able to furnish organs in sufficient numbers to meet the pressing public demand.

The ESTEY ORGAN MANUFACTORY is now the most extensive in the world, and gives constant employment to more than five hundred workmen. No other organ has gained an equal popularity, or been produced on such an extensive scale. Step by step, Messrs. ESTEY & Co. have advanced in the rapid march of progress, until it may be truly said that

The Estey Organ Leads the World!

Figure 22

Jacob Estey served in both houses of the state legislature, and died in Brattleboro on April 15, 1890. Jacob Estey himself never built an organ and couldn't play the organ. He was the first of a new breed in the reed organ business in the United States—the professional manager and entrepreneur. His son Julius J. (1845-1902), who succeeded him as President of Estey Organ Company, served in the Civil War as a Captain and later Colonel of the Vermont Militia. He commanded the First Regiment of the Vermont Militia and was later promoted to Brigadier General. He served as a state senator in 1882.

Levi K. Fuller also was a Colonel in the Militia and served as a senator, as Lieutenant Governor, and Governor of Vermont. He had started with Estey as an engineer and machinist in 1860, and married Abby, the boss's daughter. Fuller was the technical brain behind the Estey success, with numerous patents on improvements to organs.

Almost every reed organ manufacturer in the United States of any consequence could trace some connection to the Estey organization, Prescott, Prince, or to a lesser extent, Mason & Hamlin. For example, E. B. Carpenter, after selling to Isaac Hines in 1853, started another melodeon manufacturing business in Brattleboro with Samuel Jones and George Woods, both of Boston. This firm was sold to Estey in 1857 or 1858, at which time Carpenter moved west. Woods went to Boston where he eventually became a factory foreman at Mason & Hamlin and later formed his own company. In 1865 Carpenter formed a company in Mendota, Illinois with a local melodeon maker, George W. Tewksbury, known as Tewksbury & Carpenter. Tewksbury left in 1873 after selling his interest to Scott and E. E. Wise. The firm then became Carpenter, Scott & Wise. In 1875 Carpenter left and the company was reorganized as the Mendota Cottage Organ Co. Carpenter began manufacturing organs on his own under the name E. B. Carpenter in 1876. In 1882 he renamed the business the Carpenter Organ Co., and in 1887 again renamed it as the Mendota Northwestern Cottage Organ and Piano Co. This business closed in 1889 and Carpenter returned to Vermont, where he died in 1891. Carpenter held a number of patents, the most important of which was on the divided octave coupler.

Edwin P. Carpenter is often confused with his father, E. B. Carpenter. Edwin P.

Figure 23: The Brattleboro Melodeon Co. factory, about 1867.

started a reed organ manufacturing business in Worcester, Massachusetts under the name of E. P. Carpenter & Co. in 1850. He went bankrupt about 1866 and was indicted for concealment of assets in bankruptcy. In 1881 he was again doing business in Worcester as E. P. Carpenter. He moved to Brattleboro, Vermont in 1884, occupying the

former Brattleboro Melodeon Co. factory on Flat Street. The business was later renamed The Carpenter Co., and remained in operation at least until 1917, when organ number 126,000 was built. E. P. Carpenter served as a judge of the musical exhibits at the World's Columbian Fair in Chicago in 1895.

In the fall of 1879, F. R. Wolfinger, John A. Comstock and Herman D. Cable started a reed organ manufacturing business under the name of the Wolfinger Organ Co., in a two story building at Randolph and Ann Streets in Chicago. Cable's experience was as a book seller, but he turned out to have a genius for modern business management and marketing. Under his guidance the firm grew rapidly. He presumably felt the need to strengthen the production side of the business, and about 1885 he brought in two highly experienced organ builders, E. E. Wise and George W. Tewksbury, who bought out Comstock's interest. Both men had previously been associated with the Western Cottage Organ Co. or its predecessors. The Wolfinger firm was then renamed the Chicago Cottage Organ Co. It continued to grow and a large factory building was acquired at 22nd and Paulina Streets to accommodate the increased demand for organs. Wolfinger sold out to G. K. Barnes and E. E. Wise sold his interest to Cable and Tewksbury. H. D.

Figure 24: The E.P. Carpenter & Co. factory, about 1885.

24

Cable then became president of what had become one of the largest, if not the largest, reed organ producers in the world. Alfred Dolge wrote:

"Cable applied the methods used in selling books, as far as possible, to the organ and piano business, with amazing success. . . . The training which he had enjoyed in the bookselling business impelled him to introduce system in his manufacturing and selling organization, with all that word implies in modern business management, and perhaps he was the first in the piano industry to profit by the application of scientific accounting. At all events, his success was so rapid, and his business assumed such immense proportions, that it became the wonder of his contemporaries."[5]

In 1889 Barnes sold his interest and Herman D. Cable brought his brothers Fayette S. and Hobart M. Cable into the business. By 1890 pianos had become an important part of the business, and Cable acquired the Conover Brothers piano company. Growth continued unabated. A second factory was built in St. Charles, Illinois as well as an office building at 21521 Wabash Avenue in Chicago. They were completed in 1899, giving The Cable Co. a capacity of 16,000 pianos and 18,000 organs per year. That same year Herman D. Cable died at the age of 50. F. S. Cable became president and at this time they renamed it The Cable Company.

In 1900 Hobart M. Cable left and the next year bought the name and property of the Burdett Organ Co. in Freeport, Illinois, renaming it the Hobart M. Cable Co. H. M. Cable decided to concentrate on his piano business located in LaPorte, Indiana, and sold the organ factory to S. N. Swan, its manager. S. N. Swan & Co. continued in operation at least until 1925.

About 1904 Fayette S. Cable left The Cable Co. and bought the Lakeside Organ Co., another Chicago business, a remnant of the breakup of Tryber & Sweetland. He renamed it the Fayette S. Cable Piano Co. and later it became the Cable-Nelson Company.

Another midwestern giant in the organ business was the W. W. Kimball Co. of Chicago. William Wallace Kimball was born in 1828 in Rumford, Maine and grew up on a farm there. At the age of 25 he followed many of his fellow easterners in their journey to the west, settling in Decorah, Iowa as that town was being laid out in 1853. A land rush was in progress, a result of the steady flow of prairie schooners full of easterners and European immigrants who, as they were passing through, got a look at the rich farm land of northeastern Iowa and decided to stay. Kimball went into the real estate business and through canny but conservative dealings managed to amass a small fortune by 1857. Possibly sensing something in the wind, Kimball liquidated most of his investments just before the panic of 1857 and headed for Chicago. There he traded some remaining pieces of land in Decorah for four square pianos and managed to sell them at a profit. He continued to deal in real estate while he taught himself the music business. While concentrating on selling pianos he also managed to sell melodeons made by Prince and by Taylor and Farley. By 1860 he had dropped real estate and devoted himself full-time to his music store.

Looking for some way to appeal to a larger and therefore lower-priced market, he built up his reed organ stock, adding the Smith American and Shoninger organs. By 1862 he became the sole agent for the Alexander organ, made in Chicago. By 1864 he had set up a string of agents throughout the midwest; business boomed for W. W.

Figure 25: W. W. Kimball

Figure 26: Edwin S. Conway in the 1890s.

Kimball. His store was burned out in the Chicago fire of 1871, but the business survived, partly from the cash flow generated by rentals and out-of-town agents. One of those agents, Edwin Stapleton Conway, a supersalesman working the Minnesota and Wisconsin area, came to work for Kimball in Chicago as head of the wholesale department in 1876. W. W. Kimball described Conway as:

> A natural born salesman, fresh from the farm himself, with the manure still on his heels. This man Conway knows the people on the farms and in the small towns out there. He's one of them. . . This is the kind of man I want to handle my trade in the field.

At Conway's urging Kimball began manufacturing organs in 1879, at first on a small scale. The actions were built in the company's repair shops and the cases were contracted out to furniture builders. The results were so promising that Kimball decided to go into full-scale production. While the factory was being organized, Kimball contracted with John G. Earhuff, another Chicago organ maker, to produce the Kimball organ. Kimball's production resumed in 1880, but sales soon outstripped the factory's capacity, and a new, larger one was constructed in 1881, located at Twenty-sixth and Rockwell. This factory was a four-story building, eighty by two hundred forty feet, with a separate engine room.

Meanwhile, Conway was busy perfecting the field sales organization. The agency system previously used was superseded by the Kimball music stores, which by 1881 were operating in Minneapolis, Kansas City, Grand Rapids, Springfield, Rock

Island, Galesburg, Oshkosh, and St. Joseph. Between thirty and forty travelling salesmen were hired as Kimball employees. In his spare time Conway had located and leased a walnut forest in Arkansas, set up a sawmill, and organized the operation as the Newport Lumber Company, a Kimball subsidiary. He was named President and general superintendent.

The Kimball enterprise was incorporated in 1882 with W. W. Kimball, Conway and Albert G. Cone, Kimball's brother-in-law, as stockholders.

The so-called "stencil" business was perfectly legal but led to some abuses which plagued the musical instrument business for some years. Organs and pianos were made by mass producers, who would stencil the name of any buyer on the instrument. Kimball made good use of stencil instruments, buying thousands of Kimball pianos made by J. P. Hale, and was himself one of the leaders in producing stencil organs. Reed organs of the same quality as the Kimball organs and almost identical in appearance were sold at wholesale with such names as Goggin, Thiery, Pacific Queen, and Great Western. These organs even carried the Kimball serial numbers.

The phenomenal growth of Kimball in the early 1880s was fueled by sales of the reed organ. At the same time, Kimball began experimenting with piano building, much to the consternation of the piano manufacturing establishment. An editorial in the *Music Trade Free Press* said, "The W. W. Kimball system is to the music trade what the Standard Oil Company is to the oil trade, and if he starts a piano factory in Chicago, as has been reported, he will become a more formidable rival than ever." A piano factory was built alongside the organ factory in 1887, and in 1888 the first Kimball-built pianos were produced. By

1889 the output was fifty organs per day and fifty pianos per week.

The center of the reed organ manufacturing industry in the United States had moved from its origins in New England to the west. The new giants in the industry were men who understood mass marketing and mass production, and who in fact participated in the development of those disciplines. They were industrialists who happened to be in the musical instrument business. The story of how they sold reed organs in huge quantities will be told in the next chapter.

The reed organ reached its peak of popularity about 1890. While sales continued to grow for a few years, piano sales were growing faster and the reed organ was losing market share, a sure sign that the end was near. In the decade from 1910 to 1920 most reed organ makers in the United States discontinued organ production and either went out of business or concentrated on the piano; only a handful survived.

Probably the largest factor in this decline was the success of automatic instruments or alternatives such as the phonograph and the radio. The effort and dedication of learning to play an instrument was no longer a barrier to enjoying music in the home. The first inexpensive self-playing tabletop organettes appeared in the 1870s, followed soon after by full-sized self-playing reed organs. After 1900 the push-up player was perfected, which would play inexpensive paper rolls containing sophisticated musical arrangements played by professionals. The earliest push-up players contained a set of reeds and could play by themselves as reed organs, but were usually used to play a piano, sometimes with organ accompaniment. Edison's phonograph had its beginnings in 1877 and eventually was improved enough to permit the reproduction of recorded music. In the 1920s radio broadcasting began to reduce the need for buying phonograph records.

Possibly, other factors in the decline of the reed organ were increasing urbanization and rising income levels. Reed organs had always been more popular in rural areas than in the cities, and one of their advantages with respect to the piano was the lower price. As the cities grew, rural population declined in relative terms. Incomes rose on average, bringing more people into the market for pianos.

At the time of World War I only a few of the reed organ makers remained in business. Estey still felt strong enough to decline on principle to build the lightweight suitcase folding organs used by the U.S. Army chaplains. Smaller companies specializing in this type of instrument, such as Bilhorn and A. L. White, were favored with the military business. Estey had gotten into the piano business but achieved only modest success; it always remained basically an organ company. After World War I it survived by adding pipe organs to its line and did very well for a time making large church organs and residence pipe organs, many of them with automatic player attachments. Their reed organ production continued, but in greatly reduced quantities.

By 1925 the *Purchaser's Guide to the Music Industries* (in the United States) listed only twelve manufacturers of reed organs. Autophone was still making the Gem and Concert roller organettes, mainly for sale by Sears, Roebuck & Co. Bilhorn, Faber and White were the principal makers of the small suitcase folding organs, and also made a few conventional reed organs. Piedmont was only making reed organs. Williams and Epworth made reed organs and pianos, and Estey made pianos and pipe organs as well

as reed organs. S. N. Swan, who had been the manager of the Burdett Organ Co. factory in Freeport, Illinois when it was owned by Hobart M. Cable, had purchased that business when Cable decided to concentrate only on pianos. Swan was still in business in 1925 making reed organs as well as phonographs under the "Swan" and "Burdett" names.

Although not listed in 1925 as a reed organ maker, the giant Aeolian Company was still making the Vocalion and the Orchestrelle, the most sophisticated of the American reed organs. Some of the familiar old names were still to be found, but were making only pianos, such as Baldwin;

Figure 27: A two-manual and pedal Vocalion.

Farrand; Jesse French; Gulbransen; Hamilton; Lehr; Mason & Hamlin; Needham; Packard; Schulz; Shoninger; Sterling; Story & Clark; Trayser; Horace Waters; Weaver and P. S. Wick. George P. Bent was still making puns for the company now run by his sons, Bent Brothers: "The Straight Bent Line." The Cable Company, successor to the Chicago Cottage Organ Company, had spawned Cable & Sons, Cable-Nelson (formerly Fayette S. Cable, the Lakeside Organ Co., and Tryber & Sweetland), and Hobart M. Cable (formerly the Burdett Organ Co.). The A. B. Chase name was to be found on a piano made by the United Piano Corp. W. W. Kimball made pianos, phonographs, and pipe organs in 1925. The son of W. W. Kimball and the two sons of his marketing genius, E. S. Conway, had combined to form Conway Musical Industries, which they built into a powerful business. In 1922 they acquired the assets and name of Wilcox & White,

Figure 29: Rubinoff sets aside his famous violin to try out the Estey Miniature Organ.

which had gone bankrupt the year before. The Malcolm Love name survived in 1925 on a piano made by the Wegman Piano Co. Lyon & Healy produced pianos, harps, and band instruments.

Many of these names succumbed during the depression years of the 1930s, but Estey bravely soldiered on, declining slowly but steadily. Their 1933 price list shows twenty-two models with nine different actions, ranging in price from $60 to $1150. The 1937 price list shows only fourteen models and seven actions, and the prices ranged from $32.50 to $1075. Some of the interesting instruments produced during this period were the New Melodeon, the Modernistic, the Children's, and a two-manual and pedal electro-pneumatic organ.

The New Melodeon had two ranks of reeds, electrically operated stops, and an electric blower, housed in a case patterned after the old square melodeons of sixty or more years before. The Modernistic had what we would now call an art deco case, was available with 11, 14 or 17 stops, 170 to 318 reeds, and was available with

Figure 28: The Estey Modernistic Organ, available with foot-pumping or an electric blower.

29

Figure 30: The Estey New Melodeon.

conventional bellows and foot pedals or an electric blower. The Children's or Miniature organ had a three-octave keyboard, one set of reeds, and was 24 inches long by 32 inches high by 12 inches deep. It sold to dealers for $16.50 and the matching bench was an additional $1.50. This organ was intended to sell for $35 to $40 at retail. Advertising featured Paul Whiteman and Rubinoff playing the organ (not at the same time). The two-manual and pedal electropneumatic was first produced in 1937. It had two five-octave manuals, a 32 note radiating concave pedal keyboard, balanced expression, and crescendo pedals and was housed in a stylish art deco case with a matching bench. With all its electropneumatic wizardry, it was still purely an acoustic reed organ.

During the 1930s there were a number of attempts to produce an electronic organ. One of the earliest made use of reeds to produce the tones, and thus was a transition between the traditional reed organs and the now-familiar electronic instruments. Frederick Albert Hoschke, who had been president of the Springfield Conservatory of Music in Hagerstown, Maryland, worked for the M. P. Möller Organ Co. in Hagerstown on player pipe organs, and by 1934 was with the Everett Piano Co. of South Haven, Michigan.[6] There he invented a novel organ using reeds which acted as variable capacitors in a vacuum tube circuit. The voltage variations across these capacitors were amplified electrically and reproduced by a loudspeaker. Everett manufactured and sold the instrument as the Orgatron. The first Orgatrons drew heavily on conventional American reed organ practices with pallet valves, mutes, and negative air pressure. The Model 5 Everett Orgatron is of this type. A later version, the STM1, appeared about 1937. This model had an enormously complex pneumatic key and stop action, based on player piano technology of the 1910s and 20s. The pallet valves were eliminated in favor of a primary and secondary valve arrangement using a separate positive high pressure system. Hoschke died in 1936 before completing his work on the instrument and it was brought to a finished form and patented by Benjamin F. Meissner. About 1945 the Rudolph Wurlitzer Co. of North Tonawanda, New York, purchased the rights to the instrument from Everett and did further development work on it. In this version the individual valves for each note were eliminated and the reeds vibrated continuously. A positive air pressure was used to operate the reeds, and the key and stop action was electrical. The Wurlitzer version of the Orgatron, such as the Model 4601, was sold with some success as late as the 1960s.

30

Figure 31: The Wurlitzer Model 4601 reed organ, 1954, adapted from the Orgatron patents.

The Hammond electro-mechanical organ was developed contemporaneously with the Everett Orgatron in the mid 1930s. It was an immediate success, quickly dominating and rejuvenating the small organ business. Other manufacturers rushed to offer something to compete, but World War II intervened.

After the war, another approach using reeds was taken in the Radareed organ. In this instrument, each reed was equipped with a qualifying tube and an individual microphone to pick up the sound. Air to the reeds was controlled by an electric action and the sound amplified electronically. The Radareed was priced in the range of $3,000 to $9,000 and was never commercially successful. During the late 1930s, Hammond produced the Novachord and the Solovox, small keyboards used in conjunction with a piano. The tones in these instruments were generated by vacuum tube oscillators. After the war, this approach was followed by other manufacturers such as Baldwin, Conn, Minshall Estey and Allen in producing complete electronic organs in competition with the Hammond, the Wurlitzer and some still-surviving but moribund conventional reed organs.

Figure 32: Ketterman Organ Co., Muncie, Indiana; reed organ with electric chimes, stop action and blower, about 1948.

Figure 33: The Mannborg Elektro-Harmonium, made by VEB Leipziger Pianofortefabrik Böhlitz-Ehrenberg, Leipzig, Germany in 1954.

Figure 34: Ann Page plays a circa 1875 Mustel Harmonium. She has made a number of highly regarded recordings on this instrument.

THE REED ORGAN IN EUROPE

At the beginning of the nineteenth century, France, Germany, and England were well provided with musical instrument makers, many of them craftsmen of the highest order and a goodly number inventive geniuses. Word of the earliest free-reed organs spread quickly and hundreds of makers were quick to see the potential of the little instruments. Many of these makers felt obliged to invent a distinctive name for their instruments to dramatize some real or supposed improvement, such as Aeoline, Choralodion, Euphonion, Aeolodicon, Physharmonica, Zieharmonica, Aeorophone, Melophone, Aeolklavier, Aeolmelodicon, Adiophone, Aeolophone, Symphonium, Aeolpantalon, Poïkilorgue, Angelophone, Aeolodion, Apollolyra, Bibel Harmonium,

Cecilium, Harmoniflute, Harmonine, Harmoniphone, Harmoniphrase, Kallistorganon, Kartonium, Mediophone, Melodina, Melodiorgue, Melophilon, Melodium, Metaphone, Normalharmonium, Orchestrina di Camera, Organino, Organovioline, Orgue Expressif, Panharmonikon, Pianon, Seraphine, Tryolodeon, Viola a Cembalo, Violoclave, and so on.[7]

Of these, seraphine, orgue expressif and physharmonica were the most widely used names for reed organs until "Harmonium" became a generic name.

Some of the old, established piano makers added reed organs to their product lines; for example, J. & P. Schiedmayer began making pianos in 1735 in Stuttgart, Germany and added harmoniums to its line of products in 1853. E. F. Walcker, the pipe organ builder established in 1820 in Ludwigsberg, Germany made harmoniums from 1838 to about 1914. Walcker is still in operation making pipe organs in the mid 1990s.

Another variation in reed organ production appeared in Europe, that of the "art" reed organ. The most celebrated maker of this category was Victor Mustel. He made his first reed organ in 1840, then in 1844 went to work for Julien Jaulin to learn reed making. Jaulin won a medal at the Paris Exhibition of 1851 for the manufacture of reeds. In 1853 Mustel left Jaulin and established his own factory in Paris where he set out to build the finest harmoniums it was possible to make. He first exhibited at the Paris Exhibition of 1855, winning a silver medal. Each instrument he built was a masterpiece of craftsmanship and the reeds were voiced to perfection. Production was small, typically twenty instruments per year, and while the instruments were near perfection the business was shaky. In 1889 he won the Grand Prize at the Paris Exhibition and in the same year was made a Chevalier of the Legion d'Honeur. After Victor Mustel died in 1890, his sons Charles and Auguste and his grandson Alphonse ran the business. They introduced some changes to increase production and control costs. Connoisseurs regard these instruments as very fine, but not up to Victor's standards. Under a contract signed in 1905, Alphonse Mustel was to move to Boston to supervise the manufacture of Mustel organs by Mason & Hamlin. Whether he did or not is unclear at this time, but Mason & Hamlin did produce some fine European-style harmoniums. The Mustel company was still in operation in Paris as late as 1938.

Certainly the most influential reed organ builder in Europe was Alexandre-François Debain. In 1832 at the age of twenty-two he had already become Superintendent of the Johann Pape piano factory in Paris, where he made many contributions to piano design.

Figure 35: A small Debain harmonium.

Two years later he established his own business making the orgue expressif. In 1842 he introduced and patented a radical new reed organ design which he called the "Harmonium." This instrument differed from its predecessor the orgue expressif in the arrangement of the casework, hinging of the various subassemblies, the addition of resonating chambers for the reeds, the stop arrangement, the designation of stops by number, name, and pitch on the stop face, the division of the reeds into bass and treble sections with separate stops to control them, and a control used to turn the expression on and off. The Harmonium was an instant success. Jacob Alexandre, who had been building the orgue expressif at least since 1829, obtained a license to copy Debain's instrument but not the name, and introduced the Orgue-Melodium in 1844. Other makers were not so scrupulous and copied it without license, even using the patented name Harmonium. Debain made a wide variety of reed instruments, mainly pressure operated, but including the Organophone, a suction instrument, and the Harmonicorde, a combination piano and organ.

The Alexandre firm, known as Alexandre et Fils and later as Alexandre Père et Fils, had its factory at Ivry-sur-Seine and its offices and showrooms in Paris. Alexandre made a wide variety of reed organ types, including portable, one-, two- and three-manual organs (with and without pedal bass), a combination reed organ and piano, and a combination reed and pipe organ. One model, called the Orgue Americaine, had a case resembling American organs but used pressure bellows. Alexandre bought the rights to the percussion action, invented in 1841 by Louis-Pierre Alexandre Martin, and known as Martin de Provins. Alexandre's had a factory capacity of one thousand organs per month in 1878.

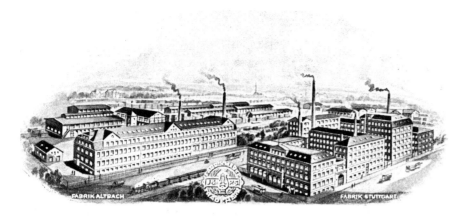

Figure 36: The J. & P. Schiedmayer piano and organ factory, Stuttgart, Germany.

Many of the top harmonium makers started there, such as Philip J. Trayser, who later started his own factory in Stuttgart, Germany, and the principals of H. Christophe & Etiènne of Paris, both of whom had been foremen at the Alexandre factory.

The great French pipe organ builder, Aristide Cavaillé-Coll, also built reed organs, one of them with the memorable name Poïkilorgue. J.-B. Napoléon Fourneaux began making free reed instruments in Paris in 1835. He was succeeded by his son J.-L. Napoléon Fourneaux in 1846. The latter was also the author of a book on the orgue expressif and a treatise on tuning. Maurice Kasriel established his factory in Paris in 1839, and became best known for portable harmoniums, harmoniflutes, and guide-chants. Kasriel continued in operation at least until 1951.

In Germany, Schiedmayer produced a broad range of reed organs, from small suction and pressure operated models for the home, large two manual and pedal models, organs with chimes, and roll operated instruments. Ernst Hinkel established a harmonium factory in Ulm in 1872. By 1883 it was listed in directories as Hinkel & Silberhorn. Silberhorn broke away and formed his own

business, located in Stuttgart, to manufacture reeds and other components for the harmonium trade, while Hinkel continued with harmoniums. The Hinkel factory produced a broad range of reed instruments, similar to Schiedmayer. Another significant German builder was the Richard Metzner Orgel-Harmonium-Fabrik in Leipzig, which also produced suction instruments under the name Deutsch-Amerikanische Orgel-Harmonium-Fabrik R. Metzner. The German reed organ industry was fairly decentralized, with concentrations of builders in Leipzig, Stuttgart, Berlin, Gera, and Dresden.

Oddly, in later years, three Swedes came to dominate the German reed organ business.

Figure 37: The Mannborg Style 97 harmonium.

Theodor Mannborg was born in 1861 in Karlstad, Sweden. He was apprenticed to J. P. Nyström's Orgel & Pianofabrik in Karlstad, then went to Germany in 1886 to take additional training with a pipe organ builder, Urban Kreutzbach. Mannborg organized his factory in 1889 in Borna, Germany where he produced the first suction reed organs to be made in Germany. In 1894 he moved to Leipzig, where he opened a new factory at Angerstrasse 38 in the Lindenau district. He was instrumental in organizing the Verein Deutscher Harmonium Fabrikanten, (Association of German Harmonium Manufacturers). When he died in 1930 the business was continued by his son Karl Mannborg until it was taken over by the state-owned piano manufacturer, Rönisch & Hupfeld in 1948, operating as VEB Leipziger Piano-fortefabrik Böhlitz-Ehrenberg. In 1911 Mannborg established the Deutsche Harmonium-Zungen-Fabrik, located in Pegau, Germany, to make "Jubilate" brand reeds and other components for the trade. This factory was eventually combined with other reed makers into the state-owned Deutsches Tonzungenwerk in Gera, Germany.

When Theodor Mannborg came to Germany, he was accompanied by two other Swedes: Lars Magnus Hofberg and Olaf Lindholm. Both men worked for Mannborg when he established his first factory. Hofberg broke away in 1891 and set up his own factory in Leipzig, where he made harmoniums and organettes. Hofberg died in 1919 and the business was operated by his heirs until 1930 when it was sold to Lindholm.

In 1894 when Mannborg moved to Leipzig, Olaf Lindholm stayed behind in Borna and established his own factory. Lindholm retired in 1911[1] and sold his factory to Gustav Weischet, who ran a successful retail music business in the Rhineland.

Weischet operated the business under the Lindholm name, and was succeeded by his son Hermann, who in 1952 was succeeded by his son Joachim. Under the Weischet management, Lindholm acquired Hofberg in 1930 and made organs under both names. During World War II, Lindholm made ammunition boxes for the German army, and after the war he made furniture for a few years. By the late 1940s the reed organ business revived and organ manufacturing was resumed. Despite heavy pressure from the by-then communist government, Lindholm somehow remained under private ownership and even managed in 1961 to buy the Mannborg business from the state-owned VEB Leipziger Pianofortefabrik Böhlitz-Ehrenberg, and in 1969 to buy from the state owned Deutsch Harmonium-Zungen-Fabrik, the reed making machinery it had acquired earlier. Ideology eventually prevailed and in 1972 Lindholm was taken over by the government monopoly, which had been renamed VEB Deutsche Piano-Union Bölitz-Ehrenberg. Reed organ manufacturing was discontinued and the machinery moved or broken up. The original factory building still exists at the time of this writing; and since the fall of the communist government the last private owner, Joachim Weischet, has recovered ownership and turned it into a harmonium museum.

One of the earliest reed organ makers in Austria was Anton Haeckel, who made the four-octave Physharmonika. This instrument was intended to be placed beneath the right side of a piano keyboard and played with the right hand while the left hand played accompaniment on the piano. Jakob Deutschman, who was already doing business in Vienna in 1825, made seraphines and harmoniums at least through 1883. Peter Titz served as an apprentice under Deutschman and in 1852 began making harmoniums under his own name in Vienna. His business was highly successful, and after his death it was taken over by and renamed for his son-in-law, Teofil Kotykiewicz (1840-1920). He was succeeded by his son, also named Teofil Kotykiewicz (1880-1971). Kotykiewicz produced a full line of harmoniums, up to an immense three manual and pedal instrument with forty stops.

In the European countries at the height of the reed organ era, the industry presented a more varied pattern than in the Americas. As in the United States and Canada there were a number of European mass production instrument makers, but in addition there also existed numerous small shops, employing only a few people, which more or less hand-built a few instruments, often to special order. Many of these shops made both pipe and reed organs, and often the more complex assemblies such as reed pans, keyboards, and stop boards were purchased from others and assembled into complete instruments. In many of the European countries both pressure and suction instruments were being made in large quantities, while American production dealt exclusively with suction instruments, with a few minor exceptions.

Probably nowhere was the European pattern of reed organ production more striking than in Britain. In London alone over two hundred reed organ makers have been identified. Some of them were large enterprises such as Barnet, Samuel & Sons and R. F. Stevens, but most of the British makers were small enterprises like John Holt of Birmingham, and J. W. Sawyer of Leeds. Holt started making reed organs in 1876 and eventually produced American organs, harmoniums, and pianos at his "Pioneer Organ & Piano Works." Holt had two sons, Wallace Groves Holt and John William Holt, and a

daughter, Doris Mary Holt, who all worked for the firm. Wallace left to work for the pipe and reed organ builder Rushworth & Dreaper; and on their father's death in 1932, John William took over the business. Doris looked after the accounts and correspondence, tuned reeds and occasionally helped out in the shop.

The Holt business declined during the 1930s and according to a letter from John William Holt he was operating in the red for the two years prior to the start of the war. Holt survived during the war by doing organ maintenance, tuning, and repair. In 1941 the Admiralty offered him a contract to build 65 folding organs, which he was forced to turn down due to lack of capital. He foresaw an upturn in the reed organ business after the war, but his health deteriorated and he died in 1946. Doris disposed of the business over the next two years. Holt organs are highly regarded, as evidenced from the following letter written

Figure 38: Holt No. 1509 in the music room at "Suncot" in Christchurch, New Zealand; Mrs. Muriel Bradshaw shown seated.

36

in 1945 by Mr. G. Faxon, who was then in the U. S. Army:

"I was most impressed with the excellence of this instrument (a 3mp belonging to Dr. M. P. Conway, organist at Ely Cathedral) and was frankly amazed at the variety of tonal colors and range possible in such a small instrument. May I quite frankly say that I've seen nothing whatsoever in America which would compare with this instrument for studio and practice use, and feel definitely that it is an instrument which would meet any of our needs in school and private studios in the States."[8]

John William Sawyer started building reed organs in 1885 out of his house at 21 Barton View, Beeston, Leeds. His organs were usually built to order for each customer, using the best of materials and careful workmanship. As his reputation became established business started to grow and he built a new shop near the Beeston Railway Station.

Sawyer was especially skillful at reed voicing and on one occasion built a three-manual organ with thirty ranks of reeds. It was said that no two ranks were exactly alike in tone color. In his new residence in front of his workshop he built an immense four-manual and pedal reed organ with sixty stops, standing twelve feet high and occupying floor space seven by seven feet. It was winded by a water motor located in the basement, along with the reservoirs and exhausters. New customers were invited to play this organ, experimenting with the various stops to determine the exact combination to be used on their own new instruments. The Sawyer shop had no electricity; the only machinery consisted of a six-inch treadle saw and a treadle drill. Lumber was cleaned, sawed, and planed to order at a mill, then the joinery was done at the Sawyer shop. The action was built up first,

Figure 39: J. W. Sawyer's Beeston Organ works, Leeds, England.

then the case built around it. J. W. Sawyer died in 1907, aged 38. His brother Percy Alfred Sawyer continued the business until his death in 1952.[9]

After World War II the reed organ still prospered in Europe for a number of years. In England, France, and Germany a number of the old manufacturers resumed production. Some of the Norwegian reed organ manufacturing companies were particularly long-lived, especially those which were family operated. Johann Cornelius Isachsen built his first harmonium in 1852 in his home in Eidesora, Skogn, Norway. He soon began making them for others, and by 1860, he moved the business to Levanger. Petter K. Renbjør joined the firm about 1880 and later married one of Isachsen's daughters. The firm was renamed Isachsen & Renbjør and Petter eventually took over the management. On his death (about 1935) his son Reidar replaced him. Reidar's son Leif succeeded him. Soon after, in 1978, reed organ production was discontinued due to the unavailability of reeds. Over 5,000 harmoniums had been produced. In the mid-1990s, Leif Renbjør was still in business servicing pianos and harmoniums.

Figure 40: The Isachsen & Renbjør workshop, Levanger, Norway, 1905.

One of Isachsen's employees, Iver Torkildsen, studied organ building in Sweden and Germany, then started his own shop in Åsen with his brother Peder under the name Torkildsen Brothers. Peder worked for a time for the Chicago Cottage Organ Co. in Chicago. About 1900 they began building pipe organs, and discontinued reed organ production in 1952. At the time of this writing, Torkildsen Brothers continues as a pipe organ maker.

Ludwig Vestre started making harmoniums in 1885 in Haramsøy, Norway, and his company became one of the most important in the country. Ludvig died about 1937 and his son Hans succeeded him. Hans died in 1955 and his wife Jennie and son Ludvig continued the business. It was incorporated in 1980, but finally went bankrupt in 1982. Vestre's originally made only harmoniums, but later expanded into pipe organs, and built a few pianos between 1947 and 1954.

Bernhard Berntzen organized the Norsk Harmoniumfabrik in Gjøvik, Norway in 1925, moved the factory to Snertingdal in 1925 and made harmoniums until 1976. As

of this writing, the company is still doing business as a pipe organ maker.

Karl Hals trained in piano manufacture in Copenhagen, Hamburg, and Paris from 1842 through 1846, then returned to Norway to work in J. W. Cappelen's piano store in Christiania (now Oslo) as a tuner and repairman. The next year he started making pianos and in 1848 his brother Petter joined him. The business was then named Brødrene Hals (Hals Brothers). Over the years, Karl's three sons, Olav, Thor, and Sigurd joined the business. In 1885 the Hals expanded into the publishing business. Harmonium production was begun in 1886, continuing until 1918, and produced a total of 1,337 instruments. Piano production was discontinued in 1925 when a total of 27,000 pianos had been made. In 1909 the publishing business was renamed Norsk Musikforlag, and in 1930 the Hals family sold its remaining interests in it. Norsk Musikforlag remains Norway's foremost music publisher and dealer in printed music.

Jergen Wright Cappelen started in 1829 as a book dealer located at Kirkeg. 15 in Christiania, Norway. In 1995, the business was still operating at that address as a book publisher and rare book dealer, publishing the authoritative *Cappelens Musikkleksikon*, a musical encyclopedia. Cappelen started selling pianos, and by 1840 had opened a separate piano department, which also sold the Chicago Cottage, Mason & Hamlin, Carpenter, Gregorian, Putnam, Mannborg, and other reed organs. Cappelens manufactured about 500 small upright pianos in the period 1953-59 and may also have made harmoniums.

In 1888 A. N. Östlind and Anton Almquist organized a factory in Arvika,

38

Sweden to manufacture pianos and harmoniums. When the Östlind & Almquist factory closed in 1913, a Norwegian, L. Eriksen, bought the factory and moved it, with machines and employees, to Drammen, Norway. Östlind's brother-in-law, a Mr. Nelson, who had taken a leading position in the Packard Organ Co. of Fort Wayne, Indiana, became the factory superintendent. By the next year they were producing three hundred harmoniums per year. In 1925 the factory was enlarged and new machinery installed.

Sweden had a total of about forty harmonium makers, the largest concentrations being in Stockholm and Kristinehamn. A number of Swedish harmonium makers became established in other countries. Mannborg, Lindholm, and Hofberg settled in Germany as previously mentioned. Peter Colseth started making American organs in Moline, Illinois in 1877 as Peter Colseth & Co. Over the years the name changed to Moline Cabinet Organ Co.; Moline Organ Co.; Moline Organ & Piano Co.; Peterson, Thulin & Co.; and finally, Peterson & Co. from 1899 until at least 1920.

Charles Oscar Hillstrom learned organ building in his native Sweden. After emigrating to the United States he worked for a while as a lumberman, then established a reed organ factory, Hillstrom and Bredshall, in Chicago in 1872. In 1880 Hillstrom moved the business to Chesterton, Indiana where he set up a new factory with his brother, John August Hillstrom, employing a great many Swedish immigrants. An 1893 photograph of workers at the factory pictures the Hillstroms, C. A. Forsberg, C. G. Ryden, Emil Nelson, Charles Holm, Gust Johnson, Eric Lafving, Charles Pearson, Fred Nelson, David Erickson, Nels Alfred Olson, Sven Grans, Albert Forsberg and Ed Sundeen. In 1887 C. O. Hillstrom returned to Sweden for a visit. While there he had an audience with King Oscar II of Sweden, who expressed a desire to see a Hillstrom organ. A special model was made in the factory and sent to the King as a Christmas present.

Finland's harmonium manufacturing was centered in the cities of Kangasala, Tampere, and Lapua. One of the earliest, Kangasalan Urkutehdas (Kangasala's Organ Factory) was begun in 1843 by A. Thulé, who had come to Finland from Sweden. He was followed in the business by his son B. A. Thulé, his grandson M. Tulenheimo, and his great-grandson P. Tulenheimo. The firm continued in operation until 1984, by which time about 10,000 harmoniums had been made. Other harmonium makers in Kangasala were Veljekset Pulkkila (Pulkkila Brothers) and Rautavuori ja Suomen Urkuhuolto.

A. A. Hedén learned organ making in Germany, returning to Tampere, Finland in the 1860s to build harmoniums. He was later joined by his brother J. E. Hedén. In 1928 the firm became Hedén ja Kumpp. Kumpp had previously been a partner in Halonen ja Kumpp, located in Jyväskylässaa. The firm later was renamed Nummelan Harmoonitehdas and finally closed in 1969. Other makers in Tampere were Yrjö Pilvinen, who made both pianos and harmoniums, and A. J. Tiainen.

In later years Lapua became the largest harmonium making center in Finland. Juho Saarimaa and Elias Sillanpää made the first harmonium there. Sillanpää began making harmoniums commercially in 1875, and was followed by his son Vihtoripoika Sillanpää, who continued in business at least until 1916. In 1879 Jussi Aho and Kustaa Niemi founded Jussi Ahon ya Kustaa Niemen Harmoonitehdas. K. W. Perälä began making harmoniums there in 1893 and A. Källmann in 1897.

Figure 41: A Nishikawa organ at the Evangelical Lutheran Church in Hiyoshi, Japan.

Japan was a latecomer to the reed organ business. Christian missionaries who came to Japan during the Meiji restoration brought organs with them, and eventually local artisans began building their own versions. Torakichi Nishikawa established his organ factory in Yokohama in 1885, and was regarded as the best of the Japanese reed organ makers. Nishikawa organs were sold by Hakubunsha in its main store on the Ginza in Tokyo and by Jujiya.

Torakusu Yamaha, assisted by Kisaburo Kawai, built his first reed organ in Hamamatsu, Japan in 1886 and the next year set up production. The business was formalized in 1888 as Yamaha Hukin Seizosho (Yamaha Organ Manufacturing Company). Torakusu Yamaha remained at the head of the business until his death in 1916. As the business prospered the name changed over the years to reflect the nature of the business. For many years it was known as Nippon Gakki Co. Ltd. (Japanese Musical Instrument Co.), but the business diversified into electronics, motorcycles, and other products and in 1987 was renamed Yamaha Corporation. In Japan Yamaha organs were sold mainly by two dealers, Kyoecki-Shosha in eastern Japan and by S. Miki in western Japan. Yamaha also made organs under other names, such as the Tiger brand made in the factory in Tenryu and sold by Zenon, the Miki brand sold by S. Miki, the Steigerman brand used on some export organs, and others. After Torakichi Nishikawa died in 1920 his business was absorbed by Yamaha, which continued to produce organs under the Nishikawa name until at least 1928. Koichi Kawai, who had been chief engineer at Yamaha, founded Kawai Gakki Kenkyusho (Kawai Musical Instrument Laboratory), in Hamamatsu in 1927 and is still in business as Kawai Gakki Seisakusho Co., Ltd., at the time of this writing.

Figure 42: Prof. Sakao Ito playing his 1932 Yamaha reed organ.

40

The Canadian reed organ industry was similar to that of the United States in that mostly suction instruments were produced in rather large mass production factories. William and Robert Bell began making the "Diploma" melodeon in the upper story of a building on Upper Wyndham Street in Guelph, Ontario in 1864. William Bell assumed management in 1865 and by 1867 they were producing eighty instruments per year. The name W. Bell & Co. was used at least as early as 1871 when a new three story factory was opened on Market Square in Guelph. An English syndicate bought the company in 1888 and changed the name to Bell Organ & Piano Co. By 1906 the factory had a capacity of 6,000 organs per year. Organ production was discontinued in 1928.

W. Doherty & Co. began as Doherty & Menzies, a furniture and musical instrument retailer in Clinton, Ontario in 1868. They made a few reed organs in 1875 and the next year built a small organ shop in which they employed eight men, located in the block bounded by Princess, Raglan and Rattenbury Streets. A second factory building was erected alongside the first in 1879, bringing the production to 100 organs per month. This factory complex burned in 1898 and was replaced by two new buildings on the corner of East and Irwin Streets with a capacity of four hundred organs per month. The changing market was reflected in the changes of name to Doherty Piano & Organ Co. in 1908, and Doherty Piano Co. in 1913. Organ production declined after 1913 but continued at a reduced volume until after World War II. William Doherty retired in 1920 and the company was acquired by Sherlock-Manning Organ Co.

Darley & Robinson was established in Oshawa, Ontario in 1872 by A. M. Darley and William Robinson, with the backing of Jesse Farwell of Detroit, a partner in Simmons & Clough of that city. In a rapid series of management changes it was renamed Darley & Hoskin and then Oshawa Organ & Melodeon Mfg. Co. In 1873 the factory was moved to Bowmanville, Ontario, by then under the management of Darley and O'Hara, and two years later renamed the Dominion Organ Co., with Messrs. Piggott, Russell and Wesley as management. When Mr. Piggott died in 1890 Jesse Farwell again resumed control until it was sold in 1895 to Alexander, Kydd and McConnel. Through Jesse Farwell, Dominion maintained close relations with Simmons & Clough, later called Clough & Warren, as indicated by Dominion's use of the Scribner patents on qualifying tubes. The company closed in 1907.

Dennis W. Karn and John M. Miller formed Miller & Karn, also known as the Woodstock Organ Factory, in Woodstock, Ontario in 1867. Karn bought out Miller in 1870 but retained the Miller & Karn name for a few years before changing it to D. W. Karn Co. Ltd. Karn acquired the S. R. Warren & Son factory in Toronto in 1896. In 1909 it was renamed the Karn

Figure 43: Dominion Style 191S.

Figure 44: D. W. Karn & Co., organ and piano factory.

Morris Piano & Organ Co. and in 1924 it was acquired by Sherlock-Manning.

In the Americas, besides the United States and Canada, the only significant producer of reed organs was Brazil. The best of the Brazilian builders was considered to be Bohm, located in Novo Hamburgo, Rio Grande do Sul. Organ production was discontinued in 1984 but Bohm continues making accordions and harmonicas, as of 1995.

There were about fifteen harmonium makers in Russia, concentrated mostly in St. Petersburg; fourteen in Spain centered in Barcelona and Madrid; Czechoslovakia had over thirty; Italy 68; Belgium 53, the largest

concentration being in Brussels; Denmark about fourteen, Estonia five, India seventeen, Hungary twelve, and China three.

ALEXANDER GRAHAM BELL AND THE PARLOR ORGAN

. . . on March 10, 1876, Alexander Graham Bell spoke, and Thomas Watson heard the first complete sentence ever transmitted by the telephone. It was, "Mr. Watson, come here; I want you." . . . On May 10, 1876, Bell read a paper before the American Academy of Arts and Sciences entitled "Researches in Telephony." On that occasion he exhibited a number of pieces of apparatus including membrane telephones, his new ironbox receiver, some circuit-breaking telegraph transmitters and tuned-reed receivers, and his liquid telephone transmitter. He had a wire connecting the hall of the American Academy with his private room in Boston University, which was almost next door, and over this wire he transmitted music from a parlor organ, the reeds of which were arranged to interrupt, in vibrating, an electric circuit. The ironbox receiver was used for listening.

Frederick Leland Rhodes[10]

Figure 45: The troops are mustered for the Civil War at Campus Martius, Detroit, Michigan, May 11, 1861. In the background, right, can be seen the Melodeon Manufactory of Simmons & Whitney, a predecessor of Clough & Warren.

Chapter Two

The Selling of the Reed Organ

Figure 46: Hortense, Georgia, about 1907.

the reed organ in its heyday. In the early days however, life was simpler and slower. The first reed organs were essentially hand-made. As the industrial revolution was then in its early phases, the instruments were fashioned by individual artisans or in small shops with two or three workers using hand tools or foot-powered machinery. The finished organs were sold out of the front of the shop, and publicity was by word of mouth and by means of displays at local fairs. The population was largely rural, and some organ makers found they could greatly increase sales by taking the instruments on the road:

"My mother's going to get a new upright piano," said a little girl to another a few days ago. "Oh, that's nothing," replied the other, "my mother's going to get a divorce." But if she had purchased one of our beautiful Bell Treble Pianos or Organs, for sale at Mackie & Co.'s., she would have led a contented and happy existence, and if she changes her mind, we will discount the money she has invested in the divorce from the price of the instrument. This offer holds good for the public at large.

Mackie & Co., Rochester, NY, ca 1880

Salesmen's blarney, hyperbole and downright fraud all came into use in selling

We suppose it would make some of the Estey agents of today smile—those, we mean, who sell the company's goods in elegant stores in the great cities—could they now see Jacob Estey as he, in those days, started out on the country roads with a load of melodeons or seraphines, making a round trip over into New York or up the west side of the state and back through the Connecticut river towns, selling his instruments for barter—butter, cheese, lumber, peltry, or what not—and reaching home finally with a load which bore little semblance to that with which he started away. The agents may smile, but that was the spirit of Yankee thrift, enterprise, and self-reliance which put the organ business on its feet in the early beginnings and made it ready to grow up to what they see it and are reaping their profit from today

The Vermont Phoenix
Brattleboro, August 19, 1892

The reed organ was obviously the right product at the right price at the right time, always a formula for success. For whatever reasons, the public found the little instruments desirable and demand grew rapidly at the same time as machinery became available to mass produce them and the railroads were built to distribute them. Production in quantity required methods of selling in quantity. Over the years the annual selling trips of Jacob Estey and others like him became the pattern for a network of agents who were hired to spend full time on the road. These sales agents were, many of them, colorful characters and their stories bring back the flavor of the events and times. Hampton L. Story, co-founder in 1868 with Isaac N. Camp of Story & Camp, a large Chicago dealership, writing in the *Indicator,* a Chicago musical trade publication, said:

We were feeling our way then in a great, almost limitless field. There was no such institution as the retail trade in the West in those days. Here in Chicago all the houses were jobbers as well as retailers—that is, we were willing to wholesale when we could, and it was a principal part of our business to establish subagencies through the Western states between Ohio and the Pacific coast. The other jobbing centers besides Chicago were Cincinnati and St. Louis.

Securing reliable agents was a still harder task then than now. Organs—which were everything in the trade, as pianos were far too expensive for any but the wealthy—cost a lot of money even at wholesale, and inexperienced

Figure 47

merchants were cautious about accepting them even on consignment. My own method of working up wholesale trade was to start out on the road with a full line of goods, ship them to a promising town, set them up wherever I could and hold a sale; then after closing out a number of instruments at good prices go around to some druggist or furniture dealer, show him what I had done and get him to take over the remnant of the stock. Then on to another town. . .

Our territory was so wide and its trade possibilities so great that naturally there was no jealousy between us here in Chicago. I never saw a more friendly lot of competitors than the half dozen Chicago jobbers. We used to visit each other, talk over what we had done and consult as to plans. Such confidence would mean business suicide today, but you see each of us had as much business as he could well handle and knew where he could get more any time he wanted it, and there was no incentive to take mean advantage of the tips your competitor dropped.

George Payne Bent was a natural salesman who had his first success in the sewing machine business, but eventually found the manufacture of Crown reed organs to be more to his liking. After he retired, he published a book in 1929 entitled *Four Score and More,* in which he gathered articles by some of his old friends in the music business. The following stories, excerpted from that book, convey the spirit and color of the times in the way that only those great salesmen could. The first one is by George P. Bent himself:

My commercial travelers had many humorous experiences while on the road. For instance, there is the story about Henry B. "Highball" Morgan, one of our travelers at the Kansas City Branch in the early days. We had him equipped with a "Crown" badge, in red, black and gold. One day, on a train near Tucson, Arizona, a gunman entered the car, evidently with the intention of holding up the passengers. When he got along to Mr. Morgan, the badge caught his eye and cowed him. Thinking that he had encountered an officer, he expressed a willingness to give up his gun and desist, promising to be good thereafter. He did desist, but Mr. Morgan did not care to continue wearing our badges. Probably he feared that he might be shot some day by a harder boiled desperado who mistook him for an officer.

Henry C. Turck, our bookkeeper at the Kansas City Branch, won the friendship of a cowboy deputy sheriff from Honeywell, Kansas, close to the line between that State and the Indian Territory (now Oklahoma). This individual's name was Steve, and on one occasion Mr. Turck was able to do him a service by saving him from the clutches of some bunco men who were trying to sell him some wildcat mining stock. Later on, Steve was of great help in collecting one of our difficult accounts.

We had a customer at Wichita who did not pay as he should and who finally undertook to get across the line from Kansas into Indian Territory, where he knew he would be safe from legal process. Mr. Turck wired Steve what was up and asked his help to collect. The customer had gotten together every dollar he could borrow or secure in any other way, and was fleeing with all of the merchandise he had been unable to sell. When Mr. Turck and Steve overtook him, he was only half a mile from the line, and Steve megaphoned him that if he did not stop, he (Steve) would shoot, and showed that he could shoot by letting off a few volleys, striking objects near the fleeing man. He finally surrendered, and after a heart-to-heart talk with Mr. Turck, settled our account in full, in cash, on the spot, whereupon he was allowed to proceed on his way. Later, this man did a large business in Vinita, selling our goods, which he obtained through a Cherokee Indian Chief, of Tahlequah, whose credit with us was high. This chief, by the way, had a daughter who was a very fine organist. We never learned how this chief fared in extending credit to the man in question, who had so nearly given us the slip in the settlement of his account, and would have done so but for the timely assistance given us by Steve.

John Fremont Salyer, writing in *Four Score and More,* recalls his early experiences in the reed organ business:

When we sold the farm in Iowa, I came into possession of a team of horses and a spring wagon; and, moving to Kansas, formed a partnership in 1878,

Figure 48: Estey's delivery wagon, made by the Kirkwood Wagon Company, Elmira, New York.

with my brother, which for eight years was known as SALYER BROS. This brother, Alfred M. Salyer, began teaching school at the age of sixteen and had graduated into agent for Whitney and Holmes organs. I often helped unload and held on to the handles while he "said a few words;" then the father of the girl would "sign here;" and that is how I learned the business.

In 1882 we began to handle exclusively the CROWN organ; and during the three years following, we made over three hundred "satisfied customers," and had the proud satisfaction of never having been beaten once in competition; although we had many a "knock down and drag out, side by each" contest. One thing that held our virtue absolute was that we never left an organ out "on trial," but always lived up to the motto "sell or take;" and two other things—not the least— were the merit of the CROWN organ and the superior brand of salesman-

ship that we all carried with us. Sometimes we were compelled to "double up;" in which case there was but one answer: "CROWN on top." It was quite the fashion in those days for near agents to place an organ "on trial." Whenever we could hear of such a case, we were there and had the money before the agent could muster nerve to go back to see the prospect.

OUR OFFICE ON OUR WAGON AND OUR WAGON ON THE ROAD

Many agents had their office
    in a store six stories tall;
But we only had an office
    and not any store at all;
Yet we sold a lot of organs
    without any fixed abode,
With our office on our wagon
    and our wagon on the road.

We would drive up to the warehouse
    and would load up back to back
Two Crown organs in the morning
    and then hit the lonely track
For a farmer who had money
    and a girl, and we'd unload
From our office on our wagon,
    from our wagon on the road.

Then we played and sang our heads off;
    and, to be entirely frank,
Our sole intention was to get
    and "shave" his note at bank.
We did not know "psychology applied"
    as a la mode,
When our office was our wagon,
    with our wagon on the road.

Having sold 't was very easy
    to the next place then to go,
Saying: "Mr. Neighbor just has bought
    a fine organ—so and so.
Don't you think your girl should have one?"
    He would buy it, I'll be blowed,
From our office on our wagon,
    from our wagon on the road.

Back we hied to Kansas City,
	buying two more CROWNS from Bent;
And this for years and years and years
	was the bally life we spent.
When we failed to sell, we jested;
	when we sold, we loudly crowed;
When our office was our wagon,
	with our wagon on the road.

		—John Fremont Salyer

At the Kansas City Inter-state Fair in 1883, we exhibited a line of CROWN organs and won the first prize. During this period there was in Kansas City a splendid wholesale branch of the CROWN ORGAN under the able management of Weston Wingate, a brother-in-law of Geo. P. Bent, and a very fine man physically and mentally. We used to back our wagons up at the wholesale house, pay cash for an organ and disappear until we had sold, discounted the note and had the money to pay for another organ.

Yes sir! We paid cash; but this was the way we did it. We went to a country bank and arranged to sell the prospective customer's note, then went to him and got it! yes, and there wasn't a neighborhood from Salina, Kansas, to Warrensburg, Missouri, in which we did not sell a CROWN, and in which we could not go and stay over night with a welcome. The only charge they made was a "charge to come again." They considered our music—we both sang and played—as more than compensation.

Our old friend, Van Ness, who sold organs in Iowa and Kansas for fifty years and who started us on the same downward path, told the following story:

'No, No! Nobody ever charges me for staying over night. My friends are always glad to have me come for my music. I always ask in the morning, "How much do you charge me for stay-ing over night?" and the only charge they make is to charge me to come again, ha! ha! ha! The only man who ever did otherwise said: "Well, Mr. Van Ness, about a dollar, I guess," and I said to him, with a laugh, "Well, well! isn't that strange! one of the most curious things I ever heard of! It just come out EVEN. That's just what I charge you for my music." And now that is one place where I am always welcome.'

Brother and I made a three-cornered partnership with a man named Harmon, who was a local agent at Wamego, Kansas; and we moved down there and rented a building on the main street, using the down stairs for a store room. We thought this arrangement would be a benefit, as Mr. Harmon had a large acquaintance, was a good salesman and had a beautiful span of black horses which attracted a great deal of attention. We soon discovered that he was having some—I should say quite some—marital troubles, and had even threatened to "shuffle off this mortal coil." Soon after this I graduated onto my own wagon and sold my first organ alone, a little single reed Mason and Hamlin, on the day I was sixteen years old. My customer, as part of the first payment was to kill, dress, and deliver a mammoth hog on the following Saturday.

On Friday we learned that Harmon had sold his horses to a deliveryman, but neither he nor his wife could be located. Saturday came, but no hog, dressed or undressed, was delivered as promised; and I began to think that my virgin sale was still to be made. Sunday evening, just after dusk, my brother and I returned from a drive; and when he tried to unlock the door to the salesroom, in some way or other the key wouldn't work; so he clambered through the window, struck a match—those were the days of kerosene lamps—and we heard him exclaim, as he backed out of the window: "I guess I want to get out of here."

By this time, I, being the brave one, had rushed up and reinforced him, asking, "WHA-wha-what's the mat-matter, Al?" He said: "There's something in there! I touched it! and it's cold and stiff and covered with a sheet! My God! Poor Harmon!"

With great trepidation, together, hand in hand, we encouraged each other into the dark room, and after several badly scratched matches, we found—belly up and feet distended, holding the white sheet high aloft, not Harmon, but hog!—just a plain dressed hog amidst the harmony of the silent CROWN organs. My first customer had delivered his hog; and Harmon was not dead! What a relief to both of us! a relief to my brother Harmon was not dead—"No, no, not dead;" and to me that I had my first payment on my first sale. I want

to say, right here, that Brother Al never could eat of that hog. He always thought it might have been Harmon.

As it turned out, Harmon did not commit suicide, but, instead, skipped the country, and I never did hear of his death. I hope that if he is still alive and reads this, he will communicate with me.

There were more things and different in Bleeding Kansas in 1878 than you can find there now. "What's the matter with Kansas" had not then been propounded. One day in early Spring, after the Hog and Harmon hoax, Brother Al loaded up two organs, back to back, on his platform spring wagon, as usual. He took our eldest brother, Dan, with him and started west to explore. One organ was sold at Abilene and the other at Salina. This was the far west then and there was public land to be "taken up" in Ness County. These lands were what

Williams Bros'. Organ and Sewing Machine Cart.

Above cut shows Cart with all coverings removed with Adjustable Seat moved forward in practicle use. **You want it. You can't get along without it** Price, $38.00. **WILLIAMS BROS., De Soto, Mo.**

Figure 49

48

were called Timber Claims. Not that there was any timber there; but the big idea was that you were to put it there. Al was something of a "taker up" in those days; and, feeling flush with the proceeds of two cash sales, he decided to take up three claims, one each for Dan, himself and "little Willis."

But, before doing this, the thriving town of Salina looked so good to him that he rented a store and telegraphed E. B. Guild of Topeka to ship a stock of small goods and sheet music up there at once. You see business was humming.

Then, as he heard there were many buffaloes in Ness County, he got a rifle and he and Dan started out with the organ wagon to go "on location." They found and filed the claims and started back without seeing anything of "The Thundering Herd;" but, about twenty miles of the return trip was made, upon mounting a rise of the rolling prairie, of Joy! There were the buffaloes, and half dozen of them, off to the south. It must have been a sight to see that platform spring wagon hump itself over the horses, mane and tail flying, galloping in pursuit, while one of the boys held a gleaming rifle ready to gleam if only they could get close enough.

However, that wasn't just the way to hunt buffalo, and soon the animals were over the rise, out of view. On gaining the next ridge, it became apparent that one cow and calf were slowing up. Then the calf fell and the mother went on. Well, anyhow, they got their buffalo, and, tenderly lifting the very young calf out of a "buffalo wallow," they put it under the organ covers and started for home. Horses were pretty well spent, not used to buffaloing, not used to galloping, not used to dragging an organ wagon over trackless prairie; but, What Ho!—I mean "Giddap"—for here came the mother buffalo looking for little buffalo bill—I mean bull. Now the boys didn't want any more buffalo; weren't

looking for buffalo; in fact they were buffaloed and wanted to go to Salina "and be quick about it, too."

But why all this hurry and distress? All the old cow wanted was what belonged to her. Should they lighten ship by throwing out the ballast?—I mean buffalo?—Never! Perish the thought. But what's to do? Ah! Safe at last! The one who could look back told the one who was looking forward that when the buffalo cow got to the buffalo wallow where the buffalo bull calf had fallen she had stopped! Lost the scent! So, "Alone at Last," the boys slowed up and congratulated themselves that there were no lives lost, neither buffalo, horses nor men. They had a buffalo and not a shot was fired!

Reaching Salina, the small goods and some organs having arrived from Topeka, a young girl music teacher was hired and put in charge of the new store. Dan was left to sell the organs and Al took the train back to Wamego to inform me of what WE had been doing.

He took the buffalo calf to the express office, but the rate appeared exorbitant and prohibitive; so he invested in the largest gunny sack he could find and placed "Billy" in it. When the east-bound train came along, he clambered into the smoker and dumped the sacked calf on the floor at his feet. Mr. Conductor came along, took tickets and passed on unsuspecting. Abilene. Junction City, Manhattan, were passed in quick succession. Al grew so confident that he let a few of the passengers into the secret, and when the conductor was elsewhere, they were allowed to come and view the buffalo calf. The conductor never knew he had carried live stock, and Al brought his gunny sack off the car in triumph.

We put a bell on Billy and he followed us just like a dog, up and down the one street of Wamego, even up and down stairs, much to the astonishment and delight of the Wamegans. We fed him on milk and he grew amazingly. About two months later, he disappeared. We found him, after three weeks hunt, tied up in the river bottom, nearly starved to death and eaten by fleas until nearly skin and bone. Some one had stolen him and some one told us—for a consideration—how to find him.

We then put him in a fenced pasture with a lot of young cattle and he had a glorious time all that summer and fall. When we visited him, he knew us, for a few months; but gradually lost his affection and became so wild that we could not manage him; so we sold him to Mr. Blood (not Captain Blood), who had a sort of menagerie in connection with his Cottage Hotel at Manhattan. Three years after, when we visited Billy, he was a regular fierce buffalo fellow and had to be kept tied in a stall.

And this is the story of how we came to have a store in Salina. How we came to discontinue it is another story.

THE TAIL OF A HORSE

When I sell a horse, I'll buy one,
And not a day before;
So it's no damn use to press me;
If you do you'll make me sore.
And I don't know when I'll sell one,
I've a plenty, as you see,
But I got to have my own price,
When they get a horse from me.
So wait until I sell one
And I'll buy a Crown of you;
But I'll sign a note at six months
Which must then be paid when due.
"That is fair enough," we told him,
We will let the organ stay.
Just sign this note, which reads like this:
"When I sell a horse, I'll pay."

He signed and time went on apace.
We saw the son of a gun,
But every time the answer was:
"I've never sold a one."

And whether he had or hadn't,
Or whether he ever did,
Was more than we could ever find out.
If so, he kept it hid.
Six months or more we waited;
Then, backing up our truck,
We got our organ back again
And thought ourselves in luck.
But we learned "time is the essence
Of a contract."—Dirty cuss!—
It was horse and horse for six months,
Then he had a "horse on us."
                    —John Fremont Salyer

The "trade-ins" which have been such a worry and problem of late were nonexistent in those early days for there were but few old organs in the West, and those who had them would not part with them. However, we did have trades—lots of trades—trade for hogs, cattle, horses, corn—anything to induce the father (who was always the one to convince) to buy an organ. I remember one German at Alma, Kansas, who said he could not afford to buy an organ, although he was reputed well off. I could not get him to pay cash, nor to give me his note. In desperation, I said, "trade me a horse." "No, I couldn't spare vun." "Trade me a cow." "No, I need all of de fresh vuns, and I vouldn't part mit vun until she vas fresh." "Well," I said, "trade me something. You know what you have, and I don't. You've certainly got something you would part with. Come now." "Vell," said he, "I'll tell you vat I vill do. I vill trade you my debts."

Always it was a struggle between the girl and her father. Some girls wept, some girls teased, but all girls wanted an organ. The best helper we ever had was a little ten year old Swede girl at Lindsborg, Kansas. She did not say much, but she said it often. Every chance she got, she would sidle up to the old man, and putting her hands on his arm, would say, "Pa, git it!" "Pa, git it!" As the scotch golfer says: "after a purity considerable struggle," Pa—got it.

Every one of you knew Billy Roberts, (W. B. Roberts), Kimball's famous agent at Kansas City. He was a shrewd salesman, both wholesale and retail. We bought a few Kimball organs from time to time from him, to fill out. One day I found down at Grain Valley, a few miles west of Kansas City, a Kimball organ placed out "on trial," and, with my usual ability—for taking advantage of the other fellow when he wasn't around—I placed my CROWN organ by the side of the Kimball and demonstrated the superiority of the CROWN sufficiently to get the lady's money. She said she had room for only one organ; so I told her that I would take the Kimball and store it at the Grain Valley Hotel and notify the Kimball Company that she had found one she liked better and bought that.

I took the Kimball to the hotel, put it in the parlor, and stayed over night. The landlord wanted me to play and sing, which I did. He said he wanted to buy an organ and asked how much the

Kimball was worth. I told him they had asked Mrs. Jones one hundred dollars for it; but I could sell him one which was a deal sight better—like the one Mrs. Jones had just bought—for the same money. Of course I blowed a whole lot about having licked this organ side by side with a CROWN at Mrs. Jones' that very day.

"Well," he said, "this Kimball organ is good enough for me; in fact, I like it; and if you only had the agency, I'd buy it from you." "Well," said I, "don't you worry one bit about that. Of course you know it is a fine organ and well worth the money; and, if I were the Kimball agent, I couldn't sell it to you for that. But as long as they offered it to Mrs. Jones for a hundred dollars, you can have it at that and I'll sell it to you. I've bought a lot of organs from Billy Roberts and I'll settle with him." And, by Gosh! that hotel man up and paid me for the organ.

Next day, after a thoughtful night, I drove my Texas ponies pretty fast into Kansas City and called on W. B. Roberts. I explained to him that his agent who left one of his Style 402 at Mrs. Jones' house near Grain Valley, was not a very good salesman; as he left it too long and I found it waiting to be licked and had licked it. I told him I had moved the Kimball to the hotel and that I could sell it to the hotel man; so, if he wanted to wholesale it to me, I'd save him and his agent the expense of bringing it back. Otherwise, I would sell my friend a CROWN organ.

Billy was shrewd as they make them; so he said; "Well, if you can sell my organ to the hotel man, I guess I ought to be able to sell it to him myself." I said: "No, Mr. Roberts, you can't do that. He is a friend of mine and will take the organ I want

Figure 50: Mr. & Mrs. David Hilton and children in rural Custer County, Nebraska, with their proudest possessions.

him to take." He said: "Not if I could see him first." "Well, my team is ready to make the return trip, and I'll take a CROWN organ down and you can come along if you like." Billy was quite hard of hearing, as you know; but he heard that and said: "Well, Salyer, that's all right. I was only joking you; but wouldn't it be a good idea next time not to sell my organ before you buy it? Here, Bookkeeper, make out a bill to Salyer Brothers on that organ at Grain Valley, and collect it now."

Driving over the prairies of Kansas in winter time, with a blizzard raging is one of the most uncomfortable outdoor sports invented. One terrible afternoon, I remember, Brother and I lost our way, and night—as it will—came on. We were apparently miles from nowhere. We got off the road in the darkness and were afraid to go farther for fear of tipping over the organ. We stopped and I climbed out and got back of the organ, out of the wind; and, after several attempts, lighted a match and held it over my head. "What are you doing, Fremont?" said Al. "Trying to get a light so I can see a house," was my innocent reply. I forget whether we froze to death that night or not.

In 1884 there lived at Greenwood, Missouri a venerable clergyman who was, I think, related to the poet Longfellow. At least, that was his name; and he had a charming daughter who very much wanted the organ I had in his house and was trying to sell to him. He had the cash to buy; but, as I wanted a hundred and twenty-five dollars, he would not make the deal. I said: "Mr. Longfellow, that is my price; but, as you are a minister, I am willing to make a concession. But what is the use of my offering to take less, unless you will accept? I would only be cheapening my goods without getting the deal. To be frank with you, I will say this: for the good it will do me—your influence in helping me to make other sales—make me an offer cash; and (I know what it costs me.) if it is above costs, I promise to accept it; and, if it is not, I will not say another word, but will load up and go." It was near midnight and I had my organ wagon outside as a gesture to close the deal.

"Now, Mr. Salyer," said he, "I shall not make you an offer; no, I shall not make you an offer; but, if you will say the lowest figure you will take, I will take it, if it suits me; but I will not make you an offer." "Well," said I, "it looks like we don't do business, for I certainly don't want to cut my price and then not get the deal. But I'll try it this way, Mr. Longfellow. I am going to come down until you say yes and, if it is enough, I will take it. So: Will you give me a hundred and ten dollars for this organ?" A prompt response "No." "Will you give me a hundred dollars?" Another no. "Will you give me ninety-five dollars, Mr. Longfellow?" Not so prompt a reply, but an emphatic NO. He had got his breath again. "Will you give me ninety dollars?" A faint "No." "Will you give me—will you take it, Mr. Longfellow, if I will sell it to you for eighty-five dollars?" Quick as the flash came the answer: "No; but I'll tell you what I will do, Mr. Salyer; I'll give you seventy-five dollars, cash."

I am wondering yet how I had the nerve to do it; but it made me angry, and I grabbed the end of the organ and started for the door. "Now, Mr. Longfellow, you said you would not make me an offer, and you have done it! It's at less than cost (I'm afraid I said this) and I will not take it." He rose to his full six feet and a quarter, his grey mane shaking with rage and his voice trembling with emotion.

"Mr. Salyer, you have tricked me into doing what I said I did not want to do. You have made me, a minister of the Gospel, disgrace myself by not keeping my word, so take your organ and yourself out of my house. I am ashamed of you—and of myself."

My salesmanship returned at this instant and I dropped my head and my hold on the organ. "I beg your pardon, Mr. Longfellow; but I am a very young man and you are too old, I know, to cut off your nose to spite your face. The harm has already been done to the price of my organ and I get no benefit from your good will, etc. I can't afford to take even eighty-five dollars; but, let's forget what has passed and I will take—I will take, if you promise never to tell others, who must pay a hundred and twenty-five dollars—I will let you have it for eighty." "Here is my hand, Mr. Salyer; and I will write you a check. I feel that we were both hasty." He was ever after one of my most devoted friends.

Along about this time, quite by accident, Brother and I, having left Kansas City by different routes, met near Independence. We had each sold two organs and I remember how we sharpened our pencils and used up all our blank notes in figuring out an Inventory of "Present worth." This is usually done by merchants once a year; but I think it was our first one. As there were not many items, it did not take us over an hour to do it; but I feel sure it gave us more satisfaction at the time to find that it footed some hundreds of dollars than any balance sheet we have ever had since. "Youth must be served" and we were young and hopeful in the early eighties.

We all have our peculiarities and the organ customers had fifty-seven kinds. The oldest one we met was a nice old fellow who had but one sentence in his vocabulary, so far as we could discover. To all and sundry advances we made, his sole reply was: "It don't suit me."

"We will sell it to you on time, if that would induce you to buy." "It don't suit me." Whether it was the organ, the price,

terms or idea that he referred to, we never knew. We didn't sell him an organ; and the last word I remember hearing from him was, "It don't suit me."

—John Fremont Salyer

Some of William Bates Price's recollections of the reed organ business also appeared in *Four Score and More:*

We moved to Sweetwater, Tenn., just at the close of the Civil War, and I was started to "taking" music lessons from Mrs. Helen M. Cooke. I was her only boy, also the youngest (aged 9) in her big class of some twenty-five pupils. Took many of my lessons before daylight, by candle-light—only time she had to spare.

Father bought me a Needham & Sons organ. In about three months I wrote Needham Organ Company I would "graduate" in music in a year. Charles H. Parsons sent me a piece of music and wrote congratulating me, saying "no one else in the world had ever graduated in music even after studying an entire lifetime." After awhile, one of the soft-toned reed notes of this Needham Organ sounded gently all the time I pumped the organ, regardless of whether I touched that particular key, or not. I wrote Mr. Parsons there was something wrong with his celebrated Needham & Sons organ, and he wrote back, "Oh no, there's nothing wrong about the organ; that's simply a delightful Aeolian murmur". Charles H. was a humorist, you see, as a very young man. I didn't know then it would last throughout life and keep him young and blythe all along the way "even unto now."

Well, my family moved again, to San Francisco, where I got a job in Philip Werlein II's piano store, 1212 Market Street, dusting off old-fashioned square Dunham & Sons pianos.

After awhile we moved back to Knoxville, Tenn., where I got another job in W. F. Cummins' Music Store, selling W. B. Tremaine's hand-grinding "Sweet By and By" Organettes, when they first came out. At that time little did Mr. Tremaine dream of the evolution of the organette into magnificent reproducing pianos (electrically operated) of today. All honor to him!

Gilbert Smith 'n me were competitors at retail down in Georgia—the land of goobers, cornfield peas and sweet potato yams—and later on we were competitors at wholesale, he traveling for W. W. Kimball Co., and I for Farrand & Votey Organ Company. Bob Howard came South in his "whole section" Pullman, representing J. & C. Fischer, and showed up at Phillips & Crew's Atlanta store with an immaculate stovepipe silk hat, so when Gilbert and I got jobs at wholesale, we emulated Bob and stole his silk hat idea, and that's the way we traveled together all over the South, in silk hats (not altogether), a bit ruffled when arriving at New Orleans or other places, 'tis true, but we ironed 'em out and showed up at our dealers' stores smiling just like "the cat that ate the canary." Yes indeed, Gilbert and I were competitors, first at retail and later on at wholesale, but in all those years we never had a cross word, except twice. The first when I found out he had been distributing his photographs to all the girls around Jug Tavern, Ga., for the young ladies to first embrace, then carefully place in their plush-covered albums; and second, when his Kimball organ had been sold for cash and my Farrand & Votey had only taken the "Blue Ribbon."

And now I recall Mr. W. W. Kimball, whom all the old-timers remember so pleasantly.

He had a delicious sense of humor too, and always an encouraging word to the beginner in business. Seemed at times he could tear the veil off the future, possessing remarkable vision and business acumen. A good, good friend.

There also was Mr. Edwin S. Conway. My! what a mountain of energy he was! I never came in contact with him without, upon parting, feeling that I had received a big charge of optimistic electricity. He was full of it, gave freely of it, and was instrumental in helping many a poor soul along life's rocky road.

Another human dynamo who fairly breathed business steam as he walked along Wabash Avenue, was Mr. H. D. Cable, founder of the Cable Company. Ah! there was a man whose business ambition knew no bounds. I had the good fortune to be associated with him several years. In that time nothing seemed too big for him to tackle and I never went to him with an expansion idea but what he was in for it, if plausible. He was a prince.

Figure 51: A load of Estey organs on the way to the railroad station.

Let us not pass by Mr. P. J. Healy. How often have I seen him with his soft hat jauntily tilted to the left side of his head, sauntering down Wabash Avenue to lunch. It usually was with "the piano crowd," in the basement of the old Wellington Hotel, and over a bottle of "Cresta Blanca" or "Clicquot." What fun he would have with Mr. George P. Bent about his celebrated "Combinola" piano attachment, which however "lest we forget," made by the aid of "the grace of God" and George P's energetic brain and indefatigability, amassed him a fortune.

. . . Granville Wood, now over 90, I believe, and living in Detroit with his daughter, was one of the first builders of Harmoniums in this country. He it was who made the reeds for the first harmonium out of a brass tea kettle his aunt let him have for that purpose because, being a shoemaker by trade, he didn't have enough money to buy that much brass.

Adam Schneider, writing in *Four Score and More,* reminisces about the music business in Chicago in the 1870s:

Business methods were different in the early days. . . . There was no such thing as large alluring advertisements reaching thousands of people and bringing them into a luxurious store. The successful man was the one who was willing to load a piano or an organ on a wagon, drive into the country, unload his piano or organ at some farm house, and play and demonstrate it in the hope of making a sale. It was literally a matter of going into the highways and the byways and compelling them to buy. In most cases, a piano or organ left in the parlor of a home meant eventually a sale. Such a plan necessitated, of course, being away for a day or two, and in many cases sleeping at the farm house where the piano or organ had been left. One such

incident I remember distinctly; as a younger man I was active as a singer, being a member of a quartette and of several musical societies. One time I had an organ shipped to Barrington, Illinois. At Barrington I got an expressman to take the organ out to a farm house. When we arrived at the house there was no one there…the farmer and his wife and children were out in the fields working. I had the expressman help me carry the organ into the parlor. Then I sent him away and waited. I could see across the fields, and after some time I saw the farmer and his family coming towards the house. I started to sing and play such

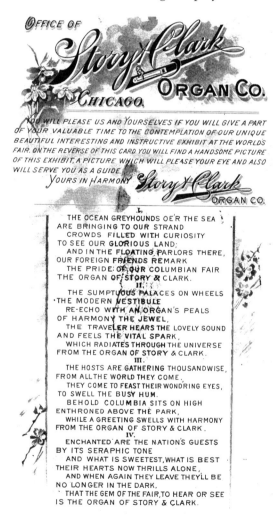

Figure 52

hymns as "Lead Kindly Light" and "Jesus Lover of My Soul," because in those days most farmers were religious and any of the old time hymns were sure to please. I kept playing and singing until they came in and sat down. When I had finished they were convinced that they needed a musical instrument. That evening I told them to invite some of their friends and we would have a musical evening. They did so and it was very successful. Before we retired the farmer's wife was very anxious to have her husband close the deal as she felt they could not afford to let the organ go. The daughter was somewhat of a musician and that helped to put the sale over.

R. K. Maynard remembers the old days in Chicago, in *Four Score and More:*

Away back when Geo. P. Bent was selling Crown Sewing Machines and Billy Bush was on the road for the Woods Organ Co., a young farmer from Wisconsin came to Chicago, and Deacon I. N. Camp of the old and well known firm of Story & Camp, 188-190 State St., gave him a job as City Collector. The young farmer's aunt advised him to be very careful not to go near the cattle pens at the Stock-Yards as those cattle were so hungry for something green they might lick him through the fence and eat him.

Mr. H. L. Story returned from a trip to California in the spring of '82 with an order for a full car load of Estey Organs to be shipped to Daynes & Coalter at Salt Lake City, Utah. When Deacon Camp saw that order he exclaimed, "Story, are you crazy? You must be to ship 60 organs all at once way out to Salt Lake City." Mr. Story calmly replied, "No, I'm not crazy, but I would have been if Ed & Wise or Conway had beat me to that order." Another time Mr. Story returned from a fishing trip and straightaway began to study the Order Book. Deacon Camp said, "Story, I notice when you come back to town the first thing you do is look at the Order Book—you never look at the Cash Book." Mr. Story replied, "No, of course I don't look at the Cash Book—there is no need of my looking at the Cash Book, that is all you do, Deacon."

In 1884, when Mr. Story decided to take up residence in California, Story & Camp dissolved partnership and Mr. Story with Melville Clark formed the firm of Story & Clark and the Estey Organ Co. with Mr. Camp formed the firm of Estey & Camp which was discontinued soon after the death of Deacon Camp in

STORY & CLARK ORGAN CO., Chicago—London.

CLUETT & SONS, 49 State St, Albany, & 265 River St. Troy, N.Y.

Figure 53

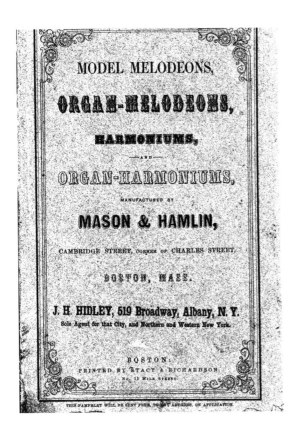

Figure 54: Mason & Hamlin published this catalog in 1856, in its first year of operation.

1896. The Esteys took over the St. Louis business and the Camp boys the Chicago business which was sold to W. W. Kimball Co. in October 1898. When Mr. Story left to live in California in 1884 Mr. Camp predicted we would be buying flowers and slow music for him in two years. Mr. Camp died in July 1896 and Mr. Story lived until October 1926.

CATALOGS

Most of the potential customers in the rural areas were unable to travel to the cities to see the various models of organs on display there, so the larger manufacturers published catalogs which illustrated and described their wares. In addition to carrying one or two organs on their wagons for demonstration, the sales agents handed out these catalogs, which served as a reminder to hesitant buyers. Magazine advertisements also offered free catalogs. The catalog became one of the standard tools for selling organs, and remained so to the end of the reed organ era.

One of the standard features of these catalogs was the testimonial, then as now highly regarded as a selling technique. Henry Mason and Emmons Hamlin founded their new organ manufacturing enterprise in 1854, and for their first catalog, dated 1856, they received strong testimonial support from the family:

> After having carefully examined the Melodeons of Messrs. Mason & Hamlin, I am enabled to say, that, in my opinion, they are decidedly superior to any others with which I am acquainted.
> New York, July 1, 1854
> Lowell Mason

> Having thoroughly examined your Melodeons, I am of the opinion that they are unexcelled—if, indeed, they are equalled—by those of any other maker. They are distinguished from all I have seen by their extreme fullness, yet mellowness of tone, and quick response to the touch of the performer. I recommend them as embracing all the essentials of a superior instrument.
> Boston, August 24, 1854
> L. W. Mason

> Having examined the Organ-Harmoniums made by Messrs. Mason & Hamlin, of Boston, I am enabled to say that I consider them by far the best and pleasantest toned reed instruments which I have ever seen. Before examining them, I had supposed it impossible to construct a reed instrument combining so many organ effects, such as power, variety of tone, expression, solos, etc.
> New York, May 27, 1855
> William Mason

57

As their business prospered they were able to obtain testimonial letters from the most celebrated musicians of the day:

The fame of the Mason & Hamlin Cabinet Organs is not confined to America; these excellent instruments are widely known in Europe, and in my opinion they deserve the warm expressions of praise which have been bestowed upon them. I know of no similar instruments anywhere, at all comparable to them.

Johann Strauss

Allow me, in thanking you for the organ which you have placed at my disposal for my series of concerts, to express my very favorable opinion on the charm of this instrument, the tones of which, both delicate and full, combine so well with the voice. I do not doubt that the Mason & Hamlin American Organ will be of excellent and valuable use in all vocal or instrumental combinations of moderate limits.

Ch. Gounod

What a magnificent [Mason & Hamlin] organ for which I have to thank you! It is a marvel, and truly praiseworthy! Even players of moderate ability will be able to create much admiration in its use.

Weimar, Germany, June 12, 1883
F. Liszt

Judging by the number of copies which have survived, Estey probably distributed more catalogs than all the other makers together. Not to be outdone, they also included testimonials from famous musicians as well as from missionaries and diplomats in far-off places:

The tone of the Estey Organs is very beautiful and noble, and gives me the greatest pleasure. My great friend Franz Liszt is also charmed and delighted with them.

Richard Wagner

I have played upon the Organs of Messrs. Estey & Co. and have been charmed with their quality of tone, which comes very near that of a Pipe Organ, and the resources it gives to the player.

Paris
Camille de Saint Saens

It gives me great pleasure to give due praise to Messieurs J. Estey & Co. for their really splendid Organs. The tone of these instruments is full, noble and charming, and has the advantage of pleasing and captivating the ear. To these artistic qualities must be added that they are of solid workmanship and of the most elegant finish, and I doubt not their having an extraordinary success in Russia.

St. Petersburg
Rubinstein

Figure 55: Estey catalogs from 1866 to the 1950s.

I am at my station; have set up and use daily in my family, and Sabbath days in my chapel, the Harmonium I bought of you last October. It answers all my expectation, and adds greatly to the pleasure of our singing. My Harmonium is highly praised by all who see it.

Umvoti Station
Port Natal, South Africa
Rev. A. Grout
Missionary of the A.B.C.F.M.
May 12, 1859

When I received your style JJ (portable) folding organ, it was on a little mission station in the heart of Africa, sixteen hundred miles from the nearest large town, thirteen days from the doctor and seventy-two miles from our nearest missionary neighbors at Dungu. The porters who came in with it said that the canoe had upset while crossing the last river and that my organ had floated around for ten or fifteen minutes.

It was necessary to take your organ all to pieces and dry it in the sun, piece by piece, for it was so swollen with the dampness that it was useless. Having a little knowledge of mechanics I did what I afterward tried to do with other makes of folding organs. In the case of the Estey, it was very easily repaired. With the others it was impossible to repair them, as the action was sealed and glued with no means left of getting at it for repairs."

Washington, New Jersey
March 11, 1921
Joseph W. Johnson

The Organ arrived here safely by the barque Jasper, from New York. It came in excellent condition, and is by far the best Organ ever sent here. It was evidently not sent on the principle to send an inferior instrument 5,000 miles away, and to real or supposed ignoramuses, rather than to customers nearer home.

Liberia College, Monrovia
M. H. Freeman, President

For some years my wife used at Marash, Turkey, an Estey Organ. It was considered by all competent judges the best instrument in Central Turkey. Will you please send me now another instrument of about the same compass, well packed for a long and rough journey?

Rev. T.C. Trowbridge

Mr. Parmelee, of Erzroom, took our Estey Organ out with him twelve years ago. After his return to America we sent to Trebiz for it. It was brought again over the mountains, six hundred miles on horseback, and was seven months reaching Oroomiah. But with all this rough treatment, and subsequent constant use it has kept in perfect tune—not a reed has failed—and no part has ever needed repairs—save only the pedal carpets and straps, although our climate is a very dry and trying one to cabinet work.

Oroomiah, Persia
Rev. G. W. Coan

[Clough & Warren Organ Co.'s] Combination Style F came through in extra time (a distance of nearly 5,000 miles) and in perfect order I may say, for not a scratch or blemish is to be seen. Now I can say to you that 'F' is the finest instrument in Washington Territory. It stands in my parlor, not only as a beautiful instrument, but a true specimen of the mechanical skill of the manufacturers, and I can assure you that all who get their eyes on 'F' exclaim, 'What a beautiful instrument,' and more that I cannot write. My parlor carpet suffers from the many feet of those who daily congregate to see it and hear it played.

Walla Walla, April 26, 1873
Wm. H. Andrews

My [Cornish] organ compares more than favorably with other instruments in this neighborhood costing $50 more. I can recommend your goods as being all and more than represented by you; I will recommend your company as being entirely reliable, kind, courteous in all its dealings. I would not think of giving my instrument for any I have ever seen, costing twice as much.

Muskogee, Indian Territory
John P. Rupert

The [Clough & Warren] Organ purchased of you in May, 1874, and shipped from New York in July for this port, per sailing ship 'Star of the West,' arrived safely on the afternoon of the first day of last January. Mrs. Hall received it as her New Year's present, and rarely has a gift been received with more gratitude, or one more worthy of gratitude and admiration, than this beautiful Organ. After nearly six months at sea, and eight since leaving the manufactory, it was unpacked here in our distant home in tone perfect, and finish exquisite. Its condition after its travels was wonderful, and can only be accounted for by its careful packing. We had in our friends the same evening to celebrate its arrival, and unite in joy, for such an arrival happens but seldom in this far-off land. The Organ is the admired of all who see it, its beautiful finish and rich tone making it worthy of all praise. An English gentleman, long a resident in China, and a fine musician, said that he believed it is the finest Instrument for home use he had ever seen in China, or out of it. It is to us a source of comfort and joy continually.

Kin Kiang, China, Feb. 25, 1875
Rev. Henry H. Hall

I should never have believed that a tone such as the Cornish Organ possesses was obtainable in an American organ; it is exactly as represented by you, and it gives me infinite pleasure in informing you that it has given me

Figure 56

entire satisfaction. I was asked by a friend of mine what sort of an organ I had, and, on telling him, he said he was wondering who was playing a pipe organ; said that he could hardly believe that such a tone could be obtained from a reed organ.

Port Elizabeth, South Africa
L. F. Monaghan

I have one of your [Cornish] organs style No. 41,000 'Imperial Chimes' with which I am very much pleased. I never saw such an excellent instrument before and I am quite delighted with the tone and many combinations.

Seydisford, Iceland
Halldor Vilhajalmsson

I am much pleased to inform you that the organ, [Cornish] Style No. 41,000, which I purchased from you in October, 1893, is in every way satisfactory, and having given it a good testing I can safely assert that your description of it was in no way exaggerated. After having it in the hot and dry climate of Mhow, Central India, for over 12 months and through the Monsoon it was packed and sent 2,000 miles to Aden (on the Red Sea, notoriously the worst climate on earth) and it was never the worse for its journey or the two years' stay in Aden, and all who heard it admired its perfect tone.

Mhow, India
J. Wharton

The [Cornish] organ came in the best condition and all who have seen and played on it are enchanted. The longer I use my organ, the better I like it.

Opalany, Bohemia
Rev. Fr. Sustr

It gives me great pleasure to state that I have purchased three [Cornish] organs from you, one thirteen years ago, and this is just as good as when I purchased it; I shall always recommend your instruments.

St. Kitts, West Indies
Edwin Hamilton

The [Cornish] organ that I purchased from you some time ago has given the best of satisfaction.

Somerset Bridge, Bermuda
A. Miller

I have often had occasion to play the Estey Organs and can testify with pleasure that they are, for fullness and beauty of tone, as well as for easy, reliable action, the best and most perfect I have ever played on or seen.

Bergen, Norway
Lauritz Grimster
Cathedral Organist

I am surprised at the extraordinary softness, fullness, and beauty of tone.

St. Petersburg, Russia
Ed. Napravnik
Director, Imperial Opera

This is to certify to Messieurs. J. Estey & Co. of Brattleboro, that the Organ furnished by them two years ago, for use in the Grand Ducal Palace, has proven itself exceedingly appropriate in the celebration of religious services, very durable, and not in the least affected by any changes in the temperature.

By the Duke's order
Von Stenglin, Marshall of the Court

I recently had occasion to give my judgment officially on reed instruments, and am confirmed in the opinion then formed that Estey's Cottage Organs are without a superior for 'exceedingly quick articulation and round tone'—the essential features in instruments of this class. I have also critically examined the new Vox Humana Tremolo, and am free to concede to it all the excellence claimed for it. In fact, it is the only Tremolo I have ever heard that is really worthy of the name.

New York
George Jardine, Organ-Builder

TELEGRAPH CODES

The Morse telegraph system was begun in 1844 and grew rapidly so that by 1856 most of the territory east of the Mississippi River, that is, most of the populated area of the United States, was interconnected by wire lines. In this period the reed organ was making the transition from a handmade curiosity to mass-production. The telegraph became the common method of placing orders on the factories, and in order to save expense, as messages were paid by the word, telegraph "codes" were eventually developed and usually included in the catalogs. In 1878 Estey published a code of 31 words, each starting with the letter F, representing the 31 styles of organ then in production. This was obviously not Estey's first

61

code, since the following footnote was appended, "This Code is to take the place of all previous Codes issued by the House."

The words presumably were selected so as not to conflict with those usually used in business communications. Judged by today's standards, sensitized as we are by advertisers to the emotional content of words, the code seems strange. While some words are neutral (*Faculties, Farina, Farmers, Financial*) and some are positive (*Fabled, Fairyland, Faithful, Famous, Fancied*) some are downright negative, such as *Fallen, Fallible, Falsehood,* and *Fanatics,* and would surely not be acceptable today. Later Estey codes added *Disfavor, Dishearten, Exasperate, Fatality, Fatigue, Fatuous, Fatty, Fawning, Flustered, Gloomy, Grasping, Glandular, Holocaust, Hopeless, Idleness, Illusion, Lifeless,* and *Lowly.*

The Dominion Organ Company also had some negative code words (*Arrest, Arsenic, Afire, Afraid, Acid*) but improved on the usefulness of the code by adding two words to abbreviate the most common inquiries: *Damask,* "When Can You Ship?" and *Danube,* "Ship As Soon As Possible." Similarly, D. W. Karn's code included: *France,* "Telegraph when organ will be shipped;" *Fox,* "Write particulars first mail," and *Fish,* "Ship by express." Estey's 1902 code permitted easy specification of the cabinet finish, for example the Style Z56 in walnut was *Zenith,* the same organ in mahogany was *Zephyr* and in oak, *Zealot.* Mason & Hamlin's code was carefully neutral, the nearest to negative words were *Baboon* and *Pagan.* Mustel favored composers' names: *Buxtehude, Scarlatti, Haydn, Haendel, Bach.*

W. W. Kimball had a more complex code in which the second letter of the code word was always a vowel representing the quantity to be shipped; A, E, I, O, U and Y

signifying quantities of 1, 2, 3, 4, 5 and 6 respectively. For example, the code words for Style 112 were *Camping, Cedarwood, Cidermill, Coaxing, Culprit, Cypress*; Style 801, *Danger, Debtor, Dictate, Doctor, Dumping, Dying*; Style 111: *Camp, Cedar, Cider, Coax, Cup, Cyanide.* A telegram worded as follows: "W. W. KIMBALL CO.: SHIP CYPRESS DEBTOR COAX" when translated back to plain English meant, "ship six Style 112, two Style 801, and four Style 111." Apparently if you wanted to order more than six you could afford to spell it out.

Another complex code was that of J. & P. Schiedmayer of Stuttgart, Germany, used to indicate the type of finish as well as the style number. The codes for their Style L158 were: *Loforelo, Lofolone, Lofredo, Lofimos, Lofradis, Lofertos, Lofasos, Lotiroso* which signified respectively: Black, Oak, Walnut, Mahogany, Rosewood, Burr-walnut, Caucasian walnut and African Pear, all in the Style L158.

MEDALS AND AWARDS

The early reed organ makers advertised their wares in the local newspapers, but counted on displays at fairs and exhibitions to reach a wider audience. Abraham Prescott won a silver medal at the New Hampshire State Fair in 1837 for his display of musical instruments and in October of that year displayed his instruments at the annual fair of the American Institute in New York, although apparently failing to win an award. Mason & Hamlin produced their first reed organ in 1855, and in 1856 won awards at nine exhibitions, including a gold medal at the Massachusetts Charitable Mechanic Association Fair in Boston. By 1859 they had received 23 awards including one gold medal. Mason & Hamlin were such

Telegraph and Cable Code

FIVE OCTAVE ORGANS

Style			A 1	E 2	I 3	O 4	U 5	Y 6
111	Wal.	Fin.	Camp	Cedar	Cider	Coax	Cup	Cyanite
112	"	"	Camping	Cedarwood	Cidermill	Coaxing	Culprit	Cypress
801	"	"	Danger	Debtor	Dictate	Doctor	Dumping	Dying
802	"	"	Dancing	Depend	Director	Document	Durable	Dynamite
803	"	"	Dapple	Desperate	Dimple	Dolphin	Duncecap	Dyeshop
151	"	"	Bank	Bend	Binding	Bomb	Butter	Bylow
152	"	"	Banked	Bended	Bindery	Bombast	Busted	Byplay
153	"	"	Banking	Bending	Birdnest	Bonded	Busting	Bying

SIX OCTAVE ORGANS

711	Mah.	Fin.	Dandy	Deaden	Dipping	Donkey	Dunce	Dynasty
712	"	"	Dandruff	Denman	Diploma	Dotage	Dungeon	Dynamic
713	"	"	Dandelion	Denmark	Diplomat	Dotting	Dubious	Dyeing
811	Wal.	"	Garden	Genesis	Gimlet	Gospel	Gumming	Gypsy
812	"	"	Garbed	Gentle	Gilpin	Gong	Gummy	Gypsum
813	"	"	Gamble	Gender	Gilt	Gold	Gumdrop	Gymnast
161	"	"	Handcar	Headache	Hidebound	Hotbed	Hunting	Hypnotist
162	"	"	Handcuff	Heartfelt	Hindmost	Honest	Husband	Hymen
163	"	"	Handling	Heaviest	Hindered	Homely	Humbird	Hymning

SEVEN OCTAVE ORGAN

681	Mah.	Fin.	Famed	Fencing	Finding	Fodder	Fuming	Fydstar

CHAPEL ORGANS

431	Mah.	Fin.	Pain	Pen	Pillow	Power	Punch	Pynacle
432	"	"	Painful	Penman	Pillage	Powerless	Puny	Pynaby
433	"	"	Painless	Penury	Pilgrim	Powerful	Pure	Pynabist
451	"	"	Rake	Rent	Risk	Robin	Rug	Rynack
452	"	"	Rakish	Rented	Risked	Robbing	Running	Rynacker
453	"	"	Raking	Renting	Risking	Robinson	Runner	Rynackist
455	"	"	Radical	Renew	Rickety	Rodent	Rudiment	Rythm
458	"	"	Radish	Renewal	Richard	Rotate	Rule	Rythmic
459	"	"	Rancid	Renewing	Rich	Rotation	Ruling	Rythmical

Key to Code

Ordered as per Code means finish mentioned.

When *oak* is desired, add the word "oak" to code word.

The vowel at the top of each column signifies the number of instruments desired.

The first letter or combination of letters preceding the vowel signifies the particular style case desired.

Examples

W. W. KIMBALL Co.: Ship Cypress, Debtor Oak, Coax.—(Ship six Style 112 walnut finish, two Style 801 oak, and four Style 111 walnut finish.)

W. W. KIMBALL Co.: Ship Cedar, Garden, Pilgrim Oak.—(Ship two Style 111 walnut finish, one Style 811 walnut finish, and three Style 433 oak.)

Figure 57: W. W. Kimball's telegraph code from their 1915 catalog.

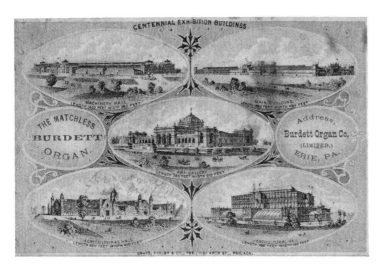

Figure 58, left: Burdett trade card from the 1876 Centennial Exhibition.

enthusiastic believers in the value of medals won at these fairs that they used illustrations of the medals on the stop-boards of many of their organs and in their catalogs.

The race for medals produced its abuses, however. For many years Estey had enthusiastically reported its successes in its catalogs, but finally in 1871 protested the distortions that had crept into the system. From that time on Estey discontinued all mention of medals and awards in its catalogs.

Figure 59: This imposing instrument was built by the Burdett Organ Co. especially for the Centennial Exhibition in Philadelphia, 1876.

Figure 60, left: Detail of carving on Burdett Centennial organ.

AT ALL THE GREAT WORLD'S EXHIBITIONS
SINCE 1867

MASON & HAMLIN CABINET ORGANS

HAVE BEEN FOUND WORTHY OF

THE HIGHEST DISTINCTIONS FOR DEMONSTRATED SUPERIORITY.

WORLD'S EXPOSITION, PARIS, 1867.

THIS WAS THE FIRST of the GREAT INTERNATIONAL EXPOSITIONS at which the Mason & Hamlin Organs were exhibited, in competition with European as well as American makers. They were awarded the FIRST MEDAL for proved superiority.

From HON. J. M. USHER,

Massachusetts Commissioner to the Paris Exposition.

Allow me to congratulate you upon the success attending your Organs at this Exposition.

I have witnessed with pride the attention arrested by the show of your instruments, and the eagerness with which the thousands gather around when your organs are played.

It is a great compliment to the mechanical taste, as well as the artistic skill, of your house in the production of such splendid organs.

The people of our State and nation will share the honor conferred upon your house by the unanimous judgment of the committee in the award rendered.

J. M. USHER

Figure 61

65

Figure 62: Exhibit of Beckwith organs at the St. Louis World's Fair.

Figure 64: Probably no one disputed the many medals won by Mustel over the years.

Figure 63: Story & Clark's display at the Centennial Exhibition, 1876.

MEDALS,

First Premiums, Diplomas, &c.

We have taken over ONE HUNDRED AND FIFTY MEDALS, FIRST PREMIUMS AND DIPLOMAS *at Fairs and Exhibitions throughout the United States. All of the principal Industrial Fairs in our country have bestowed upon our Organs the highest Premiums. We thought of publishing herewith a full list of them, but of late this class of testimonials has fallen into such disrepute, that we have concluded not to do so. Some manufacturers have had the audacity to advertise that they obtained a* GOLD *medal, when in point of fact they received a* SILVER *one; a* FIRST—CLASS *prize, when they received a* THIRD—CLASS *one; a* FIRST *premium, when they received a* SECOND, *or none at all; and even to announce that they have withdrawn entirely from competition at all exhibitions, when in reality we meet them constantly, and learn that their withdrawal in several instances has been in this wise:—finding a jury could not be packed or bought, they boxed up their instruments and announced them as* WITHDRAWN FROM COMPETITION! *For more than ten years we have not seen a day that our order-book did not contain orders for weeks ahead of our capacity to fill them; and for the past three years, although we have been constantly enlarging our works, we have refused to take a large number of orders for our Organs on account of our inability to furnish them; but with our new factories and increased facilities we hope to be able to meet the demands of the public.*

We desire to let our Organs speak for themselves, and all of the encomiums embraced in these pages are over the full signature of the writers. We prefer to make our statements plain and explicit, without insinuations or confusion.

Figure. 65: From the J. Estey & Co. catalog of 1871.

DIRECT SALES

The growth of the railroads and the telegraph made possible a new method of distribution of goods— direct sales from the manufacturer to the customer—described with perhaps a little exaggeration in a Beckwith (Sears Roebuck & Co.) catalog as "The Old Way" and "The New Way."

THE OLD WAY

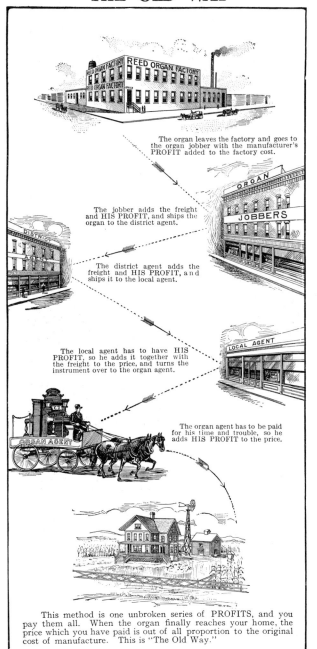

The organ leaves the factory and goes to the organ jobber with the manufacturer's PROFIT added to the factory cost.

The jobber adds the freight and HIS PROFIT, and ships the organ to the district agent.

The district agent adds the freight and HIS PROFIT, and ships it to the local agent.

The local agent has to have HIS PROFIT, so he adds it together with the freight to the price, and turns the instrument over to the organ agent.

The organ agent has to be paid for his time and trouble, so he adds HIS PROFIT to the price.

This method is one unbroken series of PROFITS, and you pay them all. When the organ finally reaches your home, the price which you have paid is out of all proportion to the original cost of manufacture. This is "The Old Way."

THE NEW WAY

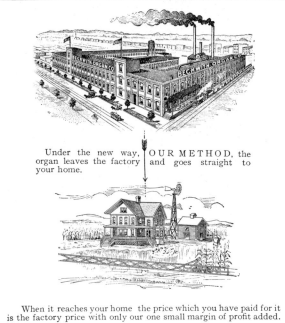

Under the new way, organ leaves the factory your home. | OUR METHOD, the and goes straight to

When it reaches your home the price which you have paid for it is the factory price with only our one small margin of profit added.

Not only do we save you a large amount in the purchase of a high grade organ, but the fact that we control the entire output of the two immense Beckwith Organ factories enables us to secure prices on these organs which are entirely beyond the reach of other organ dealers. As we take the entire output of these factories and handle the Beckwith Organs exclusively, you will see how impossible it is for you to procure a Beckwith Organ from any other dealer. We, however, do not seek to take advantage of this monopoly at the expense of our customers by placing high prices on these splendid instruments, but, on the contrary, we give our customers the full benefit of every advantage we obtain in this way by selling these instruments at the actual cost of material and labor at the factory with but our one small percentage of profit added. As we simply desire to make a uniformly small margin of profit on our organs, every advantage that we can obtain in buying, and every expense that we can save in selling goes into the pockets of our customers in the shape of a reduction in the prices of the organs. While we have reduced the prices on these organs to a point which makes competition absolutely impossible, we have steadily refused to reduce the prices where such a reduction would necessitate a sacrifice in the quality of the instrument. Were we to do so we would find it impossible to guarantee them.

Another important point in this connection is that these organ factories have been established at Louisville, Ky., and St. Paul, Minn., as these two points are admirably located in regard to shipping facilities. By making our northern and western shipments from our St. Paul factory and our southern shipments from our Louisville factory, we can place these organs in the hands of our customers at the very least possible expense in freight charges. This is a great advantage to our customers because it enables us to make the freight charges on each shipment from $1.00 to $5.00 lower than they would otherwise have to pay. It will pay you to consider these facts when you are ready to purchase an organ.

Figure 66

Figure 67: Daniel F. Beatty, proprietor of Beatty's Piano & Organ Co.

NOTHING CAN BE FAIRER.

Your money refunded after one year's use, with interest at 6 per cent.

To take effect March 1, 1882.

Washington, New Jersey, United States of America, March 1st, 1882.

To Whom it may Concern:

☞ If the Beethoven Organ, after one year's constant use, does not give you perfect satisfaction in
every particular and is in any way not as represented
in this circular, I hereby bind myself to take it back
and refund you your money, paid in current funds,
with legal interest of New Jersey (six per cent). I
further agree to pay freight charges on the instrument both ways, the money to be refunded immediately upon receipt of the instrument at Washington,
New Jersey. I further agree, if requested, to exchange it for any other organ or piano as shown in
my catalogue.

*Given under my hand and Seal
this First day of March, 1882.*

DANIEL F. BEATTY.

Figure 68

➤✳WASHINGTON, NEW JERSEY.

*If you live within the limits of the map below, I extend to you a cor-
dial invitation to visit my factory at Washington, New Jersey, and
select an instrument in person. As an inducement, I will pay your
travelling expenses both ways. I do this because I like to take my customers by the hand, and know that they are satisfied and find everything as I represent it. Come and see me.*

Figure 69

One of the pioneers of the direct sales technique in the reed organ business was the flamboyant Daniel F. Beatty of Washington, New Jersey. Beatty began selling melodeons as a traveling agent in Hunterdon County, New Jersey about 1870 when he was twenty-two years old. The following year he took a partner, probably Ed Plotts of Washington, New Jersey. About 1875 he developed his ideas about direct sales, bypassing the various intermediaries and dealing directly as a proprietor with the buyers. Initially the organs were built with the Beatty & Plotts name by the Bridgeport Organ Co. of Bridgeport, Connecticut. About 1879 he organized the Beatty Organ Co.[11] and built a factory building located at Railroad Ave. and Beatty Street, characteristically named after himself. This factory burned in 1881 and a much larger one was built to replace it. Later he built an office building at Broad Street and Washington Avenue, which still stands.at this writing.

69

BEATTY'S

Music Hall

Headquarters of the

BEATTY VETERAN GUARDS,

WASHINGTON,

New Jersey.

Even this Lion Wanted a Beatty Organ.

The Largest, Most Commodious, Best Seated and Best Ventilated Hall outside the large cities, with capacity of seating over 1000 people comfortably.

GOOD STAGE AND BEAUTIFUL SCENERY.

FOR RENT upon the Most Reasonable Terms to First-class Theatrical and Concert Troupes, or for Lectures and Addresses. A Beatty Grand Piano is connected with the Hall. The Beatty Grand Orchestra (20 Pieces) can be Engaged at a Moderate Sum.

For Terms and Particulars, address,

DANIEL F. BEATTY, Washington, New Jersey.

Figure 70

Beatty's sales methods were usually ingenious and often shady. The organs were characterized by the large number of stop knobs. His basic instrument had twenty-seven stops, of which many were soft stops, knee levers, or other mechanical devices. The instruments were said to have ten "full" sets of reeds, but some of the sets were only of one octave.

Beatty offered to pay the round trip travel expenses by rail for anyone within sixty miles of Washington, New Jersey to visit the factory and purchase an organ or piano. Within this sixty-mile circle are locat-ed the cities of New York, Philadelphia, Scranton, Wilkes-Barre, Reading, Trenton, and others.

At Washington, N. J., a coupe will be waiting for you at the station. You will have TWO WHOLE HOURS AT WASHINGTON, giving you a chance to go through Beatty's Organ Factory, where you will be shown how organs are built, from beginning to end. You will have time to visit the Mayor's offices, (Beatty was also mayor of Washington, N. J.—the 'Honorable' Daniel F. Beatty) printing rooms,

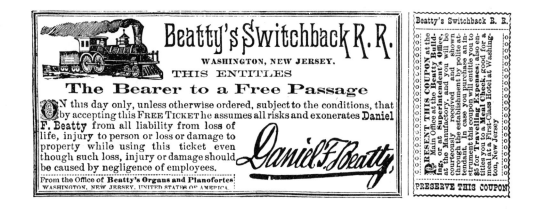

Figure 71: Visitors from New York also were given a free dinner during the two-hour visit.

newspaper rooms, counting rooms, advertising rooms and letter department, where over a million letters are on file from all parts of the world. In the newspaper department are papers in all languages and from all nations. A visit will be made to the Beatty Music Hall, Beatty Orchestra Rooms, and the Beatty veteran Guards' Armory, in charge of Captain and Sergeant Beatty."[12]

BEATTY'S SWITCH BACK RAILROAD

In the rear of the great buildings a railroad of standard gauge connects the dry houses, yard and factory station with the Delaware, Lackawanna and Western Railroad, so as to load instruments and receive materials without the great expense of cartage. A narrow gauge road over 2,000 feet long leads to all parts of the yard for convenience in handling lumber, etc. This is the most convenient arrangement possessed by any factory in the world."[13]

Such offers, while unusual, seem to be harmless in themselves. Some of Beatty's other practices were not so harmless. In their 1880 catalog, Estey printed the following warning, without identifying the party:

A . . . glaring fraud is perpetrated by a 'manufacturer' in New Jersey, who displays some of the choicest cuts of the Estey Organ on multitudinous 'confidential' circulars, and then foists an absolutely worthless article on his unsuspecting customers. The public should be on their guard and not allow themselves to be imposed upon by such unprincipled sharpers.

Beatty frequently used bait and switch methods, advertising an organ at a very low price and, when orders came in, shipping a more expensive one along with a bill for the difference in price, saying that the instrument ordered was out of stock. He also received money for orders and never shipped the organ. When he received a complaint he would reply that the instrument was temporarily out of stock and would be shipped soon. Sometimes it was not shipped at all. In 1884 he went bankrupt, then was convicted of using the mails to defraud.

While Beatty was the most flagrant of the sharp operators, others were active. As the largest and most visible organ manufacturer, Estey was always a target, as reported in this excerpt from their 1880 catalog:

FRESH DEVELOPMENTS OF FRAUD

The disposition of dishonest sharpers to take advantage of hard times and scarcity of money appears in new forms daily. We have recently discovered frauds in the Organ trade so flimsy that they should not for a moment escape detection. Defective or refuse material is thrown together, haphazard, as it were, liberally coated with varnish, and then put forth in the guise of secondhand instruments, to be sold at an immense sacrifice. On the other hand, real *secondhand* Organs, often of irresponsible make, worn out and 'played' out, which have been let, or sold on the installment plan and taken back, are 'fixed up' and palmed off as new. The cheat in either case is fatal and in view of such developments, it goes without saying that the only safeguard for buyers is to patronize reliable dealers or agents, and select instruments that bear the names of first-class, wholly responsible manufacturers.

An irresponsible party in the West has put the name of our firm—spelling it Estee—on a lot of cheap instruments, with the intention of deluding buyers into the belief that they are genuine Estey Organs.

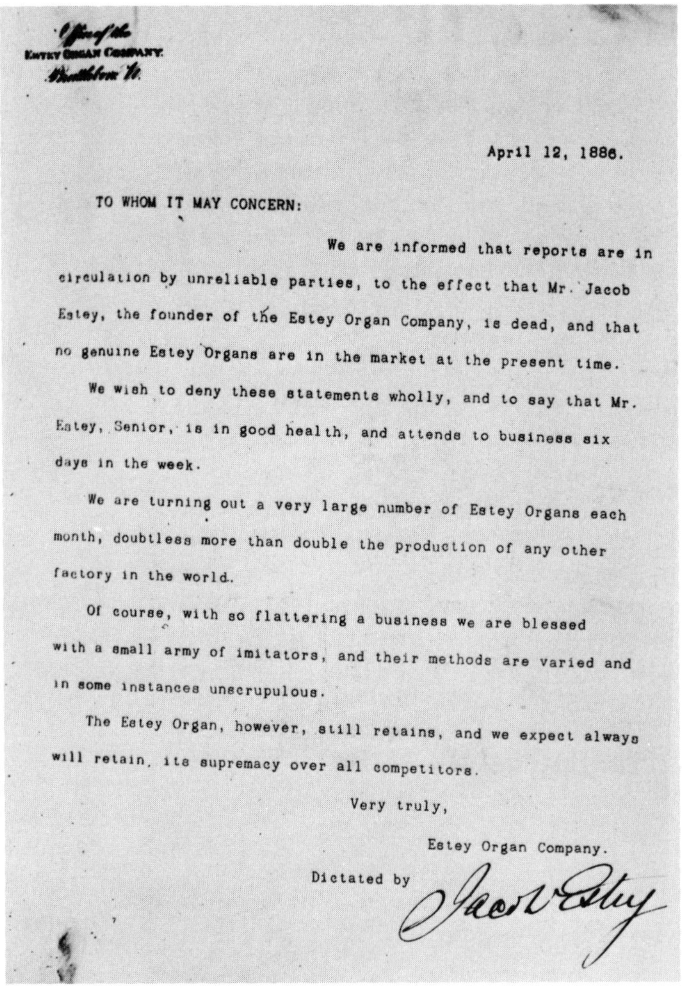
Office of the
Estey Organ Company.
Brattleboro Vt.

April 12, 1886.

TO WHOM IT MAY CONCERN:

We are informed that reports are in circulation by unreliable parties, to the effect that Mr. Jacob Estey, the founder of the Estey Organ Company, is dead, and that no genuine Estey Organs are in the market at the present time.

We wish to deny these statements wholly, and to say that Mr. Estey, Senior, is in good health, and attends to business six days in the week.

We are turning out a very large number of Estey Organs each month, doubtless more than double the production of any other factory in the world.

Of course, with so flattering a business we are blessed with a small army of imitators, and their methods are varied and in some instances unscrupulous.

The Estey Organ, however, still retains, and we expect always will retain, its supremacy over all competitors.

Very truly,

Estey Organ Company.

Dictated by Jacob Estey

Figure 72

While Beatty gave the mail order organ business a bad name, others managed to prosper, selling honest instruments at an honest price. The Cornish Company, also of Washington, New Jersey, was one of these. Joseph B. Cornish was a sales agent for organs in the 1870s, working for a time for Beatty. In 1879 he bought out the Dawes & Wyckoff organ factory in Washington. John M. Wyckoff then became the factory superintendent for Daniel F. Beatty. Cornish and Beatty both started to manufacture organs for the direct sales market in 1879. Johnston Cornish, son of Joseph, was a partner with his father. Johnston was elected mayor of Washington in 1884, defeating Beatty. Both Joseph and Johnston Cornish served as state senators in later years.

The Cornish organs were similar in many respects to those made by Beatty; in particular they had an excess of stop knobs. In contrast to Beatty, Cornish was explicit in stating the number of reeds in each stop, and did not count the knee levers as stops. Cornish bought the organ actions, keys and other components from others and assembled them into cases which were made in his factory. Cornish produced tasteful catalogs with full color covers, printed on heavy paper, giving an impression of quality. Cornish was careful to spell out its terms of credit, and always required credit references. It was said that Cornish was the only one of the Washington organ builders who made money.

Figure 73

Figure 74: Interior of the Cornish Factory

Figure 75: Employees of the Cornish Piano & Organ factory, Washington, New Jersey.

During the nineteenth century most large businesses distributed "trade cards" as a low-cost way of keeping their names in front of potential buyers. Most of the cards were of post card size and often had color engravings of instruments on one side and information about the company on the back. Several examples of such cards appear on this and the following pages.

Figure 76

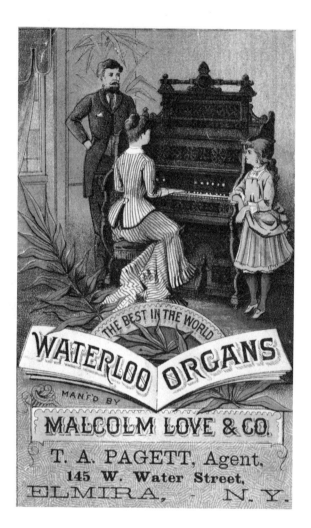

Figure 77

Figure 78

Figure 79: Another novel advertising item is the card puzzle distributed by the Farrand Organ Company. This puzzle was composed of ten pieces which, when properly fit together, formed a seven by seven inch square.

75

Figure 80: Blasius & Sons, the Philadelphia music dealer, gave away a small hand mirror with advertising for the Packard organ on the back. The original was 1.5" in diameter.

Figure 81 (two views, above): Horace Waters & Son issued this souvenir Centennial coin in 1876.

Figure 82: Estey offered to send a set of five die-cut paper dolls representing the United States, Cuba, Hawaii, Puerto Rico and the Philippines on receipt of two two-cent stamps. This example represents the United States in a Rough-Rider uniform.

Figure 83: This book mark, with an appropriate advertising message on the back, was distributed by the Carpenter Company of Brattleboro, Vermont.

Some manufacturers provided large wall posters for display by their dealers. These posters were typically about twenty by thirty inches (100 by 150 cm).

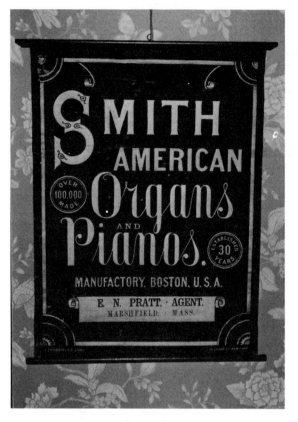

Figure 84

Figure 85

Figure 86: Julius J. Estey, Levi K. Fuller and Jacob Estey with the 100,000th organ, 1880.

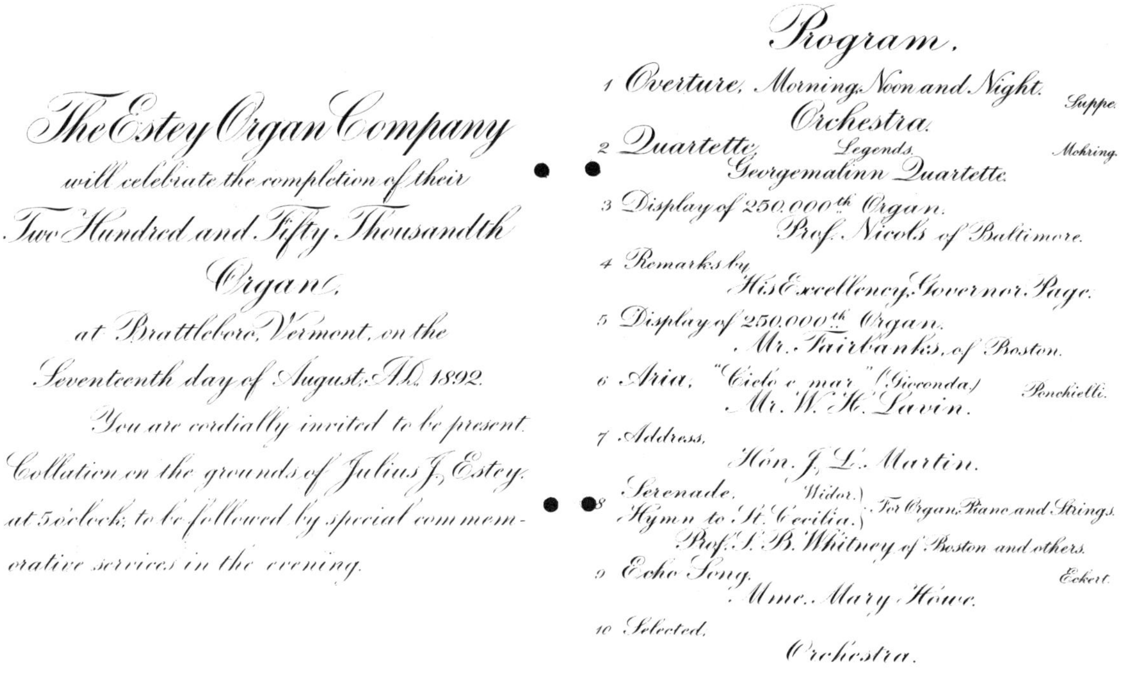

The Estey Organ Company

will celebrate the completion of their

Two Hundred and Fifty Thousandth

Organ,

at Brattleboro, Vermont, on the

Seventeenth day of August, A.D. 1892.

You are cordially invited to be present.

Collation on the grounds of Julius J. Estey,

at 5 o'clock; to be followed by special commem-

orative services in the evening.

Program.

1 Overture, Morning, Noon and Night. *Suppé.*
   Orchestra.

2 Quartette, Legends, *Mohring.*
   Georgematinn Quartette.

3 Display of 250,000th Organ.
   Prof. Nicols of Baltimore.

4 Remarks by
   His Excellency, Governor Page.

5 Display of 250,000th Organ.
   Mr. Fairbanks, of Boston.

6 Aria, "Cielo e mar" (Gioconda) *Ponchielli.*
   Mr. W. H. Lavin.

7 Address,
   Hon. J. L. Martin.

8 Serenade, *Widor.* } For Organ, Piano and Strings.
   Hymn to St. Cecilia. }
   Prof. S. B. Whitney of Boston and others.

9 Echo Song, *Eckert.*
   Mme. Mary Howe.

10 Selected.
   Orchestra.

Figure 87

Some reed organ makers made a special effort to produce outstanding instruments for great occasions. As previously mentioned, the Burdett Organ Company displayed a magnificent three manual and pedal instrument for the Centennial Exhibition in Philadelphia in 1876. To commemorate its 100,000th organ, Estey introduced its New Salon Organ, Style 900 in 1880. This instrument was intended not as a single example produced for a special occasion, but to become a part of the regular product line, and as such it appeared on the cover of the 1881 catalog and every catalog thereafter for ten years. The Style 900 had fourteen speaking stops. In 1887 the Style 910 was introduced with nineteen speaking stops. The case was identical in appearance but slightly enlarged to accomodate the larger number of stops. At the time of this writing, the actual 100,000th organ is now in the collection of Robert J. Yates of Glenshaw, Pennsylvania.

In 1892 Estey produced an extravaganza for the occasion of its 250,000th organ. A special edition of Brattleboro's leading newspaper, the *Vermont Phoenix*, published on August 19, 1892, carried a full account. The streets of Brattleboro were decorated with flags and bunting. Levi K. Fuller's collection of tuning forks was displayed in a large downtown show window. The company gave its five hundred employees the day off and invited them all to a reception held on the grounds of Julius J. Estey's house. Also invited, by engraved invitation, were the Governor of Vermont and his staff, Estey representatives and agents throughout the country, officials of some of the major organ manufacturers, and officials and citizens of Brattleboro. In the center of the garden the band of the First Regiment of the Vermont National Guard played its stirring music, while a caterer from Springfield, Massachusetts offered a generous collation under the Estey Guard mess tent. Lemonade stands, made to look like organ packing crates and stenciled with exotic destinations, were set up at various places around the grounds.

Among those present were: Geo. G. Saxe of Estey & Saxe, New York; I. N. Camp of Estey & Camp, Chicago; Edward M. Reed of the St. Louis branch and Geo. S. Cheney of the Boston branch, agents of the company; and Henry Kirk White, of Wilcox & White, Meriden, Connecticut, a former longtime Estey employee. Also attending was Lorin F. Deland, a well-known advertising expert, and A. Mugford of Hartford, Conn., one of New England's leading engravers. Perhaps most significant was the presence of Estey's first employee, Joseph L. Jones, who came to Brattleboro with his brother, Samuel H. Jones in June of 1846 to begin the predecessor of the Estey firm. Julius J. Estey, a Colonel of the Vermont Guard and Levi K. Fuller, also a Guard Colonel and soon to become Governor of Vermont, circulated among the guests making them welcome.

At 7:00 p.m. the festivities continued in the auditorium of the Baptist church, where the employees and out-of-town guests were seated on the main floor and first gallery. All others were accommodated in the second gallery and in the chapel at the rear of the auditorium. The citizens of Brattleboro presented a resolution of their esteem as did the Estey employees. An orchestra played and several gifted musicians demonstrated the capabilities of the 250,000th organ. The

principal speaker was the Hon. J. L. Martin, Levi K. Fuller replied, and Gov. Page made the final remarks.

After the formal events, carriages were provided to take everyone to the meadow below and in front of the Estey factory for a fireworks display:

"The great row of factories were brilliantly illuminated from the ground floors to the top, and the entire plant was surrounded with lines of Chinese lanterns, presenting a beautiful effect, which was greatly increased by the handsome illumination made by the residents of Organ Street just above the shops, forming an effective background for the picture, and the whole presenting a magnificent spectacle. The pyrotechnic display was the finest ever seen here, and was a succession of novel and beautiful effects, lasting upward of an hour. The grand finale was a large commemorative piece showing across the top the figures

ESTEY ORGAN 250,000.

Figure 88: Estey's 250,000th organ, shown at the Columbian Exposition in Chicago, 1893.

250,000, on either side the dates 1846, 1892, and in the centre a portrait of Jacob Estey, surrounded by a wreath of laurel. . . . Throughout the display the First Regiment band entertained the spectators with another outdoor concert."[14]

The Estey company continued for a few years at the same level of activity, but in 1897 factory production, which had averaged over 12,000 instruments per year, dropped suddenly to half that, never to recover. The three men who had built the company were to die within a few years of each other: Jacob Estey in 1890, Fuller in 1896, and Julius J. Estey in 1901. While some of the other large manufacturers such as Mason & Hamlin and Kimball maintained their production for a longer time, the decline of the industry had begun. In retrospect, the magnificent Estey celebration of 1892 represented the high point, not only of the company, but of the reed organ era itself.

SPECIAL OFFER No. 6, 1904-5

THE LITTLE BEAUTY

No. 30,000

THE POPULAR CORNISH AMERICAN ORGAN

On the other side of this circular you will find, accurately depicted and fully described, our popular Style No. 30,000, The Little Beauty. A great number of these desirable instruments are sold for home use, where a large and powerful organ is not necessary. The case is neat and durable, and the beautiful actions fitted to it make it a perfect organ for home use. The demand for this particular style of organ has increased so much that we have decided to make it the subject of a special offer, and we therefore direct your attention to the following

TERMS OF SALE

1. We are willing to sell on our easy payment plan, and we offer Style No. 30,000, The Little Beauty Organ, upon an easy payment plan of **$10.00** down, balance **$5.00** per month, for only ☞ **$34.25**

2. Or, we will sell this desirable organ, **if all cash** is paid after one month's use, for only ☞ **$32.75**

3. Or, if those interested wish to take advantage of our cash discount and will send money in advance with order (saving all bookkeeping and other expenses in connection with credit accounts), we will allow a cash bonus of 5 per cent., bringing the total cost of The Little Beauty Organ down to only $31.12, cash with order. This pays in full for the organ, stool and book, in either walnut or oak case, boxed and delivered free here, with safe delivery guaranteed. (Freight prepaid by us in advance, if desired, we to add cost of same to price of organ.)

$31.12
CASH WITH ORDER

Prices above quoted are for the organ fitted with The Little Beauty Action, 10 Stops, 98 Reeds. If a larger action is desired, we will supply Century Chimes Action, 12 Stops, 122 Reeds, at an additional cost of **$1.75**. The organ is only made in 5 octaves—that is **full size,** all organ music being written for 5 octaves only.

P. S.—Please use our regular form in sending your order—you will find one with catalogue. If cash is not sent in advance, don't omit reference if such is necessary. Remember that Cornish Organs are Cornish quality throughout. Nothing quite so good is made in the United States to-day. We manufacture only HIGH-GRADE GOODS, and are never in competition with sellers of cheap, flashy instruments. Get a Cornish and you will have it as long as you live, and then you can leave it in your will. We build for posterity.

ESTABLISHED 50 YEARS. CORNISH CO. WASHINGTON, N. J., U. S. A.

CORNISH AMERICAN ORGAN

THE LITTLE BEAUTY

STYLE No. 30,000

Specially Suitable for Parlor or Cottage Use. Made in Black American Walnut or Quartered Golden Oak Case.

DIMENSIONS: Height, 61 inches. Length, 48 inches. Width, 22 inches. Weight, boxed, 300 pounds.

DESCRIPTION. 5 octaves, 10 stops, 2 octave couplers, 1 tone swell, 1 grand organ swell and 4 sets orchestral toned resonatory pipe quality reeds as follows:

MELODIA, One Set of 37 Reeds
      Exquisitely pure and sweet
CELESTE, One Set of 24 Reeds
      Charmingly brilliant
DIAPASON, One Set of 24 Reeds
      Rich, mellow and smooth
DULCIANA, One Set of 13 Reeds
      Pleasing, soft and melodious

NAMES OF STOPS:

Diapason Forte, Bass Coupler, Piano, Diapason, Dulciana, Celeste, Celeste Forte, Treble Coupler, Echo, Melodia.

NOTE.—If a larger and more powerful action is desired, this organ can be fitted with Century, Chimes Action, 12 stops, 122 reeds, for $1.75 extra.

Fully Warranted for 25 Years

THE case can be of solid black walnut or quartered oak, handsomely ornamented with original designs in embossed and carved wood work. The top of the case contains a heavy French plate oval bevelled mirror. The action is one of our multiple tone combination actions, fitted with our orchestral toned reeds, and is perfect in purity of tone and volume of sound. This organ is in every sense a valuable musical instrument, capable of filling a worthy place in any home where good music is appreciated and desired.

Complete with stool and instruction book, boxed and delivered on board cars.

ESTABLISHED 50 YEARS. CORNISH CO. WASHINGTON, N. J., U. S. A.

83

84

Chapter Three

Stops and Voices

The most distinguishing characteristic of a reed organ, as with a pipe organ, is that it produces a continuous tone as long as a key is held down, as opposed to a piano that produces a tone rapidly decaying in intensity after the key is struck.

The pitch of a set of reeds is given as 8', 4', 16' or 2', following pipe organ usage.

When a stop is labeled eight feet it simply means that the longest pipe of the stop, known as CC, is eight feet long and the pitch will be the unison or normal. That is, middle C on the organ keyboard will correspond with the middle C of the piano keyboard. A sixteen-foot stop will sound an octave lower, a four-foot stop will sound an octave higher. These measures refer to pipes which are open at the top. . . [15]

The reeds in a reed organ are much shorter: a reed with a 16' C pitch is only about five inches long. Thus a reed organ can have the same compass as a pipe organ but it can be contained in a relatively compact, lightweight, and therefore inexpensive console.

Also following the usual practice in pipe organs, the keyboard of a typical reed organ has 61 chromatic notes, or five octaves plus one note, starting and ending with either C or F. The F-scale keyboard starts with the F in the next lower octave than the C-scale keyboard, thus giving a small organ some effect of a pedal bass. A few reed organs were made with six-octave keyboards, and some smaller instruments had as few as three octaves. A reed organ with ranks of 8', 16', and 4' reeds would have a total compass of seven octaves, all played from a single five-octave keyboard or *manual.*

The different ranks of reeds are brought into play on most organs by pulling out the draw knobs or *stops.* Some piano-cased organs had no stop knobs, and the various ranks of reeds were brought into play by progressively moving the *full-organ* knee lever. Reed organ stops can be divided into three categories: speaking, mechanical, and derived stops.[16] The term *speaking stop* refers to a stop which, when drawn, enables a group of reeds to sound when the keys are depressed. The basic *mechanical stops* operate the swell shutters or connect the tremolo or octave couplers. The *derived stops* are either speaking or mechanical or a combination of both, which modify the tone quality of the related speaking stops. In a simple reed organ with two sets of reeds, two speaking stops would be sufficient, one for each set, and in fact some early melodeons were so equipped. To permit splitting the keyboard on a single-manual instrument, these stops are usually duplicated on the bass and treble sides, giving four basic speaking stops for an organ with two ranks of reeds.

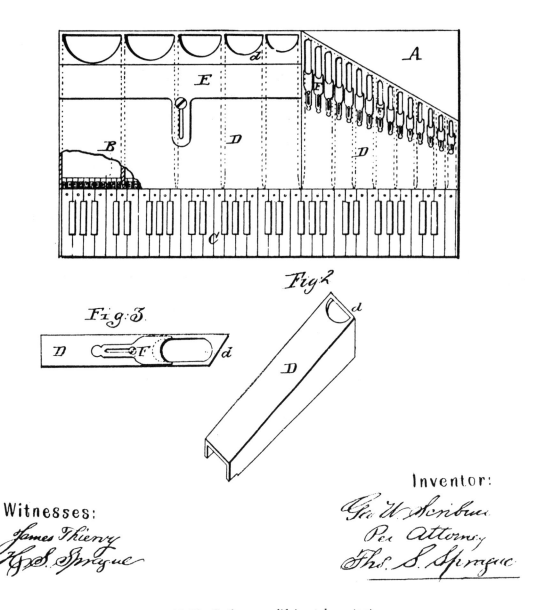

G. W. Scribner.
Reed Organ
Nº 104,653.   Patented Jun. 21, 1870.
Fig. 1.

A

E

B

D

D

C

Fig. 3.

D F d

Fig. 2.

d

D

Witnesses:
James Thierry
H. S. Sprague

Inventor:
Geo. W. Scribner
Per Attorney
Thos. S. Sprague

Figure 90: The Scribner qualifying tube patent.

86

The purpose of splitting the keyboard is to permit using different stop combinations for the bass and the treble, thus approximating the flexibility of a two-manual instrument. The majority of American parlor organs are divided between E and F in the octave below middle C, although sometimes the split falls between B and middle C or even between the E and F above middle C. Because of this variation in different instruments, music as written for American-made organs often does not take into account the location of the split between the bass and treble parts of the keyboard, requiring some rearrangement by the organist. Many American organs use different names for the bass and treble portions of the same set of reeds, leading to some confusion when one is first getting acquainted with an instrument. Some later instruments, particularly those intended for professional musicians, use the same stop name on the treble and bass sides.

Another characteristic of the reed organ is that it has a slow *attack,* that is, the sound of the reed builds up somewhat slowly after the key is depressed. This characteristic together with the continuous tones produced by the organ lead the performer to *legato* fingering, in which successive notes are played without a break between notes. Of course this style of playing limits the type of music that can be played. To get around this limitation, the percussion stop is used.

The earliest reed organs had a raspy quality described by H. F. Milne as:

> . . . A highly composite clang containing a large series of overtones (up to the sixteenth or more being recognizable.) . . . Unfortunately, the particular

kind of interrupted impulse which produces these sounds has to a maximum degree the tendency to create an excessive development of the higher dissonant overtones which by more or less smothering the fundamental or prime cause the harshness and peculiar snarling quality.

The first attempts to modify the tone quality of reed organs used qualifying chambers or tubes, as typified by Maelzel's Panharmonicon in 1807 and Grenie's Orgue Expressif of 1810, an instrument similar to a small pipe organ with free reeds in the pipes. A similar approach was used occasionally throughout the life of the reed organ but the high cost of the tubes usually prevented their use on inexpensive instruments for the home. Nevertheless, Clough & Warren and Empire Organ Co. in the United States and the Dominion Organ Co. in Canada made parlor organs using Scribner's Patent Qualifying Tubes, U. S. Patent number 104,653. Other American reed organs with qualifying tubes were made by James A. Bazin, H. N. Goodman's Cabinet Pipe Organ Co., Davie & Jackson, William Allen Johnson, J. Schleicher & Hochstuhl, Seybold Reed-Pipe Organ Co., C. E. Stevens of New York, and Stevens & Klock. Both the Vocalion and the Aeolian Orchestrelle made use of qualifying chambers to give those instruments their characteristic tone. In Europe, harmoniums with reed-pipes or qualifying chambers were made by Alexandre, Dumont & Lelievre, Klotzsch, and many others. Debain used qualifying chambers to impart distinctive tone qualities to the reeds in his Harmonium. Typical dimensions he used are shown in the table that follows.

DIMENSIONS OF DEBAIN'S RESONATING CAVITIES, IN MM.				
	Length	Width	Height	Timbre
8' C	120	12	28	Bourdon
2nd C	110	12	28	Bourdon
3rd C	106	12	28	Bourdon
4th C	95	12	28	Clarinet
5th C	68	12	28	Clarinet
1st C	115	12	25	Cor Anglais
2nd C	105	12	25	Cor Anglais
3rd C	95	11	25	Cor Anglais
4th C	80	11	25	Flute
1st C	75	10	18	Clarion
2nd C	60	9	18	Clarion
3rd C	43	8	18	Clarion

Debain's use of resonating chambers was followed by many European builders and became the standard for high quality harmoniums.

The Compensating Pipe Organ Co. of Battle Creek, Michigan and Toronto produced an organ with free reed pipes. The idea of this organ was that the reeds helped to hold the pipes in tune under varying temperature and humidity conditions, and the pipes lent a better sound to the reeds. John Green used a different technique in the Royal Seraphine, introduced about 1833. By means of curtains or shades dropped over an opening in the case, the tone quality was modified to imitate various instruments. A later approach used on some harmoniums made use of a board covered with swansdown placed over the pallets and as close as possible to them.[17] This device was said to improve the tone and take away some of the metallic sound.

In looking for a simple way to improve the tone, Jeremiah Carhart found that by using a suction bellows instead of the then-standard force bellows he could achieve a more satisfactory tone quality in a small reed instrument. He received a patent on the suction bellows in 1846, and although his patent was later declared void, he was, if not the inventor, undoubtedly the popularizer of the suction bellows in America.

Figure 91: Alfred Little, musician, reed tuner and voicer.

Later developments, particularly those attributed to Charles Austin and Emmons Hamlin, permitted an even better approximation of the organ tone quality and, significantly, those of the three other families of tones in a pipe organ: strings, reeds and flutes. The technique used was to slightly bend and shape the reed. Both Austin and Hamlin may owe their inventions to Major Alfred Little, who began working for Austin in 1840. J. D. Cheney wrote:

I was at A. Prescott's, Concord, N.H., from the winter of 1845-6 to 1850, and I am sure that Alfred Little, who was then tuning for Charles Austin, used to bend the points of the reeds, as he said, 'to take away a part of the snarl!'[18]

The organ tone is usually described as full and round and is the basic pipe organ sound, found on such stops as Melodia, Diapason and Bourdon. The string tones resemble the sounds of the orchestral stringed instruments. Typical pipe organ stop names are Violoncello, Gamba, Viola and Violin. The reed family includes the sounds of the orchestral reed instruments as well as the brass or horn sounds. The flute sound refers to the sounds of the flute pipes of a pipe organ, such as the gedackt and stopped diapason. None of these sounds is reproduced exactly in the reed organ, but they are similar enough so that they can be identified, at least in the better instruments.

In many of the less expensive models, particularly some of those intended for home rather than professional use, a great deal of salesmanship entered into the naming of stops, and frequently, derived stops were added which were impressive in appearance but added little to the musical qualities of the instrument. These stops were usually mechanically derived, and acted to raise or lower the volume of the related speaking stop, as well as to affect the celeste as will be described later. While many buyers of reed organs may have been swayed by fancy stop names, anyone who could read could be set straight, as in the following excerpt from *Clarke's New Method for the Parlor Organ:*

There is no standard in the names placed upon the draw-stop knobs of various reed organs, as each manufacturing company attach appellations to suit their own fancy... There is not so much variety in the quality of tones produced from the various reed organs as the names appear to suggest. They are based upon the standard registers of the pipe organ; but the only resemblance is in the name itself.

THE FREE REED SOUND

The characteristic free reed sound is a complex wave whose components are the fundamental frequency together with many higher-order harmonics. An appreciation of the physical basis of reed sounds can be had by looking at the spectrum of the sound produced by the reeds, using a spectrum analyzer, as shown on the following page. In the spectrum of a typical A440 reed (A above middle C), it is interesting to note that the second, third, and fifth harmonics are stronger than the fundamental. It is also possible to appreciate how much of the sound produced is dissonant. The third, fifth, sixth, seventh, and ninth harmonics in this example are all dissonant. The combination of all these harmonics and their strengths are what give the reed its particular tone quality. (The harmonics above 4000 Hz are physically present but at a much lower level.)

At very slight vacuum (or pressure), say one-half inch of water,[19] the air flow is so slight that it produces no perceptible sound by itself. The only sound is that of the simple reed motion, and an almost pure sine wave results, as seen on an oscilloscope. As the vacuum is increased, the higher harmonics begin to be noticeable. At one inch of water the wave form is made up of the fundamental plus the second harmonic, contributed by the air flow past the reed. At higher vacuum the third and higher harmonics appear.

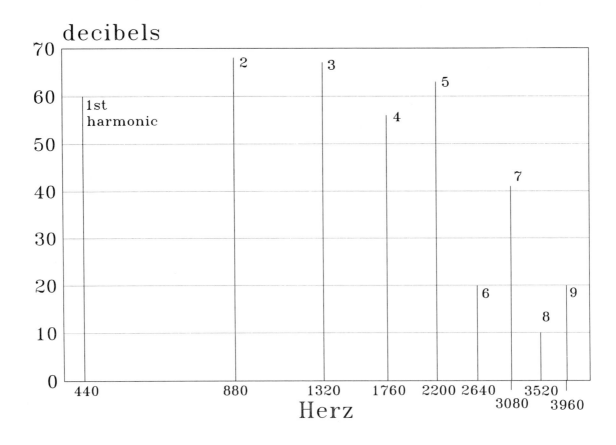

Figure 92: The spectrum of a typical A440 reed.

The low bass reeds have a different wave form, probably caused by the thickness at the free end, which reduces the bending toward the free end of the reed. This produces a waveform with a high initial peak, giving rise to a sort of clicking sound. In the better organs the sub-bass reeds are placed in a separate chest with a qualifying chamber to make the sound more pleasing.

Helmholtz observed that varying wind pressure affected the low- and high-pitched reeds differently. "The stronger blast flattens deep reeds and sharpens high ones, and from this cause arises much of the painful dissonance. . ."[20]

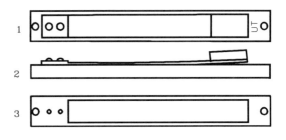

Figure 93: Harmonium bass reed. (1) top view, (2) side view, (3) bottom view.

It is also possible to visualize some of the reasons for the various effects obtained by reed voicing. Curving the end of the reed will cause the air pulse to be longer, since parts of

90

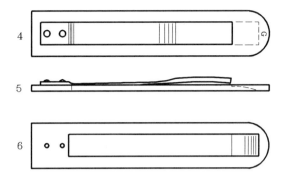

Figure 94: American organ sub-bass reed. (4) top view, (5) side view, (6) bottom view.

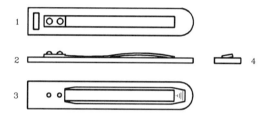

Figure 95: American organ reed. (1) top view, (2) side view of reed showing curvature, (3) bottom view of reed showing shaving of block, (4) end view of reed showing twist.

the reed will be within the block for a longer period during the cycle of the reed motion. Also, because of the curvature, there will always be considerable air leakage around the reed as it passes the block, limiting the pressure differential that can be developed, and making the pulse lower and its sides less steep. All of these effects—a longer pulse duration, lower height, and more sloping sides—tend to reduce the harmonic content of the pulse, making the tone more mellow sounding. Shaving the inside of the block, typical of the reeds used in the American organ, shortens the air pulse, reducing the power in the pulse. This tends to keep the reeds more in tune as wind pressure changes, but makes the expression stop less effective.

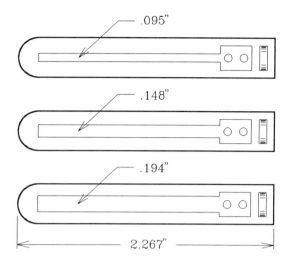

Figure 96: Top to bottom: narrow, normal and wide scale reeds for 2' C, (from Estey factory drawings).

Changes in the width or *scale* of the reed are said to have an effect similar to scale changes in organ pipes. The wide reed is supposed to have fewer harmonics, while the thin reed has more harmonics than the reed of normal scale. Be that as it may, the most noticeable effect is that the wider reed is louder and the narrower reed softer than the standard reed.

In the American organ the reeds are mounted in individual *cells.* If the cell is made large enough it becomes resonant to the pitch of the reed or to one of its overtones and is called a qualifying chamber. The typical cell, however, is too small to have much effect on the tone quality, and seems to act mainly to concentrate the sound. The cells on the bass reeds, however, act to increase the amplitude of the characteristic sharp peak of the waveform of those reeds and reduce the third harmonic, making the clicking sound even more noticeable. For this reason sub-bass reeds are usually located in a separate housing with a qualifying chamber to reduce the click and produce a more musical tone.

91

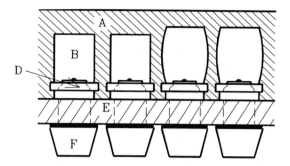

Figure 97: American organ reed cells: front view

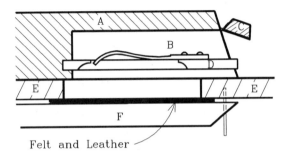

Figure 98: American organ reed cells: cross-section. A: cavity board, B: reed cell, C: mute, D: reed, E: soundboard, F: pallet valve.

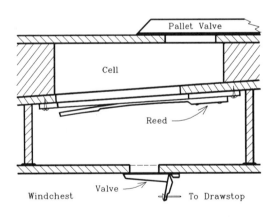

Figure 99: Cross-section of harmonium reed pan.

Swell

Control over the volume of the reed organ, often called *swell*, is usually provided for by enclosing some or all of the reeds in a box with a shuttered opening. Unfortunately for this arrangement, the reeds require an ample flow of air even when the swell is closed, so there is always a path for the sound to escape. Also some manufacturers were not careful in the design of the swell shades, and as a result, the swell control frequently has only a very limited effect on the volume of sound.

The typical American organ uses the right knee lever to control the swell. Some organs also have one or more stop knobs, usually labeled *Forte,* which when drawn, open the swell shades completely and hold them open. On some organs the swell is split to provide separate control over the bass and treble sections by means of Treble Forte and Bass Forte knobs. Other organs have separate control over the front and rear set of reeds, in which case the knobs may be labeled Forte I and Forte II, although other names are often found. If the swell is split, the knee swell opens all swell shades. On larger organs the swell is sometimes controlled by a foot pedal. A really effective volume control, called *Expression,* is used on some harmoniums, but was all but ignored by makers of the American organ.

The *expression stop* is an arrangement of the bellows such that the feeders are connected directly to the wind chest and the reservoir is connected separately to the wind chest through a valve which can be opened or closed by the performer. With the valve in its normal or open position, air from the feeders flows into the wind chest and then into the reservoir which maintains a steady air pressure. When the valve to the reservoir is closed the air pressure depends on the force exerted by the performer on the pedals, and can vary from a very light pressure with minimum pedaling to very heavy pressure with vigorous pedaling, with the result that the performer has complete control over the volume of sound.

Some idea of the difficulty of playing the organ with the expression stop can be inferred from the instructions for its use:

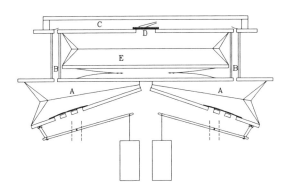

Figure 102: Cross-section of harmonium bellows and wind-chest. Air from the feeders (A) flows through windways (B) to wind chest (C). If the expression valve (D) is closed, pressure in wind chest is controlled by feeders. If D is open, reservoir (E) stabilizes the air pressure.

In playing with the Expression Stop drawn, then there must not be an instant in the blowing without one foot, at least, moving downwards. The following is the method of moving the feet:—Beginning with one foot, let the downward pressure of the pedal board be slowly and STEADILY performed. Just before the moving foot has reached its lowest level, the other foot must begin to move, so that for a second or so both feet will be moving downwards at the same time. Then the first foot will be returned upwards smartly, without disturbing the downward progress of the other, so as to be ready for its next descent before the second foot has become quite exhausted. In this way the pressure of wind is kept continuous. It will require some practice to perform this operation easily; but, after it has been acquired, its benefits will be so manifest, that the student will readily acknowledge the great value of the Expression Stop. By its use the gradual increase or decrease of tone is under the immediate control of the performer, and an instantaneous change from loud to soft or soft to loud can be obtained, which without the Expression Stop is quite impossible.[21]

The expression stop in the reed organ can be traced back to the very beginnings of the instrument in the first part of the nineteenth century. One of the first reed organs about which we have clear information was the orgue expressif made by Gabriel-Joseph Grenié in Paris. His objective was to add expression to the pipe organ.

Many reed organs made in France after that were referred to by the generic name "orgue expressif," indicating that expression was a standard feature. Indeed, many of them did not have a reservoir, so that the organs were inherently expressive. DeBain's Harmonium, which was so widely copied that its name became the universal term for that type of organ made in Europe, included an expression stop.

EXPRESSION STOP IN THE AMERICAN ORGAN

It is not a little singular that the American makers of free reed organs, or organs without pipes, notwithstanding their numerous inventions to improve the internal structure of the instrument, making it more firm or organic, and in so modifying the general quality of the tone by which the very objectionable nasal quality is removed or reduced, have neglected to make use of two of the most valuable features of the English instruments, namely, in the employment of the 'expression' stop and the 'percussion action.' For, by the former arrangement, the slightest change in the mode of pressing the wind pedals causes a corresponding change in the vibrations of the reeds, the wind going directly to them.

The Musical Courier,
Vol. III page 243, 1881

We will probably never know what motivated the editor of the *Musical Courier* to make this statement, since he must have known better, but while it was then and still is commonly believed that the American manufacturers did not make use of the expression stop, the facts are quite different. Almost from its very beginning Mason & Hamlin made organs with the expression stop. The company was organized in 1854 and probably began production in 1855. On May 27, 1856 they were granted United States Patent No. 14955 on an expression stop in a vacuum driven reed organ, a feature which first appeared in their then-new Organ-Harmonium. This

Figure 103: Mason & Hamlin's Organ-Harmonium of 1856.

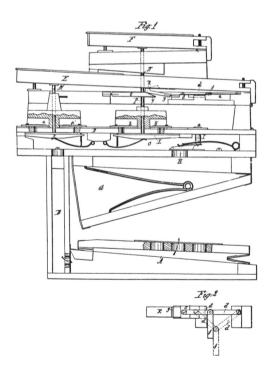

Figure 104: Emmons Hamlin was awarded U.S. Patent No. 14,955 for an expression stop on an exhaust reed organ on May 27, 1856.

organ was first exhibited at the eighth Exhibition of the Massachusetts Mechanics' Charitable Association held in Boston in September of 1856, and received the following comments from a newspaper, the *Boston Traveler*, on Sept. 22:

> Of the new musical instrument, the 'Organ Harmonium' invented and patented by Messrs. Mason & Hamlin, we need only to say that the general structure of this instrument exhibits good taste, as well as great mechanical skill. It is contained in a neat rosewood case, having two banks of keys—four complete sets of reeds, and, including the coupler and the expression, it has eight stops. The arrangement for working the bellows is such that the performer seems to have entire control of the instrument with apparent ease to himself, and as a piece of mechanism, the instrument evinces every sign of substantiality and durableness. The tone of the Organ Harmonium is at once prompt, firm, sweet, and flexible, answering as quickly to the touch as the finest piano forte, and moreover, it is capable of producing every variety of light and shade—the opposite degrees of force may be given in two consecutive chords, or the force may be graduated more or less quickly with uniform evenness from the boldest fortissimo to the most delicate pianissimo or vice versa.

Extracts from the *Report of the Committee on Musical Instruments*, at the Fair of the Massachusetts Charitable Mechanic's Association, at Boston, 1856:

> One instrument in particular, from the establishment of Mason & Hamlin, of Boston, stands out so preeminently amongst all on exhibition, that a more detailed description is here given, as well to inform the public what has been attained, as from its intrinsic value it was thought worthy of being thus noticed. The Committee refer to the Organ-Harmonium, of which two were contributed by the same firm. One of these has a Pedal Bass, the other has none; and both have two banks of keys. . . .The 'Expression' stop is peculiar to this instrument, and is the invention of the makers, by whom it has been patented. This is an entirely new and valuable improvement, and under the control of a skillful performer must be a desirable addition. . . .The Committee recommend that to Mason & Hamlin, for their great and valuable improvements in the Organ-Harmonium exhibited by them, be awarded a GOLD MEDAL.

Mason & Hamlin's catalog published in 1856 gives the following description of the expression stop:

> The Expression Stop is one of our own invention, and patented,—and is found in no other instrument made in this country. The French Harmoniums, made at Paris, have a stop somewhat similar, and of the same name, but the effect is much less, and the principle of its construction is totally different. This stop required considerable skill and practice, (in the management of the feet upon the pedals,) in order to bring it completely under the control of the performer; but when mastered, it is exceedingly beautiful and effective, producing the most perfect crescendo, diminuendo, sforzando, tremolo, affetuoso, etc., all being done by the action of the feet upon the pedals. When the Expression stop is drawn, the main bellows (or wind-reservoir with which the instrument is provided) is shut off, so that the slightest motion of the feet upon the pedals (which operate the two exhaust-bellows) affects the power of tone. Therefore, if the pressure (of the feet upon the pedals) be gentle, the tone produced will be gentle and soft, and vice versa. If the

pressure be sudden, the power of tone will be sudden also, or a sforzando effect be the result. A trembling of the feet upon the pedals will produce a tremolo effect in the tone. Thus, each different motion of the feet will produce a corresponding effect in the tone,—so that, in using the Expression Stop, the tone is, in a certain sense, entirely under the control of the feet. The foot always AT PRESSURE upon its pedal. The instant that BOTH feet leave the pedals, or discontinue the pressure, (be it greater or less, gradual or sudden, equal or unequal), the sound ceases. Therefore when one foot stops its pressure in order to let the pedal rise, care must be taken that the other foot be at pressure. This will come somewhat awkward, at first, but with a little careful practice, and attention to the above directions, it will not be long before the Expression stop may be used with its best effects; and when such is the case, no one can fail to appreciate and admire it. We would strongly recommend and urge the purchasers and players of the Organ-Harmonium to practise and study the management of this beautiful stop, and they will not fail in bringing out its full resources.

The claim by Mason & Hamlin that their expression stop was more effective and that

Figure 105: 1874 Mason & Hamlin Orchestral Organ, Style 1400.

its principle of construction was totally different from that of the French Harmoniums must be attributed to nineteenth century advertising hyperbole, since a comparison of the Mason & Hamlin patent drawing with the cross-section of a typical European Harmonium shows exactly the same principle, with the exception of the use of a vacuum bellows instead of pressure bellows. All of the Mason & Hamlin organs with the expression stop had a vacuum bellows with the exception of the Style 1400. The 1880 catalog listed the Orchestral Organ, Style 1400, with both expression and percussion, which they called Pizzicato, as well as a pressure bellows.

When Mason & Hamlin introduced what we now call the flat top organ with two exhausters, two foot-pedals, and a reservoir set below and to the rear of the action, they at first called it a Harmonium. The two-manual instrument was called an Organ-Harmonium, while the two-manual melodeon was called an Organ-Melodeon. The name Harmonium in the Mason & Hamlin usage did not refer to the use of a pressure bellows, since these were all suction instruments but, rather, referred to the physical shape of the case in its resemblance to the European Harmoniums. They continued this nomenclature until 1861 when they renamed it the Cabinet Organ. Mason & Hamlin continued to offer the expression stop over the years. In the 1874 catalog the Resonant organ, Style 43, a two-manual instrument, is shown with the expression stop. Alexander R. Koerber, a Canadian inventor, received U.S. patent no. 206,250 on July 23, 1878 for an expression stop for the American organ, but it was not widely used.

Helmholtz said that shaving the underside of the reed frame produced a softer, smoother and more flexible tone but rendered it less suitable for expression. For whatever reasons, the expression stop never became popular in the United States and the American organ builders generally ignored it. Mason & Hamlin eventually dropped it and in 1901, when he published *The History and Development of the American Cabinet Organ,* Henry Lowell Mason found no need to mention it at all. Thus the record shows that the expression stop was used successfully on suction reed organs, was introduced in America at an early date and made available over many years, but was eventually dropped, possibly due to lack of interest on the part of the buying public.

European makers, however, found a demand for the expression stop in suction organs:

> We are pleased to announce that the principal objection to the so-called 'American' harmoniums, that is the absence of the 'Expression' stop, is no longer valid. ...we have created several models, veritable salon organs, which have Expression of the same quality as in the pressure instruments. . .
>
> catalog of Les Petits-fils de M. Kasriel, ca 1928.

Frequently a performer will add a wavering effect to musical tones for the purpose of adding interest, warmth, poignancy, or some other effect. At least four methods have been found to achieve this result on the reed organ: the *celeste,* the *beater tremolo,* the *fan tremolo,* and a special use of the expression stop. The first three of these are put into operation by drawing the appropriate stop, typical names of which are

Tremulant, Tremolo, Vox Humana, Celeste, Vox Angelicus, and so on. As described previously, a tremolo effect can also be accomplished by jiggling the foot on the foot pedal with the expression stop drawn.

THE CELESTE STOP

To produce the celeste stop, two reeds of slightly different pitch are sounded together. Because they are slightly out of tune, one with the other, the sound waves alternately reinforce and cancel each other, giving rise to *beats* in the same way as a celeste stop on a pipe organ. (Details on tuning a celeste stop are given in the chapter on tuning.) Three types of reed organ celestes are used: *independent, fully-derived,* and *half-derived,* [22] with a number of variations. The celeste stops are usually found only in the treble part of the split keyboard, although bass celestes are sometimes encountered. The names given to the celeste stops, particularly by American and Canadian makers, vary widely.

To create the independent celeste, two sets of reeds devoted only to that stop are used. One set is usually tuned slightly sharp and the other slightly flat of unison so that when sounded together the combination appears to be in tune. Examples of this type are the 8' treble Vox Angelica and the 2' bass Vox Humaine, both used by Karn. Since two sets of reeds are devoted only to this stop it was the most expensive of the reed organ celestes.

THE VOX JUBILANTE

Is a new and beautiful stop, peculiar to the ESTEY ORGANS. The character of the tone is marked and wonderfully effective, giving a style of music hitherto unattained in instruments of this class. This is accomplished by an extra set of reeds, ingeniously arranged, after long and careful experiment, to meet this special and hitherto unsupplied want. It is considered by competent judges a great success.

Figure 107

In the half-derived celeste, one set of reeds is dedicated to this stop and tuned off-unison, usually sharp, although occasionally an organ is found with this set tuned flat. When the celeste stop is drawn, mechanical linkage also draws an in-tune stop, creating the celeste pair. The in-tune set of reeds can also be used alone by drawing the stop knob for that particular set. As an example, the Aeolian Orchestrelle uses the 8' Eolian Harp linked to the Muted Strings stop in the treble. The latter stop can also be drawn by itself without the Eolian Harp. The Orchestrelle also has a rarely-seen 8' celeste in the bass, using the same stop names.

The fully-derived celeste is similar to the half-derived except that there is no mechanical linkage to the in-tune reed set: both stops must be drawn manually. This arrangement gives more flexibility in registration at the expense of having to draw two stops to get a celeste. As an example, some Packards have an 8' treble Celeste stop with an associated soft stop called Celestina. The Celeste is normally played with the 8' Melodia or its soft stop Dulcet Treble. The availability of the soft stops yields a number of celeste combinations, (using the Packard stop names): Celeste/Melodia with a normal beat rate, the slightly softer Celestina/Melodia or Celeste/Dulcet Treble with a slower beat, and the soft Celestina/Dulcet Treble combination with a normal beat. The adventurous could also draw the Celeste or Celestina with the 16' Cello stop or with the 4' Flute or Flutina, at the risk of being condemned for using what Ian Thompson refers to as a "Vox Purgatorius" stop. From the name Celestina given to the soft stop we infer that the original tuning of this organ was as described above. Some modern tuners would modify this stop

arrangement by tuning the Celestina in unison, thus permitting its use to strengthen the 8' treble section, and allowing the Celeste then to be a slow celeste when played with the Melodia.

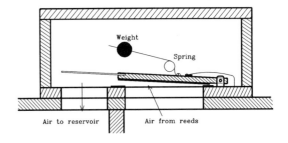

Figure 108: Mason & Hamlin beater tremolo, 1871.

THE BEATER TREMOLO

The beater tremolo as used in the American organ[23] is a mechanical valve placed in the air path between the reeds and the bellows, alternately opening and shutting off the flow of air from the reeds, thus imparting a fluttering effect to the sound. The illustration above shows a typical tremolo of this type, made by Mason & Hamlin in 1871 and used in their Style G organ. With the Tremulant stop closed, air leaving the reed chest must pass through a valve which is normally open. When the Tremulant stop is drawn, the valve is closed, forcing the air from the reeds to pass through the beater mechanism. The air flow causes the beater valve to open until it contacts a spring which limits the valve travel and helps return it to the closed position. The coil spring and weight cause the valve to oscillate open and shut. In this particular arrangement air from all the reeds flows through the beater, but its effect is most noticeable in the treble portion of the keyboard. Other beater tremolos act only on the air flow from the treble section of the reed chest. This type of tremolo is very difficult to adjust, and its effect is not pleasing to most people. A variation of the beater tremolo patented by R. W. Carpenter and used on some Burdett organs uses a cylindrical fan in an enclosed box through which air from the reeds passes.[24] This device looks something like an enclosed fan tremolo, but the principle of operation is similar to that of the beater tremolo. The beater tremolo was eventually replaced by the fan tremolo described below.

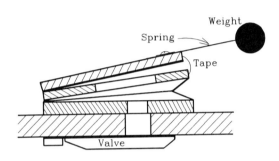

Figure 109: Harmonium tremolo.

In the Harmonium, the beater tremolo consists of a pneumatic motor with a relief valve which opens and closes, allowing pulses of air to enter a reed chamber, imparting a tremulant effect to the sound. The figure above shows a typical beater tremolo of this type. When the tremolo stop is drawn, the lower valve opens and air flows into the pneumatic motor, causing it to move upward. The relief valve is normally closed. When the motor has opened fully, the hinged relief valve opens due to its momentum, until stopped by a short tape connecting the tips of the motor and the relief valve. With the relief valve open the motor loses pressure and collapses. Then the relief valve closes and the cycle is repeated. The spring and weight establish the rate at which this oscillation occurs. The pulses of air flowing

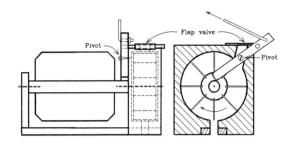

Figure 110: Typical fan tremolo. The fan is shown shortened for clarity.

through the pneumatic motor to the reeds cause the tremolo effect.

THE FAN TREMOLO

The third type, usually referred to as the fan tremolo or the vox humana, had patents dating as early as 1856 and was licensed by A. H. Hammond & Co. as the Louis Patent Tremolo. This device operates in quite a different way than the other tremolos. As it rotates, the large fan blades repeatedly change the geometry of the space inside the organ case, thus causing the standing wave pattern of the sound of the reeds to fluctuate and repetitively change the quality of the sound. It consists of a large two-bladed fan operated by an impeller, and is mounted on the outside of the chest near the treble reeds. In the figure above, when the tremolo stop is drawn, the flap valve is opened and at the same time the lever imparts an initial spin to the fan. Air flows through the flap valve, through the impeller to the chest causing the impeller to continue to rotate. The speed of rotation is limited by the air resistance on the fan. When the tremolo is shut off the spin lever acts as a brake, preventing the fan from rotating. The fan tremolo produces a rather pleasing tremolo effect, but it is often too shallow to be very noticeable. Nevertheless, it eventually became the standard tremolo mechanism used on American reed organs.[25]

99

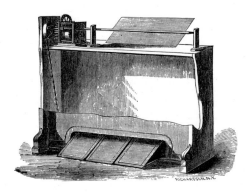

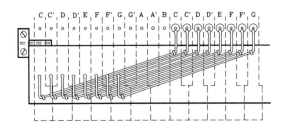

Figure 113: Octave Coupler—Top View

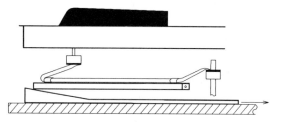

Figure 114: Octave Coupler—Side view.

Figure 111: The Carpenter Vox Humana tremolo used on Estey organs.

Another version of this device, patented by R. W. Carpenter in 1865 and used on Estey organs, was operated by a third foot pedal. About 1869 Estey abandoned this device in favor of the fan tremolo described above.

The *Octave Coupler* is a draw stop used to mechanically connect one key with another an octave away. There are several variations, but the most common arrangement consists of a Treble Coupler which couples an octave higher (super-octave coupler) on the treble portion of the manual, and a Bass Coupler which couples an octave lower (sub-octave coupler) on the bass side. Another type has a single draw stop, coupling up across the keyboard in most cases, although Mason & Hamlin made one which couples downward. The Octave Coupler is sometimes seen on the Harmonium.[26]

One disadvantage of the conventional super-octave coupler is that the highest octave on the keyboard cannot be provided with coupler action. There is a sudden loss of brilliance when a melody is played in the top octave with the coupler drawn. To remedy this, the Jenkinson Super-Octave Coupler was devised by the Jenkinson Organ Co. of London. An extra octave of reeds which come into play only when the coupler is drawn are provided for one stop.

American reed organs are almost always

equipped with a lever operated by the left knee which brings on all or most of the speaking stops together. Typical names for this apparatus are Full Organ, Grand Organ, Grand Jeu and Full Orchestra. In some organs the linkage is arranged so that as the lever is moved from its normal position toward the left, the high-pitched stops come on first, gradually followed by the lower ones, the treble side first, then the bass. Full Organ is occasionally found also as a stop knob.

Since its introduction by the Mason & Hamlin Company several years since, this instrument has been a continual surprise to organ music-lovers. . . . The latest improvement in the Liszt Organ, seen by us at the Company's warerooms last week, is the 'Pedal Point' attachment. By means of an original mechanism, set in operation by the knee of the performer, any one of the keys in the lowest octave, when depressed, remains down after the finger is removed until any other key in that octave is touched, the latter key then remaining down in place of the former; thus allowing the player to manipulate as much of or as little of the remaining portion of the keyboard as he wishes, and at the same time affording him an excellent 'organ point,' which may be varied as he sees fit. A slight movement of the knee will at any moment easily disconnect the mechanism, the lower octave keys then acting in their usual and regular manner. Several notes, instead of one, may be made to continue sounding by depressing their corresponding keys, and some remarkably charming and striking effects are thus afforded when some 2-feet or 4-feet stop is drawn. (A somewhat similar mechanism was used by the Mason & Hamlin Company years ago, but the new arrangement is a decided improvement on the old, and is peculiarly desirable in the Liszt organ on account of the extraordinary pipe-like quality of tone of this particular instrument.)

The Musical Courier,
New York, June 17, 1885

The original invention of the prolongment device is credited to Martin of Provins, then in the employ of Alexandre in Paris. Edward Snell of London invented one in 1861 as did William Dawes of Leeds. The Mason & Hamlin version was originally put into operation by means of a knee lever and was later changed to a stop knob. Cancellation of the effect was by means of a small knee lever. In the pedal bass versions of the Liszt organ the pedal point action was omitted.

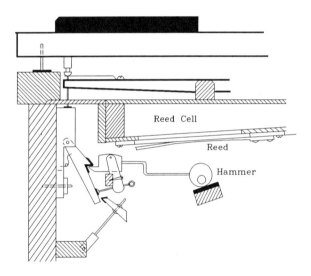

Figure 117: The harmonium percussion action

To get around the problem of slow speech of the reeds, Louis-Pierre Alexandre Martin of Sordun, Provence, France (known as Martin de Provins) invented a device in about 1841 which he called the *Percussion stop.* By means of this device,

. . . not only is all sluggishness of speech removed, but a very pleasant percussive accent is given to each note, so that the instrument partakes in some degree of the nature of the pianoforte. The invention consists of a small hammer so operated that on touching a key it strikes the reed instantaneously, causing it to vibrate at once, the wind keeping it in vibration subsequently. This 'percussion stop' allows the instrument to be used without wind, for each little tap is sufficient to give the performer the sound of the note, and thus he may practice without annoying persons who may require silence.[27]

In 1844 Alexandre et Fils of Paris announced that the percussion stop would be available in their organs as an option. The percussion mechanism is mechanically rather complex and was therefore expensive to manufacture. Alexandre charged 600 francs for a two-rank organ and another 300 for the percussion option, which tended to limit its popularity. In 1855 Jeremiah Carhart patented a percussion stop for exhaust organs but it was rarely used by American manufacturers, Mason & Hamlin being one of the few.

The *Sourdine*, or Surdine, is a mechanical stop used in harmoniums, usually in the left side of the keyboard, to limit the flow of air to a group of reeds, thus giving a soft effect. It is similar in effect to the soft stops in American organs created by partial opening of the mutes.

AMERICAN ORGAN STOP NOMENCLATURE

The names given to the stops of American organs broadly follow pipe organ usage, although there are numerous differences, some of which are wildly improbable. Unfortunately, each maker

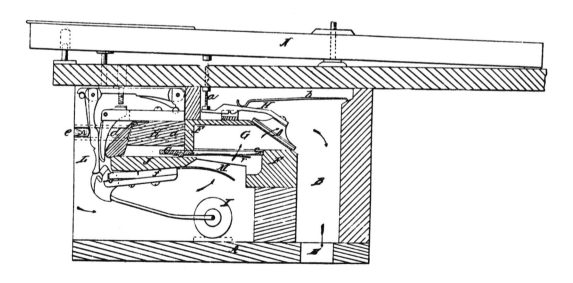

Figure 119: Carhart's percussion action, U.S. Patent No. 12,713, April 17, 1865

had his own favorite stop names, and many used different stop names for different models. Furthermore, organs with split manuals often had different stop names for the treble and bass portions of the same set of reeds, the most common of these being Diapason, usually used for the bass portion of the diapason reeds, and Melodia for the treble, although some makers reversed them. Because of this confusion, reed organ registration was not usually included in published music, since that would limit its use to a few organs with that particular stop list. Registration was a matter left to the ability of the organist.

The basic Harmonium stops are fairly well standardized, permitting the registration to be shown in the printed music. Also the basic four Harmonium stops were numbered 1, 2, 3 and 4 further simplifying the notation. Thus an organist could easily move from one instrument to another without having to re-learn the stop list, and a beginner could follow the written registration.

Some American organs built in the latter years of the instrument, particularly those made by Estey, Mason & Hamlin, Hinners and a few others, began to be more disciplined in the stop names used and also used the same name in both parts of the keyboard. Organs made especially for professional use, such as two-manual-and-pedal instruments, frequently followed pipe organ stop nomenclature.

A Stop Dictionary for the American Organ

NAME	PITCH	TONE	DESCRIPTION
Aeolian	8	string	Softest stop on organ.
Aeolian Harp	8, 2	string	Harmonium celeste stop.
Aeoline	8	string	Same as Aeolian.
Baryton	32	reed	Harmonium soft treble stop.
Bass Coupler			Mechanical stop; see discussion above.
Bass Flute	16	flute	Foundational, round tone.
Bassoon	16	reed	Resembles the orchestral instrument.
Bourdon	16	flute	Foundational, round tone.
Celeste	8	string	Wavering tone, see discussion above.
Celestina	8	string	Derived soft celeste.
Cello	16, 8	string	Broad toned.
Choral	8	diapason	Bright, forceful tone; sometimes reedy.
Clarabella	8	flute	Big flute sound.
Clarinet,	16, 8	reed	Resembles the orchestral instrument.
Clarinette	16, 8	reed	Same as Clarinet.
Clarion	4	reed	Octave of the Trumpet.
Clarionet	16	reed	Cross between Trumpet and Clarinet.
Contra Bass	16	diapason	Bright diapason on stringy side.
Cor Anglaise	8	reed	English horn.
Cornet	8	diapason	Usually a derived stop.
Cornet echo	8	diapason	Usually a derived stop.
Corno	16, 8	reed	Combination of horn and reed.
Cremona	8	string	Derived stop, smooth and soft.
Diapason	16, 8	diapason	Pure organ tone with body, brightness.
Diapason Bass	16	diapason	Most powerful 16' pedal stop.
Dolce	8	string	Soft string, may be derived.
Double Bass	16	diapason	Diapason Bass.
Double Diapason	16	diapason	Same as 16' Diapason.
Dulcet	8	string	Soft string, usually derived.
Dulciana	8	diapason	Echo diapason, may be derived.

Echo, echo horn	8	diapason	Derived stop from diapason.
English Horn	8	reed	Resembles the orchestral instrument.
Eolian Harp	2	string	Bass Celeste.
Fife	4	flute	Strong, octave diapason.
Flute	8, 4	flute	Flute tone.
Flute d'Amour	4	flute	Soft flute, smooth.
Flutina	8, 4	flute	Derived soft stop of Flute.
French Horn	8	reed	Resembles the orchestral instrument.
Gamba	8	string	Big, robust string tone.
Gemshorn	8, 4	hybrid	Neutral tone on stringy side.
Harp Aeoline	8	string	Softest of celestes, ethereal.
Harp Aeolienne	8	string	Same as Harp Aeoline.
Harp Eolienne	8	string	Same as Harp Aeoline.
Hautbois,	8	reed	Oboe, resembles orchestral instrument.
Hautboy	8	reed	Same as Oboe.
Horn	8	reed	Derived stop of trumpet.
Melodia	8	diapason	Continuation of the Diapason stop in the treble (or bass) half of a split manual.
Musette	16		Harmonium
Oboe	8	reed	Resembles the orchestral instrument.
Octave Coupler			Mechanical stop; see discussion above.
Open Diapason	8	diapason	Same as Diapason.
Pedal Bourdon	16	flute	Medium power foundational tone.
Pedal Dulciana	16	string	Softest 16' pedal stop.
Pedal Point			Mechanical stop, holds bass notes.
Percussion	8	diapason	Harmonium: Diapason stop with percussion action.
Piccolo	2, 4	flute	Full, smooth, liquid tone.
Pizzicato	8	diapason	Percussion action used by Mason & Hamlin.
Principal	4	diapason	Full, strong octave diapason.
Prolongment			Mechanical stop, same as Pedal Point.
Salicional	8	string	Soft, thin string tone.
Saxaphone	16, 8, 4	reed	Resembles the orchestral instrument.

Saxophone		reed	Same as Saxaphone.
Stop Diapason	8	flute	Round foundational tone.
Sub Bass	16	diapason	Strong diapason, usually one octave on bass part of manual.
Sourdine	8		Harmonium. Soft stop.
Surdine	8		Same as Sourdine.
Treble Coupler			Mechanical stop; see discussion above.
Tremulant			Mechanical stop, Tremolo.
Trumpet	8	reed	Bright, open tone.
Viola	4	string	Resembles the orchestral instrument, sometimes a derived soft stop of Principal.
Viola Dolce	8, 4	string	Soft, well-bodied sound; sometimes a 4' derived soft stop of Viola.
Viol d'Gamba	8	string	Big, robust string tone, see Gamba.
Violetta	4	flute	Soft flute, may be derived.
Violin	4	string	Thin, brilliant, cutting tone.
Violina	4, 2	string	Bright string, sometimes a derived soft stop of Viola.
Voix Celeste	8	string	String celeste.
Vox Angelica	8	string	Soft celeste.
Vox Humaine	2	string	Bass celeste
Vox Humana			Mechanical stop, Tremolo.
Vox Jubilante	8	diapason	Big toned diapason celeste; sometimes a mechanical Tremolo.
Wald flute	2	flute	Clear, full tone.

Harmonium Stop Arrangements

One of the great advantages of the European approach to the reed organ was the standardization of stops. By following a single system, it was possible to include registration in printed music for the harmonium, and a musician could easily move from one instrument to another with only a minimum of familiarization required. The uniformity was not absolute, but was generally followed by all harmonium makers at least for the first four stops in both treble and bass. These stops were numbered 1 through 4 to facilitate registration in printed music. The German and French makers generally followed the same stop names, and the British had some variations as shown below.

NO.	PITCH	ENGLISH	FRENCH	GERMAN
BASS SPEAKING STOPS				
1	8′	Diapason Bass	Cor Anglais	Englisch Horn
2	16′	Bourdon	Bourdon	Bordun
3	4′	Principal or Clarion	Clairon	Clairon
4	8′	Bassoon	Basson	Basson
5	2′	Aeolian Harp	Harpe eolienne	Aolsharfe
TREBLE SPEAKING STOPS				
1	8′	Diapason Treble	Flute	Flöte
2	16′	Double Diapason	Clarinette	Clarinette
3	4′	Principal	Fifre	Fifre
4	8′	Oboe	Hautbois	Oboe
5	16′	Musette	Musette	Musette

(The keyboard starts at C and splits between E and F.)

Ph. J. Trayser & C̲ie̲.

Harmonium-Fabrik, Stuttgart

100 Rothebühlstrasse 100.

Gegründet 1847. ——————— Gegründet 1847.

Stuttgart 1881 Goldene Medaille (Höchste Auszeichnung).

New-York 1853.

München 1854.

London 1862.

Paris 1867
Silberne Medaille.

London 1872.

Wien 1873
Fortschritts-Medaille.

Stettin 1865.

Santiago 1875
Goldene Medaille mit
extra Auszeichnung

Philadelphia 1876
Grosse Medaille.

München 1876.

Sidney 1879
Silberne Medaille.

London 1884
Goldene Medaille.

Altrenommirtes grösstes Etablissement,

prämiirt auf allen Weltausstellungen, liefert

Harmoniums als Specialität

in allen Grössen für

Kirche, Schule und Haus.

[1232]

Kataloge gratis und franko.

Ernst Erich Liebmann

Gera (Reuss)

Harmonium- u. Musikwerke-Fabrik

mit elektrischem Betrieb.

Orgel-Harmoniums

für

Schule, Kirche, Haus, Concert, etc.

Edler Ton, gediegene und solide Arbeit.

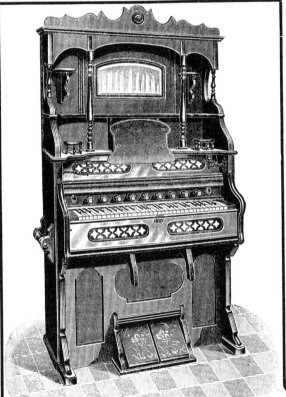

Mech. Musikwerke

mit auswechselbaren
langen Noten.

Specialität:

Kalliston-
Musikwerke

mit
Glocken- und mit Glocken-
und Trommelspiel.

Kalophon- und Erica-
Drehorgeln.

Melodion- und
Strassenorgeln.

Export nach allen Welt-
theilen.   [30

Verlangen Sie Cataloge.

109

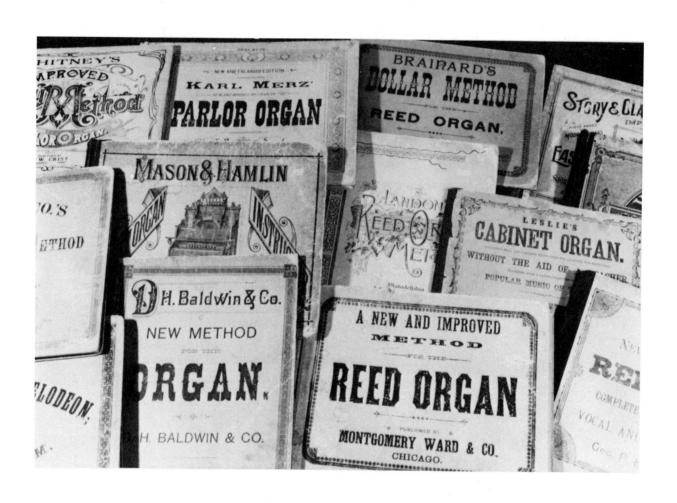

Figure 121

110

Chapter Four

Music for the Reed Organ

METHOD BOOKS

When the earliest reed organs were being built, musicians wishing to play them were either self-taught or had to rely on instruction books intended for other instruments, such as *Instructions in Thorough Base, a New and Easy Method for Learning to Play Church Music upon the Piano Forte or Organ*, by A. N. Johnson, published in 1844 by George P. Reed & Co., Boston. As reed organs became more popular, music teachers began to demand books tailored for that instrument, and publishers were quick to respond, for example, with *Winner's Melodeon Primer*. Sep Winner eventually produced at least eight different reed organ method books, some published under manufacturers' names, such as D. W. Karn.

Oliver Ditson, Boston's foremost music dealer, along with Dr. Lowell Mason, was one of the backers of the fledgling reed organ manufacturing firm founded by Mason's son, Henry, and Emmons Hamlin, so he was closely attuned to the growth of the reed organ industry. Ditson already had found a brisk business in publishing and selling books and sheet music for the piano

With the
BEETHOVEN
is sent a
Music Book,
SUITABLE for ORGANS
No extra
Charge is Made.

Figure 122

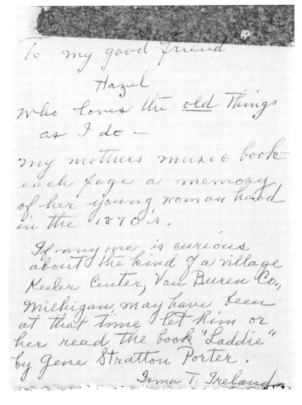

Figure 123

111

and other instruments, and soon made available J. Eliot Trowbridge's *Mason & Hamlin Cabinet Organ Instructor,* as well as William H. Clarke's *Dollar Instructor for Reed Organ,* followed by Clarke's *New Method for Reed Organ.* Other Boston music publishers offering reed organ method books were G. D. Russell & Co.; White, Smith & Co. and George P. Reed & Co. Method books were also available from Theodore Presser and F. A. North & Co. of Philadelphia, John Church & Co. and D. H. Baldwin & Co. in Cincinnati, Otto Sutro & Co. in Baltimore and S. Brainard's Sons in Chicago. W. W. Whitney's various method books became highly popular and were also published under the names of various reed organ manufacturers such as Loring & Blake, Newman Bros. and Story & Clark. Whitney did so well in publishing that in 1881 he became president of the reed organ manufacturer, Loring & Blake.

Figure 125

SUMMER HOME OF ANNA ADAMS.

Figure 124

Collecting old method books brings some hidden benefits, such as notes, names and signatures of the teachers and students. The art work by Anna Adams shown at left was done, one assumes, when she should have been practicing the organ. She also showed the family home, but it is too faint to reproduce here.

112

The following table shows a list of some of these old method books. They occasionally can still be found at flea markets and used book stores, although most of them were printed on the cheapest paper and are now badly deteriorated. In order to make them more easily available to reed organ enthusiasts, I gathered together the best parts of several method books in 1977 and reprinted them under the name *Playing the American Reed Organ*.

REED ORGAN METHOD BOOKS FROM ANDREWS TO ZUNDEL

Andrews' Complete Method for the Parlor Organ, H. T. Andrews, 1892.

Method for American Reed Organ, Frederic Archer, ca 1889

D. H. Baldwin & Co., *New Method for the Organ*, 1886.

The Eclectic Teacher for the Parlor Organ, by J. G. Barnett, 1883.

Beatty's Piano and Parlor Organ Instructor, 1882. $0.25.

Bellak's Method for Reed Organ, by J. Bellak. $0.75.

Bent's New and Improved Method for the Reed Organ, 1883.

Bentley's Dollar Method for the Parlor Organ, ca 1888.

Blake's Dollar Instructor for the Reed Organ, by C. D. Blake. $1.00

School for the Reed Organ and Melodian, C.D. Blake & C. A. White.

Harmonium Schule by Heinrich Bungart, ca 1904.

Carhart's Melodeon Instructor, by T. E. Gurney, 1881.

Century Co.'s *Excelsior Method for the Parlor Organ*, 1884.

A. B. Chase Co., *Complete Instructor for the Parlor Organ*, 1878.

Chicago Cottage Organ, *New & Improved Method Book for the Organ*.

Clarke's Dollar Instructor for Reed Organ, by Wm. H. Clarke.

Clarke's New Method for Reed Organs, O. Ditson, publisher.

Cornish's Modern Method for the Reed Organ. $1.50.

Méthode pour Harmonium, A. Desjardin. Choudens Dils, Éditeurs, Paris.

Harmonium-Schule, by Friedrich Eckhardt, Frankfurt/M, (current).

Ecole d'Orgue, Méthode complète d'Harmonium, Switzerland 1890.

Emerson's New Method for Reed Organ, by Emerson & Mathews.

Root's Easy Reed Organ Method, by J. S. Fearis, 1903.

School for the Parlor Organ, Melodeon & Harmonium, J. Getze, 1869.

Getze's School for the Parlor Organ. $1.50.

The Rapid Instructor and Chord Book for Organ, E. N. Guckert, 1903.

The Harmonium by King Hall. Novello's Music Primers, No. 4.

Heppe's Music Instructor for the Piano or Organ, 1888.

Méthode Êlémentaire pour HARMONIUM ou Orgue expressif, Carl Hoffman.

Johnson's Parlor Organ Instruction Book, by A. H. Johnson. $1.50

Leslie's Cabinet Organ, 1867.

D. W. Karn, *Winner's New Method for the Reed Organ*, 1872.

Kimball's Excelsior Method for the Parlor Organ, 1888. $1.50.

W. W. Kimball Co.'s *New Easy Method for the Cabinet Organ*, 1878.

New Kimball Method for the Reed Organ, ca 1905.

Kinkel's New Method for the Reed Organ. $2.50.

Landon's Reed Organ Method, 1891. $1.50.

Praktische Orgel- od. Physharmonica Schule, by J. R. Lindeman.

Loring & Blake Organ Co. Palace Organ Instructor, 1886.

Mack's Dollar Analytical Method for Cabinet Organ. $1.50

Mason & Hamlin Cabinet Organ Instructor, by J. E. Trowbridge, 1878.

Karl Merz New and Improved Method for the Parlor Organ, 1876.

Montgomery Ward. New and Improved Method for the Reed Organ, 1892.

Newman Bros. Improved Easy Method for the Parlor Organ, 1886.

Harmonium-Schule, Opus 22 by Herman Protze, 1917.

Nouvelle Méthode de Clavier, Harmonium ou Orgue, Pierront & Bonfils.

Putnam's New Method of Instruction for the Reed Organ, 1905.

Grosse Harmonium-Schule, opus 16 by August Reinhard.

School for the Cabinet Organ, by George F. Root, $2.50.

Sears, Roebuck & Co.'s Dollar Organ Method, by C. H. Gabriel, 1900.

Theoretisch-praktische Harmonium-Schule, by Dr. C. Seeger.

The Royal Method for the Parlor Organ, by Chas. E. Shenk, 1895.

Dr. Stainer's Tutor for American Organ, J. B. Cramer, London (current).

Praktische Anleitung zum Harmonium-Spiel, opus 5 by E. Stapf.

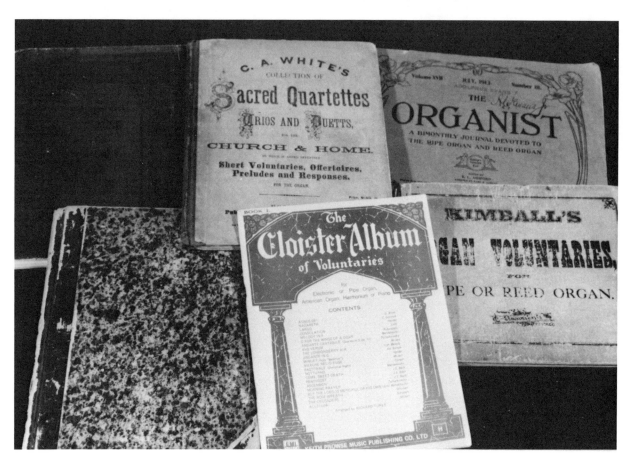

Figure 126

Schule fur Harmonium od. Cottage-Orgel, Joh. G. Stehle, ed.

Story & Clark's Improved Easy Method for the Parlor Organ, 1886.

The National Guide to Reed Organ Playing, by W.F. Sudds, 1882.

Méthode pour Orgue-Harmonium, Rene Vierne, ca 1913.

Taber Organ Co.'s Improved Method for the Organ, 1878-90-92.

Méthode complète d'Harmonium, by Renaud de Vilbac, (current).

Weaver's New Improved Method for the Organ, 1878-90-92.

Western Cottage Organ Co.'s Improved Easy Method for the Parlor Organ.

White's Excelsior Method for the Organ, 1896.

White's School for the Reed Organ, by C. A. White & C. D. Blake, 1875.

Whitney's Simplified Instructor for the Reed Organ. $1.50

Whitney's One Dollar Method for the Cabinet Organ. $1.00

Whitney's Improved Easy Method for the Parlor Organ, 1886. $1.50.

Whitney's Complete Instructor for the Parlor Organ, 1878. $2.50.

Winner's New School for the Cabinet Organ

Winner's New School for the Melodeon

Winner's Perfect Guide to Melodeon

Winner's Perfect Guide to Cabinet Organ

Winner's Easy System for Reed Organ or Melodeon

Winner's Melodeon Primer.

Winner's Ideal Method for the Cabinet Organ, by Sep Winner. $0.50.

Winner's New Method for the Reed Organ, 1872.

Wright's New Method for the Cabinet Organ, by Rodney P. Wright.

Zundel's Reed Organ Instructor. $2.00

Collections of music arranged especially for the reed organ were widely available during the reed organ era. Some examples are:

Album for kammarorgel, by Gustaf Hagg, Stockholm.

Album for orgelharmonium, 3 volumes by Gustaf Hagg, Stockholm.

The Young Organist's Album, by G. Blessner, 1869.

Clarke's Reed Organ Companion by Wm. H. Clarke. $2.00.

Clarke's Short Voluntaries for Reed Organ. $1.00.

The Cornish Collection of Modern Melodies for Pianos & Organs.

Favoritsmarscher for orgelharmonium, Stockholm.

Folio of Music for the Piano-Forte or Cabinet Organ, Thos. Hunter, 1883

Kimball's Organ Voluntaries, Vol. I, by Horace E. Kimball, 1871.

Kimball's Organ Voluntaries for Pipe or Reed Organ, 1874.

Sur des Noëls Français, by Pierre Kunc, Switzerland, 1890.

Parlor Organ Gems, Vol. I, by H. Maylath, 1884.

Royal Organ Folio, by James R. Murray, 1895.

The Organ at Home, Organ Pieces for Reed Organ. $2.00.

Recreations for Reed Organ.

The Reed Organ at Home. $0.50.

Reed Organ Folio. $0.50.

Ryder's Short Voluntaries for Pipe or Cabinet Organ.

6 Latta Tonbilder, Opus 32 by Gustaf Hagg, Stockholm.

Stamningsbilder vid orgelharmonium, Opus 37 by Gustaf Hagg, Stockholm.

COLLECTION LITOLFF.

No. 880.

The

Estey-Organ School

by

VINZ. MICKO.

Edited by

DR. WESTBROOK.

With the revival of interest in the reed organ in recent years, collections of music for the reed organ have become available. In most cases, local music dealers will often not have them in stock but will make special orders on request. Some of the currently available books are:

Heures Mystiques, Op. 29 by Leon Boëllman; Belwin Mills, Publisher.

The Cloister Album of Voluntaries for Harmonium or American Organ, 6 volumes, Keithe Prowse 1935.

Universal Edition of Franz Liszt's Complete Organ Works, Vol. 6: harmonium music.

The Organist at Home, by P. A. Schneker.

Seventy Solos for the Hammond Organ or Reed Organ, G. Shirmer, pub.

Two Staff Organ Book, Books I & II by U. S. Leupold, 1948, 1953.

Six Little Fugues A3 by Handel, Kenneth Roberts, ed. Concordia.

In Joyous Praise, Organ Music in the French Tradition, Jon Spong, ed., Broadman Press, 1971.

Partita for Organ, by Jan Bender. Augsburg, 1981.

Two Pieces for Organ, Manuals Only, by Herbert Howell.

The Church Organist's Library, Easy Organ Music from all Historical Periods, for Manuals Only and for Manual and Pedal, Vol. I. Wayne Leupold, ed. Belwin Mills 1983.

Eight Short Pieces, Old and New, Oxford University Press 1960.

Sixty Short Pieces for Pipe or Reed Organ, by Flor Peeters. Belwin Mills, 1955.

The Best of Organ Voluntaries for American Organ, Book I, Allans, Melbourne, Australia.

l'Organiste by Cesar Franck, 59 pieces for harmonium.

Portraits and Impressions by Karg-Elert.

Karg-Elert Album for Organ, Marks Music Co.

Karg-Elert Sketch Book by Hinrichsen.

Ave Maria for Piano or Harmonium by Liszt. Editio Musica Budapest.

Music for Manuals by Peter Pindar Stearns. Coburn Press.

116

Twenty-four Pieces in Free Style by Louis Vierne.

Lyric Suite for Reed Organ by Craig Penfield. Belwin Mills 1984.

Preludes for Reed or Pipe Organ, P. H. P. Rynding, ed. Augsburg 1909.

Because of the American organ's lack of uniformity of stop names, the use of keyboards beginning with either C or F, differences in the break points between the treble and bass portions, and the variety of octave coupler arrangements, published music for that instrument was generic in nature and depended on the organist to arrange the stop registration and make whatever other adjustments were required by the configuration of each particular organ. One of the few exceptions was *The Estey Organ School* by Vinz. Micko, edited by Dr. Westbrook and published by Henry Litolff's Verlag, Braunschweig, Germany about 1876. This collection includes stop registrations for a typical Estey organ of the time, and with only minor changes could be used with almost any American organ. It seems that this approach could have been used by the American publishers, but obviously they were not interested.

Explanation of the Stops which are used in the pieces following.

The sign when surrounded by a circle means that the stop is to be drawn: when the sign is crossed through it is to be shut off.

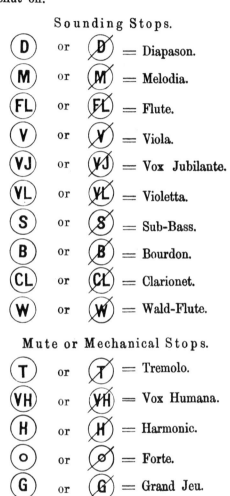

Figure 128

117

GOD SAVE THE KING.
ENGLISH NATIONAL ANTHEM.

Figure 129: God Save The King

NORTH AMERICAN POPULAR AIR.
YANKEE DOODLE.

Figure 130: Yankee Doodle

LA MARSEILLAISE.

FRENCH NATIONAL AIR.

Figure 131: The Marseillaise

119

Figure 132: Spanish Hymn

120

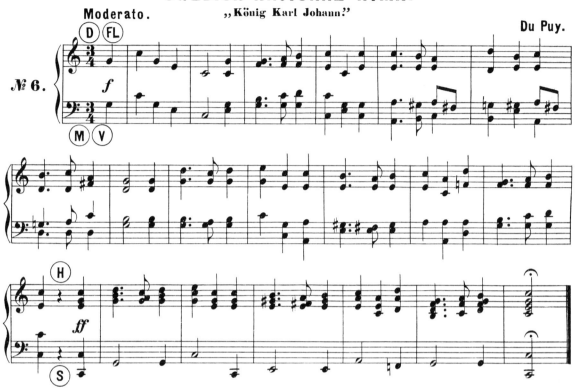

Figure 133: Swedish National Hymn

RUSSIAN NATIONAL HYMN.

Collection Litolff No. 880

Figure 134: Russian National Hymn

CHRISTMAS TUNES.

Figure 135: Christmas Tunes (continued on following page)

122

Figure 136: Christmas Tunes (continued from previous page)

123

Figure 137: Norwegian Popular Air

124

RECORDED MUSIC

Another indication of the increasing popularity of the reed organ is the recent availability of recorded reed organ music. These recordings are not likely to be found at record stores, but most merchants will be willing to order them.

Angels' Visits and other vocal gems of Victorian America, K. Battle, et al, The Harmoneion Singers; Lawrence Skrobacs, piano and harmonium. New World Records NW 220.

Bagatelles, Dvořák, Op. 47; Members of the Juilliard Quartet, R. Firkusny, harmonium. Columbia 34515. Also on Troy 41.

Franck: Complete Harmonium Music, Arturo Sacchetti on the harmonium. Four CDs. Available from Koch International, 177 Cantiague Rock Rds., Westbury, NY 11590.

French Music for Harmonium, Ann Page playing a Mustel Harmonium. Music of Franck, Vierne, Langlais, Lefebure-Wely and Dupre. Cassette. Cambridge Reed Organs, 1988.

French Music for Harmonium, Vol. 2, Ann Page playing L. Vierne, Tournemire, Hakim, Litaize, Langlais, R. Vierne. Voix Celeste Recording CEL 002 CD, ca 1990.

Sigfrid Karg-Elert: *Music for Harmonium,* Ann Page playing a 1905 Mustel, 1897 Mustel and a 1929 Mannborg suction reed organ. Cassette CEL-003 MC. Voix Celeste Recordings, 18 Hill Close, Newmarket, Suffolk, England CB8 0NR.

Sigfrid Karg-Elert: *Harmoniumwerke,* Vol. I, Johannes Matthias Michel playing a 1913 Mustel, 1992. Available from Bodensee Music, Markus Bilger, 1401 Maureen Drive, Santa Rosa, CA 95401.

Harmonium & Company—French Salon Music, Quartets, Trios, Duets of Gounod, Guilmant and Saint-Saens. Cassette available from F. Lee.

l'Harmonium Français—music of Bizet, Berlioz, Rossini, Lefebure-Wely, Boellman, Guilmant, Mouquet, Mustel—played on an 1860 Debain and a 1920 Mustel. Joris Verdin's impeccable playing and use of Expression demonstrate how the best of reed organs sound. CD: RIC 123111.

Late Chamber Music, Liszt, "Elégie I" cello, piano, harp, harmonium; plus other works.

Liszt Ferenc, Works for Harmonium; works for Cello and Piano, Zsuzsa Elekes on Liszt's harmonium (sic. Mason & Hamlin) CD, Hungarotone HCD 12768, ca 1987.

Mahler-Schreker-Schoenberg-Busoni; Camerata de Versailles, CD, Classique Auvidis 6110, ca 1986.

Mechanical Memories, The Authentic Sound of Mechanical Musical Reproducing Instruments Recorded at the British Piano Museum. *Aeolian Orchestrelle: See the Conquering Hero Comes;* Everest Tradition 2117.

Music for Harmonium, played by Germain Desbonnet on an Alexandre, music by Boellman, Franck and Berlioz. LP, MHS 4192.

Le Nouveau Salon, The Salon Orchestra, Classic Caféhaus Music, Pro Arte PAD-136.

Le Nouveau Salon, Wiener Salon, Salonorchester Cölln, EMI 16 9563 1; cassette 16 9563 4.

Le Nouveau Salon, Russischer Salon, Salonorchester Cölln, EMI 27 0530 1; cassette 27 0530 4; CDC 747672.

Music of the Grand Salon, the Salon orchestra, Pro Arte PCD-135 (cassette).

Oeuvres pour Harmonium, by Franck. Played by Joris Verdin, harmonium and Jos van Immerseel, piano. CD, Ricercar RIC 075057.

Old Pump Organ, Naomi Barfield. LP, FORUM 7G510.

l'Orgue Cavaillé-Coll Poïkilorgue (1835), LP, Motette M 10760.

A Reed Organ Anthology by Earl Miller. AFKA Records LP, SK-286.

Le Salon Parisienne, the Salon orchestra, Pro Arte PCD-222 (cassette).

Petite Messe Solonelle, by Rossini. Everest LP, S-441 1-2. Also by the King's College Singers with harmonium accompaniment on CD: EMI/Angel DSB-3976. Also on DG EMI-Electrola J1003/4 by Martin Lucker on the harmonium. Also on Argo ZRG 893-4 by The London Chamber Choir, L. Heltay, conductor, John Birch, harmonium; ca 1985, (this is said to be the best version.) Also by the Ambrosian Singers, C. Scimone, conductor, Richard Nunn on the harmonium, Philips 412 124-1/2.

The Romantic Harmonium, Franz Haselbock playing a two-manual Bruckner harmonium and a 30 stop suction bellows harmonium. Music of von Weber, Kienzl, Reger, Bruckner, Bizet, Franck, Liszt, Berlioz and Smetana. LP.

Souvenir d'Amour, popular music (salon, Gypsy and Viennese) from the age of elegance played by the London Salon Ensemble. Strings, piano and unidentified harmonium. CD, BOCD 171. Bosworth & Co., 14/18 Heddon St., London W1R 8DP, England.

A Traditional Christmas at the Harmonium, with R. Frederick Henry at the Hörügel harmonium; ca 1981.

Waltzes by Strauss for String Quartet, Piano and Harmonium, by Ensemble 13, Baden-Baden; Pro Arte LP PAD 179. Also Pro Arte Pal-1011. Also on cassette.

Figure 138

126

GOLDSCHMEDING'S

aanbevolen fabrikaten

Piano's en Orgels:

Ernst Kaps	**Packard**
Schiedmayer	**Estey**
Rich. Ritter	**Karn.**
Sponnagel	**Burdett**
Neumeyer	**Doherty**
Mann	**Peerless**
Adam	**Cabel**
e. a.	*e. a.*

Vraag Catalogus en Prijzen

van

GOLDSCHMEDING'S

Pianospeler Simplex.

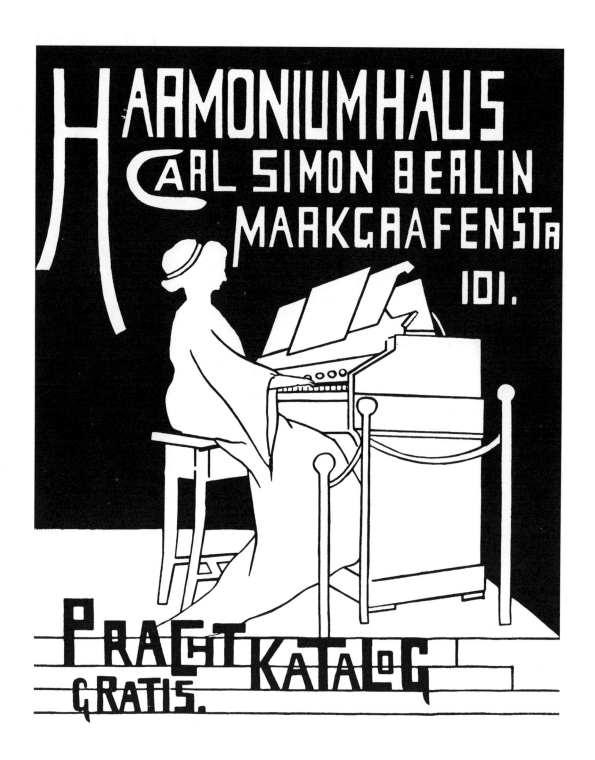

128

Chapter Five

Portable Organs

Figure 139: A camp meeting near the Redeye River, Wadena County, Minnesota in the early 1900s. The couple on the left are Henry and Mary Kiehl; the preacher, John Turnbull, is on the right; the two men in the middle are probably John and Rube Kiehl, sons of Henry and Mary. The organist is unidentified.

The earliest free reed organs tended to be massive devices, as for example Grenié's Orgue Expressif and Greene's Royal Seraphine, mentioned in Chapter 1. Previously, however, regals and even small pipe organs had been built in a light weight, portable style and, within a few years of the appearance of the first free reed instruments, portable versions were being made. These little organs eventually became important far beyond the relatively small quantities in which they were produced, as they became a standard part of the equipment of traveling preachers and

camp meetings and, later, as the fondly-remembered "chaplain organs" of the World Wars.

Perhaps the prototype of the portable reed organ is the lap organ or rocking melodeon, as shown in Figure 14. The Prescott lap organs were inspired by those made by James A. Bazin, who was making them as early as 1836, and who may have been the originator of the lap organ style of instrument. Daniel B. Bartlett and others made similar models. Very few lap organs have survived to the present.

Another early reed organ that could be considered a portable instrument is the folding-legged melodeon shown below with the legs folded and extended. This type was probably intended for use in the home, as the rosewood veneer case will not take the wear and tear of being moved about. Its light weight and small size when folded made it easy to store on a shelf or beneath a bed when space was at a premium. The example shown here was made by Jones & Burditt in 1847. It has a four-octave C-scale keyboard, a foot-operated swell, a single foot-operated exhauster and two sets of reeds, 4' and 8'. The 4' rank is controlled by a stop lever to the right of the keyboard. Virtually identical instruments, usually with only a single set of reeds, were made by many different makers in the 1840s and 50s, and a fair number still survive.

One of the pioneer reed organ makers in the United States was Geo. A. Prince & Co. of Buffalo, New York, founded in 1846. Prince made portable organs from an early date, as the following testimonial from one of their catalogs shows:

New York, March 5th, 1865

In conclusion, I would say that I have had one of your Portable Melodeons in constant use nearly thirteen years. It has been transported to California, Australia, China, the Sandwich Islands, and many of the principal Polynesian Islands, in the South Pacific Ocean, also throughout South America and the West Indies, besides being in regular use at all our concerts in the United States. During the whole time, the instrument itself has needed no repairs, and notwithstanding the many 'hard knocks' incidental to transportation, and the great variety of climates to which it has necessarily been subjected, its tone has continued excellent, and is now in as good tone as when first purchased.

J. M. Boulard, Director
The Alleghanians

Figure 140, a & b: Jones & Burditt melodeon.

130

The so-called lyre-legged melodeons were available in a portable style with hinged legs and a fitted carrying case. The illustration shown below is from the George A. Prince & Co. catalog of 1874. The popular Mason & Hamlin Baby Organ was also available with folding legs and a fitted case.

Figure 141: Prince Style 76 Portable Melodeon, 1874.

The Chautauqua movement began after the Civil War as a summer training camp for Sunday school teachers and religious workers at Chautauqua Lake, New York. It was a great success and became the pattern for other so-called "Chautauquas" located throughout the country. The original purely religious orientation was gradually broadened to include adult education and entertainment. Portable reed organs were widely used to accompany traveling musical groups who performed at these meetings, to provide accompaniment for hymn singing and for solo concert performances. Since many reed organ builders such as Jacob Estey and Riley Burdett were deeply involved in religious activities they were quick to take notice of the need for rugged but light weight organs suitable for frequent shipment from place to place. The foreign missionary movement also became very active during this period and every missionary was equipped with an organ before leaving.

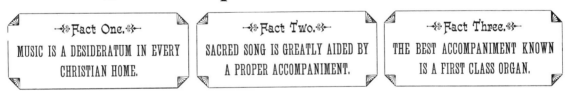

Three Facts known to all Chautauquans!

❖ Fact One. ❖	❖ Fact Two. ❖	❖ Fact Three. ❖
MUSIC IS A DESIDERATUM IN EVERY CHRISTIAN HOME.	SACRED SONG IS GREATLY AIDED BY A PROPER ACCOMPANIMENT.	THE BEST ACCOMPANIMENT KNOWN IS A FIRST CLASS ORGAN.

HAVING STATED THREE FACTS KNOWN TO ALL, WE WANT TO STATE

Three Facts which <u>ought</u> to be known to all Chautauquans!

1. No other Organ will so well bear out the title of "first class" in every respect,

2. No other Organ has so well stood the test of years—over a third of a century,

3. No other Organ has in its Construction such combined Excellence and Superiority in DESIGN, WORKMANSHIP and TONE QUALITY, as the

ESTEY ORGAN, Manufactured at Brattleboro, Vermont, by J. ESTEY & COMPANY.

ILLUSTRATED CATALOGUES MAILED FREE.

Figure 142

Perrinton, New York, Aug. 7, 1867

Mr. Geo. W. Clark, Rochester, N. Y.:

The Melodeon (Prince & Co., makers, Buffalo,) which I purchased of you in 1850, after sixteen years of constant and hard usage, is yet as good as new, except the ordinary wear of the case. It has been used at concerts and shows, carried about in the night air serenading, and so far from being impaired, the tones retain their original fullness, and have improved in richness and sweetness. Not one of the reeds have needed tuning or failed. It has never cost me one cent for repairs.

Yours truly,   I. G. ALDRICH

Peter Philip Bilhorn as a young man studied with the famous evangelist Dwight L. Moody, then traveled west to work as a missionary among the cowboys. As a result of that experience he decided that the portable organs then available were too heavy, so he designed a very light weight organ which folded up to look like a suitcase. In 1885 he formed the Bilhorn Organ Company in Chicago to manufacture it. By 1887 he was traveling with Moody and Ira D. Sankey as a composer, organist and singer, while his brother C. F. Bilhorn ran the business, now known as Bilhorn Brothers. The lightest Bilhorn organ was called the Suit Case Folding Organ, Style S, and had a 3 1/4 octave F-scale keyboard with a single set of reeds. It weighed only seventeen pounds.

The little organs became very popular, and eventually a competitor appeared. A. L White had worked for the Bridgeport Organ Co., Farrand & Votey, Story & Clark, Williams Piano & Organ Co. and the M. Shulz Co. In 1900 he formed the A. L. White Mfg. Co. in Chicago and began to make similar lightweight or folding organs. One of the more elaborate White models was called the Chautauqua Pipe-Tone Folding Organ. This model had a five-octave F-scale keyboard, with two octaves of 8', 16' and 4' reeds in the bass, and three octaves of 8' and 16' reeds plus an 8' celeste stop in the treble. This organ weighed 63 pounds and was probably the most versatile of the folding organs. Other makers of folding organs were Loduca Bros., Hans Faber, N. Kiessling & Son, C. G. Conn, Rodeheaver Co., Beckwith, Marshall Bros., and in Canada, W. Doherty & Co. Folding organs bearing the names Oliver Ditson & Co. and Lyon & Healy are occasionally seen, and it is likely that they were made by others with the appropriate stencil attached.

During the latter part of the nineteenth century and early part of the twentieth the northern parts of Minnesota, Wisconsin and Michigan were the scene of intense logging activity. The loggers spent months each year in the isolated camps working from sunrise to sunset. Their religious needs were served by traveling ministers and priests who walked from camp to camp carrying a portable organ. One of them, Rev. John W. Sorenberger, used the Bilhorn Style H folding organ now on display at the St. Louis County Historical Society Museum in Duluth, Minnesota.

At the time of World War I the U.S. Army used the lightweight portable instruments already available on the market for Chaplain's organs. A. L. White was a major supplier, but one of Bilhorn's catalogs of that era says "The Bilhorn organ . . .is the only Folding Organ awarded the United States Government Contracts for many years." Neither Estey nor Mason & Hamlin made the lightweight style, and after the war Estey attempted to interest the Army in their Style JJ portable organ, (presumably named after J. J. Estey, son of Jacob Estey,) as the following exchange of correspondence shows.

Fig. 143: Bilhorn portable organ carried by the Rev. John W Sorenberger on his rounds of the logging camps in northern Minnesota.

Brattleboro, Vermont
March 24, 1921

Colonel John T. Axton,
Chief of Chaplains,
War Department,
Washington, D. C.

Dear Sir:-

We have your valued favor of March 21, and we are sending you under separate cover a catalog showing the Estey folding organs.

We supplied over 600 of these instruments to the YMCA, Salvation Army and other Welfare Organizations that did work during the late world war and we have a number of very flattering testimonials as to the service these little organs gave.

Unfortunately we are not able to sell the United States Government as evidenced by reports that we have here in our office. They are apparently interested in a lower priced organ, lighter in weight.

Now, we take the stand that we cannot afford to put out an organ that will not give years of satisfaction and, therefore, it is not our intention to see how light an organ we can construct but rather one that will give thorough satisfaction.

You may be interested in a letter we have just received showing the hard treatment an organ sometimes receives and how the Estey stands up in comparison with some other instruments.

We should be much pleased to serve your department and await your favors. We might say that our present price on the JJ is $50. and within a reasonable distance we deliver express paid at this figure.

Yours very truly,
Estey Organ Company
By (s) M. Austin

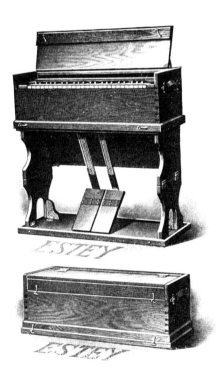

Fig. 144: The Estey Style JJ Folding Organ weighed 90 pounds in its carrying case.

Washington, New Jersey
March ll, 1921

Estey Organ Company,
Brattleboro, Vermont

Gentlemen:-

When I received your style JJ (portable) folding organ, it was on a little mission station in the heart of Africa, sixteen hundred miles from the nearest large town, thirteen days from the doctor and seventy-two miles from our nearest missionary neighbors at Dungu. The porters who came in with it said that the canoe had upset while crossing the last river and that my organ had floated around for ten of fifteen minutes.

It was necessary to take your organ all to pieces and dry it in the sun, piece by piece, for it was so swollen with the dampness that it was useless. Having a little knowledge of mechanics I did what I afterward tried to do with other makes of folding organs. In the case of the Estey, it was very easily repaired. With the others it was impossible to repair them, as the action was sealed and glued with no means left of getting at it for repairs.

Allow me to congratulate the designer of the JJ Portable.

Yours truly,
JOSEPH W. JOHNSON

Washington, D.C.
March 26, 1921

Estey Organ Company
Brattleboro, Vt.

Gentlemen:

This will make grateful acknowledgment of your letter of March 24th relative to the Estey folding organ model JJ.

We have today recommended that this instrument be made a standard article of equipment for army chaplains.

Very sincerely yours,
JOHN T. AXTON,
Colonel, U.S. Army,
Chief of Chaplains

Colonel Axton's recommendation apparently was disregarded, as the Army continued to use the light weight folding organs. In 1932 the Army decided to make a formal procurement of a new type of Chaplain's organ. The Quartermaster Corps had a sample organ built which satisfied its requirements and then issued specifications on March 18, 1932 based on that instrument, as follows:

SPECIFICATION
Quartermaster Corps,
U.S. Army

CHAPLAIN'S ORGAN, Reed

General: This specification is intended to describe the sealed standard sample of Chaplain's Organ, actually on file at the Philadelphia Quartermaster Depot, and which it is desired to reproduce. In any points, such as general appearance, workmanship, and finish, not covered by these specifications, the standard sample will govern. The standard sample may be inspected by prospective bidders at the place indicated herein or stated in the Invitation for Bids.

Materials: Wood—Bass or gum wood, oak, cedar or spruce, Rubber, steel, Nickel, Aluminum, Brass, Webbing, Gauze, Glue, Ivory or Celluloid (White), Keratol (imitation leather) black

Description: Folding or telescopic; thirty (30) inches high, when open and

134

ready to play; eleven (ll) inches deep at wind check; twenty-nine and one-quarter (29^1/4) inches long. Nineteen and one-half (19^1/2) inches high, when closed, eleven (11) inches deep and twenty-nine and one-quarter (29^1/4) inches long. Approximate weight thirty-five (35) lbs. Two (2) sets of reeds as follows:- one (1) set, front—Diapason and Flute; and one (1) set back—Melodia and Jubilante. Four (4) Octaves "CC" to "C", chromatic—forty-nine (49) notes. Ready to speak when set up—no stops required. Alternating bellows and pedals with web strap connection and one and one-half (1^1/2) inches wide; an aluminum strip as a heel rest, to be placed on the outside bottom of the case the entire length of both foot pedals. Case: board three (3) ply veneer not less than " in thickness, covered with heavy black grain keratol imitation leather; corners and other points protected by heavy hardware, nickel plated. Brass plate, nickel plated, with letters, "U.S.Q.M.C.," one-half (1/2) inch high engraved thereon, to be firmly attached to center of case, outside back section. Folding top with collapsible music rack attached in such a manner as to hold music in proper position when ready to play. Two (2) metal, leather covered, carrying handles placed on top of case, in center, whereby the organ can be carried in an upright position; handles must be secured by plates to prevent pulling out. When folding or telescoped, the entire unit to be held securely in place by four (4) metal thumbscrews, two (2) in front and one (1) on each side.

Packing: All packages shall be in accordance with usual commercial sizes, (except where special sizes may be required or specified) and packed in commercial containers or packages which will insure delivery in perfect condition.

This specification appears to be essentially that of Bilhorn's Model G, with the addition of the aluminum strip below the foot pedals taken from the A. L. White Colonial Case Folding Organ Style 2 and the possibility of telescoping taken from the Bilhorn Model C. The rather low overall height of 30 inches must have been accomplished by using an articulated cover as used on the Bilhorn Style O. This requirement must have been changed later, perhaps in the interest of making it more rugged, since the model eventually procured had a single piece cover and an overall height of 42 inches when open.

By this time (1932), the reed organ business was all but finished and the country was at the bottom of the depression. Estey's business must have been abysmal and they apparently were having second thoughts about their previous refusal to build a light weight organ during and after World War I. On March 19 Estey wrote expressing interest in the new procurement to the Chief of Chaplains. He replied on April 5, and Estey responded on April 6, 1932 as follows:

Brattleboro, Vermont
April 6, 1932

Chief of Chaplains,
War Department
Washington, D.C.

Dear Sir: *Attention Edwin Burling, Executive*

We very much appreciate the courtesy of your reply of April 5th, and your promise to call attention to the Estey line whenever purchases are made by the proper department.

As we stated in our first letter dated March 19th, we know we have lost a little business in the past by being unable to care for the demand for a very light weight dress suit case type of organ. As we do not intend to lose out on any call which may arise, we are now developing an organ of this type, and expect to have it ready for the market say 60 days later.

We just wish you to know if this particular type of organ must be furnished, the Estey Organ Company will be able to take care of the demand in about sixty days.

Yours very truly,
Estey Organ Company, Inc.
By (s) M. Austin

At the same time, correspondence was also being exchanged with Bilhorn Brothers and A. L. White, both specialists in light weight folding organs. On May 5 Burling wrote to all three companies inquiring about packing methods and requesting metal shipping cases and received replies as follows:

Brattleboro, Vermont, May 6, 1932

Chief of Chaplains,
War Department,
Washington, D.C.

Dear Sir: *Attention Edwin Burling, Executive*

We have your favor of May 5th.

It is our intention when we build the new type of folding organ, to be prepared to ship same in strong boxes, water proof lined, and iron strapped, so as to guarantee as far as possible safe delivery in transit.

We have always made it a practice in shipping organs across the water to use a box made of $13/16$" lumber. In the home market we ship in light veneered cases, but for the foreign field we use the old type of heavy boxes, and believe it is advisable.

We do not consider it necessary to use a metal box. For one reason, it would be rather difficult to secure the organ to the inside of a metal case, but in the wooden cases we are able to block it thoroughly with pieces of wood. When the box is lined with water proof paper there is no necessity of damage from dampness.

The model JJ folding organ which we are now building can be furnished in a heavy box, but we understand that organ does not appeal to you, on account of the weight, which is about 60 lbs.

The other type of organ has not been developed to a point where we can show you any illustration, as we have only completed making the drawings. We are hoping to be able to meet the price competition in the market.

We are making a record you are interested, and just as soon as we have an illustration of the organ, we will be glad to make you a quotation.

Yours very truly,
Estey Organ Company, Inc.
By (s) M. Austin

Chicago, Ill. U.S.A.
May 7, 1932

War Department
Office of the Chief of Chaplains
Washington, D.C.

Attention: Mr. Edwin Burling, Chaplain.

Gentlemen:

Your valued correspondence of May 5 is at hand. We take pleasure in giving you the information required.

First, our method of packing for foreign shipment has proven quite satisfactory for more than 40 years in shipping organs to all parts of the globe. Each model of the Bilhorn Organs has boxes made especially to their measurements, reinforced covers, panels cleated, making box almost air tight.

All organs are carefully wrapped before placing in the boxes and all foreign shipments are first wrapped in oil paper, then heavy express paper and the folding ends sealed with heavy three inch tape, which prevents any dampness from penetrating the inside wrapping. The covers are not only tightly nailed but also steel strapped and sealed.

As to the organs themselves, we have for a long time been using an indestructible veneer in the manufacturing of our instruments, especially prepared to withstand climatic conditions either dryness or dampness.

We firmly believe that you need not give this matter any further concern as we think our present method of packing completely efficient and satisfactory. However, we are in a position to consider any suggestions you may have in regard to further security in packing.

If there is any further information you desire, please command us at any time; we will consider it a privilege to hold ourselves at your service.

Very sincerely yours,
Bilhorn Brothers.
(s) P. P. Bilhorn

P. S. The cost for the packing and boxing on the different models you will find quoted on price list herewith enclosed.

Chicago, 5/10/32.

The Chief of Chaplains,
War Department,
Washington, D.C.

Re: Shipping Cases for Folding Organs.

Dear Sir:

In reply to your inquiry in regard to shipping cases for Folding Organs such as we have furnished for use of Chaplains in the United States Army, will say that we can furnish these cases in wood but not in metal. We have wooden cases made to fit these organs and use them in our foreign shipments. We can quote you on these plain wooden cases such as we carry in stock: $1.00 each.

We can furnish this same case fitted with a hinged top, and fastened down with screws, so that the screws can be removed, the top lifted and the organ removed from the box, and again replaced, the screws put back in place, and the organ can be reshipped in the same box as often as desired. The price of this would be $2.50 each.

We line the box with corrugated paper, or use a paper carton inside the box.

We trust this will meet with your approval.

Respectfully yours,
A.L. WHITE MFG. CO.
(s) A. L. White

All three companies recommended wooden packing boxes. Estey and White refused to provide metal boxes; Bilhorn left the door open.

The organs eventually produced by Estey and Bilhorn were the Model 42 and Style G, respectively. From the illustrations

Open—Ready to Play

Closed

Figure 145: Estey Model 42 Folding organ.

Fig. 146: Bilhorn Model G folding organ.

above it can be seen that they are virtually indistinguishable except for the name. These organs did not differ in any significant way from the light weight organs previously produced by Bilhorn and White.

The surviving files contain no records as to purchases made by the Army after the design of the Chaplain's Folding Organ in 1932 until World War II in Europe caused the U.S. Army to begin a buildup. By means of Procurement Directive P-E-67, dated December 11, 1940, the Army made a major purchase of portable organs of the 1932 design. It was reported publicly on February 4, 1941 by the *Washington Times-Herald*, which printed the following article:

> ### 1,200 FOLDING ORGANS PURCHASED BY ARMY
>
> There will be plenty of church music for the United States Army. The War Department today bought 1,200 folding organs from the Estey Organ Company, Brattleboro, Vt., for $41,191. They will be distributed to Army Chaplains.

This price was just under $35.00 each. Almost immediately some problems arose. Chaplain Paul M. Meikle, Morrison Field, West Palm Beach, Florida wrote in his June, 1941 report:

> "Would suggest that the quality of our portable organs purchased from Estey be investigated. The new Estey Portable Organ that I have has received most careful treatment. An expert organ man has examined it, but in this weather the keys flop down and several of them want to play at once. The valves are sticky. The organ repairman says that this organ is poorly made and of the very cheapest materials."

138

The Chief of Chaplains notified the Quartermaster General, who requested the Philadelphia Quartermaster Depot to report any problems. The Depot replied on August 27, 1941 that no complaints had been received. On September 3 the Chief of Chaplains told Chaplain Meikle to take the problem to his local Quartermaster, and if the conditions warranted it he in turn should make a complaint to the Philadelphia Quartermaster Depot. Problem solved.

Not quite. On September 24, 1941 the Commanding General of Camp Croft, South Carolina notified the Commanding General, Fourth Corps Area, Atlanta that a number of the new Chaplain's organs were defective. Fourth Corps bucked the problem to the Adjutant General in Washington who sent it to the Quartermaster General who in turn sent it to the Philadelphia Quartermaster Depot. The reply, by fourth endorsement, was as follows:

413.3 Camps SD-BI
Philadelphia Quartermaster Depot
Philadelphia, Pa.
October 22, 1941.
To: The Quartermaster General.

1. Reference is had to inclosed report of Chaplain's Organs dated September 22, 1941.

2. It is the opinion of this Depot that the difficulties listed are of a minor nature due to atmospheric conditions which may be overcome by keeping the organs in a dry place, if possible. If, however, these minor adjustments cannot be made at the post by someone who is mechanically inclined, the organs may be shipped to this Depot, charging cost of transportation against Procurement Authority 669 QM 1443 P 63-07 A 0525-2.

For the Commanding General:
(Sgd) E. S. DeLong, Jr.
Captain, QMC Assistant

One of the mechanically-inclined individuals who came to the rescue was Chaplain (1st Lt.) Henry B. Fairman, 136th Infantry, 33rd Division, Camp Forrest, Tennessee. Chaplain Fairman had for several years made a hobby of the reed organ and, with this background, was in a good position to solve the problems. He wrote up a series of notes on care of the field organs and sent them to the Chief of Chaplains, who had them mimeographed and distributed to all Chaplains. Unfortunately, whoever removed the notes from the file for mimeographing neglected to return them and we are unable to reproduce them here.

Other recommendations were soon forthcoming. The Chaplains of the 79th Division recommended replacing the wooden pitmans with metal. Chaplain (1st Lt.) Burr Millican on his arrival at Camp Stewart, Georgia found the folding organ in the Chapel unserviceable. Obviously no beginner, he sanded down the pitmans and lubricated them with graphite and the organ worked fine. He then requested an organ for his own use and was told there were two in stock which couldn't be issued because they didn't work. Showing a fine grasp of the way things work in the Army he offered to fix them both if they would issue him one.

The sticking pitman problem didn't go away, particularly in the tropical Pacific, and novel solutions continued to be reported: replace the wooden pitmans with large nails with the heads cut off; use aluminum welding rod; use steel welding rod, plastic, and so on.

Estey must have been chagrined by the uproar and offered to repair free all Chaplain's Organs shipped to them by freight collect and to return them without charge. The Quartermaster General's office pronounced on the matter as follows:

OUTFIT, CHAPLAINS'

Stock No.—Christian-Faith—36-O-800

Stock No.—Jewish-Faith —36-O-810

These outfits are alike, with the exception that the flag may be either Christian-Faith or Jewish-Faith.

Figure Number	Stock Number	COMPONENTS	Quantity	Expendable
1	36-C-1287	**CHESTS**, Container, Hymnal, Music-Edition................................	1	
2	26-D-140	**DESKS**, Field (Empty), Fiber, Headquarters..........................	1	
		FLAGS, Chaplains'		
3	5-F-980	Christian-Faith...	1	
4	5-F-985	Jewish-Faith...	1	
5	36-M-657	**MUSIC BOOKS**, Hymnal, Chaplains' Outfit, Song-and-Service (150 to the Set)...	1 Set	X
6	36-O-580	**ORGANS**, Folding, Chaplains'...................................	1	

— NOTES —

A portable typewriter was formally a component of the Chaplains' Outfit. The Chaplain requires a typewriter and authority for its issue to the Chaplain will be found in applicable Tables of Equipment or Table of Allowances No. 20, Equipment for Posts, Camps, and Stations.

These outfits are not stocked complete. Each component is procured, stored, requisitioned and issued individually.

Refer to Table of Allowances, Equipment for Post, Camps and Stations for "Hymnal (36-M-656), Army-and-Navy (1 book to every two seats in chapel)".

January, 1944

Figure 147

"... this trouble may be remedied in the field if a practical man would proceed in the following manner:

Lift out the keyboard. Remove the pitmans (wooden dowels), sand paper them lightly, and if convenient, cover them with graphite or heavy black pencil. If any sticking is due to the key puncture under the front of the key being too tight, freeing up the puncture would overcome this difficulty. Occasionally sticking keys are caused by the front board of the organ warping and laying too close to the key when key is depressed. This could be overcome by removing the front board and bushing out with medium thickness cardboard until board is free from keys. By giving greater tolerances in the parts indicated in the foregoing, this difficulty will be overcome.

It is the opinion of this office that the construction of this type of organ is sufficiently strong to permit continued use by exercising the moderate care that a musical instrument requires.

Often there has been speculation as to the total quantity of Chaplain's Organs produced during World War II. Copies of procurement documents have been preserved in the National Archives, and the table at right summarizes them.

While the original quantity of Purchase Order 12551 is unknown and there may have been other orders which are not in the files, the total of 10,421 shown above is reasonably close to the total of Chaplain's Organs produced during World War II. Of these, Estey made 9,592, Gulbransen made 476 and White made an unknown number, probably a few hundred at most. The World War II purchases were made under the Joint Army-Navy procurement program, so that the instruments used by the Navy are probably included in the above figures.

On April 1, 1944 the Chief of Chaplains sent Circular Letter No. 283 to all Army Chaplains requesting comments on the strong and weak points of the existing folding organ, looking forward to an improved organ to be procured in the future:

WHAT SUGGESTIONS
HAVE YOU TO MAKE
ABOUT THE FOLDING ORGAN?

A study is being made by this office relative to the strong and weak points of the Folding Organ (field) with the idea of looking forward to an improved and more effective musical instrument for future use in the field. Chaplains are requested to write this office, submitting any suggestions which they may have to offer toward the improvement of the organ. These suggestions may include pertinent information about climatic effect upon the organ, weight, size, improvement in general, defects, tonal

CONTRACT NO	QTY	COMPLETED	COST	SUPPLIER
W669qm-13944	243	24 Nov 1942		Estey (a)
W669qm-16621	758	1942		Estey (a)
W669qm-18356	250	1942		Estey
W669qm-20177	801	1942		Estey
(same)	753	30 June 1943	$84144	Estey
P.O. 12551				White (b)
P.O. 15994	476	15 July 1943	$22766	Gulbransen
P.O. 15995	300	31 Aug 1943	$14355	Estey
P.O. 16780	353	15 Aug 1943	$16891	Estey
(same)	800	30 June 1944		Estey
(same)	2687	30 June 1945		Estey
TOTAL	10421			

(a) Presumably the procurement of 1200 announced in April of 1941 is included in these contracts.
(b) The quantity is unknown. Apparently A. L. White Mfg. Co. was unable to complete the order, as the uncompleted portion was awarded to Estey under Purchase Order 16780.

quality, the range of the keyboard and the general stability of the instrument. The chaplains are reminded that quick changes in producing an improved organ cannot be expected because of the lack of priority materials, manufacturing problems, patent rights, and the present need for an increased output in order to supply requisitions."

Replies came back rapidly. It seems everyone loved the little organ but had ideas about how to improve it.

APO 610, New York, 2 May 1944
To: The Chief of Chaplains, US Army.

1. As requested in the last circular letter it is my purpose to suggest that if possible the Field Organ be pitched lower than it is. I use the organ three times each Sunday and every piece found in the Army Field Hymnal must be played in a lower key than written otherwise we have solos by a few tenors. After enquiring, other chaplains in this Sector observe the same condition. Otherwise the organ is perfect not only for religious services but to loan to outfits with no musical instruments when occasion presents itself.

(s) Gerald J. Whelan
Captain, Chaplains Corps

As Lee Chaney has pointed out[28], the problem was not with the organ, which is pitched at the international standard of A440, but with the key signatures of the hymns in the Army Field Hymnal. Other comments from the field:

. . .make it sturdier. —Herman L. Driskell, Chaplain, USA Hospital Ship Acadia.

. . .make it more stable, it walks away from the organist. . . .place a han-

dle at each end. . . .it is very difficult for one person to unfold the organ and hold it so while at the same time to place and insert the two screws which are necessary to keep the organ in upright position. —Ernest W. Moyer, Chaplain, Fort Sill, Oklahoma Station Hospital.

. . .I have been well satisfied with the Field Organ. It is a wonderful little instrument. The only weakness in it that I have found is that little piece of wood which lies between the bellows and supports the spring for the bellows. . . .I am submitting a diagram showing the construction of a strap iron which has been installed very satisfactorily on our organ here. This "repair part" was designed and installed by Sergeant Alvin Schubkegel and Corporal William Phillips, Chaplain's Assistants here. —Chester E. Chandler, (Capt), Base Chaplain, La Junta Army Air Field, Colorado.

My organist, Cpl. Norman Eberlin, submits the following: 1. Change the metal in the reeds in treble cleff notes to improve tone quality. It seems to be out of proportion to the bass notes. 2. Add octave of eight notes -five to treble cleff and three to bass. 3. Improve tone quality of treble cleff, so that solo work can be done. 4. . . .provide space for rack to carry music. 6. . . .give more leg room to player. 7. Change book holders from top to bottom. 8. Change screws in case, as phillips screw driver is very hard to obtain overseas. 9. Dampness plays a large part in tone quality, especially in Florida. Definite damage done. Salt water has no noticeable effect. —William O. Hope, (Capt), Chaplain, Army Air Base, APO 964.

. . .put a screen in front of both sets of reeds to prevent sand and other particles from clogging the reed.

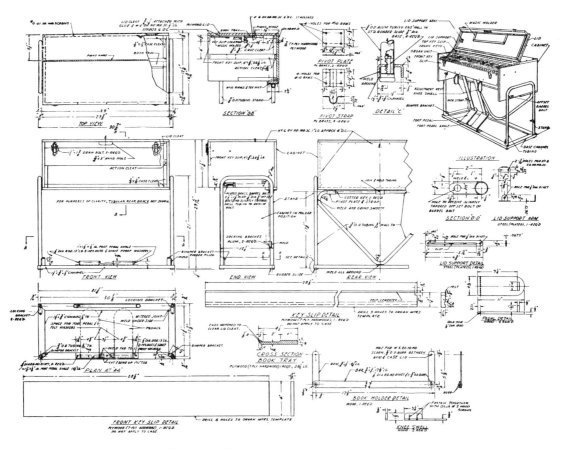

Figure 148: Organ, Folding, Chaplain's, M-1945.

. . .Pins [pitmans] . . .should be turned about one third smaller to allow for expansion in wet climates, as in Pacific area. Pins might be of non-expanding plastic This is main cause of keys sticking and notes sounding continuously. A painted or enameled cabinet would be more practical than the leatherette. . . The organ, as it is, has a fine tone and adequate volume; it is serving capably, but the above would make it more trouble-free and more satisfactory for mobile units. —Howard D. Gould, Chaplain, 41 Bomb Gp.

. . .their size is as compact as they can be made. The weight should be kept at a minimum, no heavier than the present instrument. The volume I have found adequate. . . instead of developing an improved field organ, I believe a small public address system . . . would be more practical. —Walter J. Bielitz,

Chaplain, 59th Fighter Group, Thomasville Army Air Field, Georgia.

In general, the folding organ has given much added help to our church services. . . Its size and weight are not out of proportion to the fine results obtainable from its tone and range. In a few rare cases, we would have desired more volume; but, on the other hand, there can really be no complaint when the men sing loud enough to drown out the organ . . .—Werner R. Saar, (Capt) Chaplain, 45th Inf. Div. Arty., APO 45 New York.

. . .A few Chaplains who are using the field organ for services in hut chapels have built a ply-wood case in which they place the unfolded organ to dress it up a bit. With a little ingenuity it gives the appearance of a small upright piano. It is a clever idea and very easily carried out. —Air Force Chaplains' Bulletin.

By 1945 the problems of organizing and prosecuting the military effort were well in hand, and time became available to work on an improved model of the Chaplains' Organ. The following memorandum summarizes the status:

Office of the Chief of Chaplains
4 May 1945

Memorandum for the Record.
Subject: Organ, Folding, Chaplains'
QM Stock No. 36-0-580.

1. Mr. Eugene E. Hallock, Ext. 74816, Office of the Quartermaster General, Military Planning Division, informed Chaplain Weber in telephone conversation this date, that experimentation and study of possible changes on subject item has resulted in extensive improvements that will be incorporated in the specifications. The basis for these studies were recommendations from this office dated 10 July 1944.

2. It is expected that a new procurement order for an additional supply of subject item will be issued by the Quartermaster General at the end of this month. Mr. Hallock stated that he will keep this office informed of developments.

(s) EDMUND W. WEBER
Chaplain (Major) USA, Assistant

Office of the Chief of Chaplains
11 September 1945.

MEMORANDUM
FOR THE QUARTERMASTER GENERAL.

Attention: Mr. Eugene D. Hallock
Military Planning Division
Research and Development Branch
Subject: Folding Organs.

Request is made that five (5) Organs, drawing No. PQD-1002A,

Quartermaster Tentative Specification and five (5) Case, Organ, Folding, M-1945, Specification No. PQD-1003 be acquired and mailed to this office for experimental use.

(s) LUTHER D. MILLER
Chaplain (Brigadier General) USA
Chief of Chaplains

This organ eventually became the new standard, and was called the Chaplains' Folding Organ M-1945, Stock No. 36-0-581. The identical organ with a rugged carrying case was designated 36-0-581-45. The new organ had the following specifications:

Range: four octaves—two above and two below middle C, 49 keys.

Reeds: two sets—diapason, 8'C to $1/2'$ C, rear set; flute, 4'C to $1/2'$ C, front set.

Bellows: the feeders have a minimum area of 132 sq. in. each with a minimum opening of 5 inches. The minimum area of the reservoir is 338 sq. in., with a minimum opening of $6^1/2$ inches.

Weight: minimum 50 lbs., maximum 65 lbs.

Measurements: Closed, not more than $30^5/8$ in. long, 12 in. wide and $10^7/8$ in. high, exclusive of rubber buttons and handles. Opened, the keys are not more than 29 nor less than 28 inches from the floor.

Stops: Solo Bass, opens the lower half of the mute on the flute reeds. Solo treble, opens the upper half of the mute on the flute reeds. Left Knee Lever, actuates the full set of flute reeds. Right Knee Lever, opens the swell on the diapason reeds.

Tools: Reed hook, secured to inside of organ case. A screwdriver is also required for maintenance but not supplied.

The Army also published a Technical Manual, TM 10-750, on the Chaplains'

Folding Organ on February 24, 1948. This manual covered both the 1932 design and the 1945 model, and for the new model included a description of the instrument, illustrations, maintenance instructions and tips on achieving special effects in playing. From the drawing in Figure 148, it can be seen that the organ was similar to the previous model in many ways, except that it had a tubular metal stand and an optional separate case instead of the combined wooden stand and cover of the old model. Presumably the M-1945 organ was never produced in large quantities, if at all, and apparently none has survived.

The same organs were used during the Korean War, but in recent years the familiar folding reed organs have been retired from active duty and replaced by even lighter weight electronic keyboards or, more often, by organ music recorded on long playing records and cassette tapes.

The aircraft carrier *USS Franklin* was hit in a bombing attack during fighting off Japan on March 19, 1945. The damage was said to be the most severe suffered by any aircraft carrier which remained afloat. The ship returned to the United States where it was repaired and returned to duty. After it passed through the Panama Canal on its way home, twenty-five men of the skeleton crew gathered beneath a gaping hole in the flight deck for a religious service. A chaplain's folding organ can clearly be seen as part of the musical group (see figure 149).

Rufus C. Jefferson carried his own Bilhorn folding organ with him throughout World War II. Serving on the *USS Menkar* in the Pacific, he provided music for religious services as attested by the program reproduced in Figure 151. Both Jefferson and the organ survived the war, including 22 months at sea and seven landings in the Western Pacific, but both were to meet an untimely end many years later. After the war Rufus pinned his military campaign ribbons on the organ in recognition of its valiant service.

Figure 149

145

Figure 150: Ensign Rufus C. Jefferson plays the Bilhorn organ at the Coast Guard Station, Pistol River, Oregon, 1943.

He was always an enthusiastic sailor, and he and the little organ had many adventures throughout the years. In 1989 Rufus lent the organ to a friend who wanted to take it with him on a sailing cruise. On July 14 of that year the schooner *Sheila Yates,* carrying four Americans, two Canadians and the Bilhorn organ, was en route to Iceland, the Faroes and the Shetland Islands when it became ice bound in a pea soup fog. The sailboat's SOS was answered by a Canadian shrimp boat which rescued the crew, but despite heroic efforts to save it, the boat was crushed by the ice and sank, carrying with it Jefferson's favorite folding organ. A little more than a year later, Rufus disappeared while sailing alone on a boat of his own design, the *Far Shore Explorer,* between Madeline and Long Islands in Lake Superior. He and the beloved organ were reunited in a watery grave.

While the organ involved was not a portable, 'The Case of the Disappearing Lindholm Organ' fits in with the other war stories. Before World War II the Italian passenger ship *SS Conte Biancamano* plied the

seas carrying those fortunate enough to afford a luxury cruise during the depression. After the United States declared war on Japan, Germany and Italy in December of 1941, the *Biancamano* arrived at the Panama Canal on its regular voyage back to Italy. As an "enemy" ship it was seized by the U.S. Navy, the passengers released, the crew taken as prisoners of war and interned in the United States. The ship was then taken to Philadelphia where it was converted for service as a troop carrier by the Cramp Shipbuilding Co. In March of 1942 it was recommissioned as the *USS Hermitage,* AP-54, and saw service throughout the war.[29]

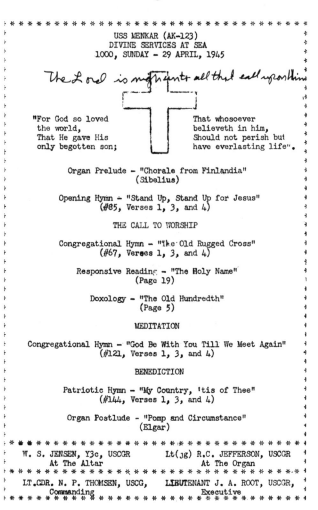

Figure 151

146

After the Italian crew had settled into their new routine the chaplain at the prison camp requested, through the YMCA's War Prisoners' Aid of the Young, that the Lindholm reed organ on their ship be sent to the camp for use by the prisoners in their religious services. A check of the ship by the Navy found no organ. The Navy base in Panama reported that the organ had been on the ship when it left there en-route to Philadelphia. The Navy Yard in Philadelphia maintained there was no organ on the ship when they received it. A search of the YMCA Archives, held by the University of Minnesota, shows no record of this incident. At this point, the paper trail comes to an end, leaving one of the great mysteries of World War II still unresolved.

Probably no manufacturer in the world produced more different portable organ styles than R. F. Stevens, Ltd. of London, including the following: Abbey Portable No. 1, Baby Organ, Models K, 18, 21, 22, 24, 25, 25a, 28, 30, 31, 33, 50, 55 and 66. Many of these models were available in several versions. The Model 25, for example, was a five octave instrument which could be had with one or two rows of reeds and with the C-C or F-F keyboard. The Model 25a was similar in appearance but had a four octave F-F keyboard with two sets of reeds.

Figure 153: Stevens Model 22.

Figure 152: The Lindholm Koffer-Harmonium, Model 20. Identical organs were sold under the names of Mannborg, Hofberg, and Cleve & Pick. A similar non-folding model was made by R. F. Stevens, London.

Figure 154: Stevens Model 66.

147

Figure 155: Stevens Model 33.

Figure 156: Stevens Baby Model

Figure 157: Stevens Model 25

Figure 158: Stevens Model 18

Figure 159: Stevens Model M

Figure 160: Stevens Model 1

Figure 161: C. G. Conn Wonder Portable Organ

Figure 162: C. G. Conn Wonder Portable Organ, closed.

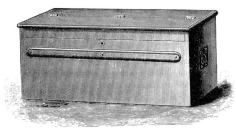

Case 106, closed.

Case 106, open and set up.

Figure 163: Mason & Hamlin Case 106, 1880.

Figure 164: Estey Style 2, 1897.

Figure 165: Kawai portable organ.

Figure 168: Prince Melodeon.

Figure 166: Gloria Harmonium

Figure 169: Miniature Harmonium.

Figure 167: Norwegian table harmonium.

Figure 170: Indian table harmonium.

Chapter Six

The Instrument Which Plays By Itself

Figure 171: Two Japanese children play an organette.

We wish to explain how an instrument is made which plays by itself continuously in whatever melody we wish, sometimes in a slow rhythm and sometimes in a quick rhythm. . .

Thus begins *Al-alat illati tuzammir binafsiha, The Instrument which Plays by Itself,* written by the Banu Musa—the sons of Musa—in the ninth century. The three sons of Musa, the

seventh imam, were the most eminent Arab scientists of the time, occupying important positions at the College of Science in Baghdad where they had been appointed by Khalif Al-Ma'mun (813-833). Among their many accomplishments they created what is the first documented automatic musical instrument. The music was recorded by means of raised teeth on a rotating cylinder, in the same way as in the familiar barrel organs, cylinder music boxes and the "cob organ." The sound was produced by a single horizontal pipe with eight holes in it, much like a flute. Authorities differ on whether a flue pipe or a reed pipe was used; of course we prefer to think it was the latter.

The holes were covered by pallet valves, weighted to keep them normally closed, and which were opened by levers in contact with the teeth on the rotating cylinder. Running water provided the motive force. The wind was generated by an adaptation of Apollonios' Automatic Hydraulic Organ, an even more ancient device which generated compressed air from running water.[30]

Athanasius Kircher (1602-80) in 1650 described an automatic hydraulic organ in his famous work *Musurgia Universalis.* This organ was similar to the Banu Musa device in that it used a pinned cylinder and that water provided the motive force. A separate pipe was used for each note, however.[31]

With the industrial revolution, more and more sophisticated automatic instruments were produced, but for many years the pinned cylinder remained the preferred recording system.[32] J.-B. Napoleon Fourneaux of Paris made his "Orchestrion" in 1844, which was an orgue expressif with both a cylinder and a keyboard. Most of the "monkey organs" used by strolling organ

grinders in the late 19th and early 20th century were small pinned-cylinder reed organs, powered by a hand crank, although pipe models were also common. Later models were usually operated by a paper roll. Because the reeds took up less space than pipes, the reed variety tended to be lighter, have more elaborate scales, more ranks and consequently better musical arrangements. Some of the European makers were Gavioli and Thibouville-Lamy in France, Fratti & Co., Berlin and Anton Okenfuss, Vienna. Currently reed monkey organs are being made by Hofbauer and Joseph Raffin in Germany and by Peter Trueman in England.

In the 19th century several inventors worked more or less simultaneously on using a punched paper roll or disc to record

Figure 173: Joseph Raffin with his 20/40 Reed Organ.

Figure 172

152

the music. This would greatly reduce the cost and size of the recording device and permit mass production. Alexander Bain received a patent in 1847 in England for a paper roll operated instrument in which as the paper roll passed over a tracker bar. Perforations in the roll allowed air to flow to the selected reeds. Apparently no completed instruments were ever produced. One of the earliest organettes to become commercially successful was a paper disc machine, the Ariston, first produced about 1876 by Paul Ehrlich of Leipzig, Germany. In America the paper roll became the preferred technique. The first successful instrument was the invention in 1878 of Mason J. Matthews, an Englishman who came to the U.S. a few years earlier. His instruments were produced by the Munroe Organ Reed Co., and sold by the Mechanical Orguinette Company. The Mechanical Orguinette Company was organized in New York in 1878 by William Barnes Tremaine to sell organettes. It became highly successful and later acquired Munroe, Vocalion and the Orchestrelle company to form The Aeolian Organ and Music Company.

The organette was a small, simple reed instrument powered by a hand crank. Through mechanical linkage the hand crank

Figure 174: McTammany Organette made by the Mechanical Orguinette Co.

turned the barrel or advanced the paper roll and also operated the bellows. The early American instruments were of the paper-as-a-valve type, based on the Bain patent, so-called because the air required to operate the reeds passed through the perforations. Of course the perforations had to be rather wide—about $1/4$ inch is typical—in order to permit enough air to flow. The number of notes which could be accomodated on a paper roll of practical size, typically $7^3/4$ inches wide, was limited to about twenty. In their heyday, these immensely popular instruments sold for about $5.00 apiece.

A similar instrument was invented about the same time as the Matthews organette by John McTammany, Jr.[33] McTammany at first manufactured his own instruments as the McTammany Organette Co., located in Worcester, Massachusetts, and later licensed the Munroe company to make them. Munroe made instruments for McTammany and others under a variety of names. Bowers[34] lists the following names just for the McTammany instrument: Mechanical Orguinette, Mechanical Organette, Automatic Melodista, McTammany Orguinette, National American Organette, New Musical Orguinette, Victoria Organette and Royal Organette. McTammany claimed to be, in his own words, "the greatest musical inventor of any age" and "the original inventor of the player piano." He did have numerous patents on musical devices and spent many years in the courts trying to prove his claims, but he never succeeded in convincing the most demanding judges of all, his peers.

Professor Merritt Gally, who initially had his office at 9 Spruce Street in New York City, in 1879 developed and patented a system of pneumatic valves which permitted much smaller perforations in the paper—about $3/16$" in width — since only enough air had to flow through the perforation to operate a

153

pneumatic valve. In Gally's system, the valve was mechanically connected to a pallet valve through which the air passed to operate the reeds. Using this arrangement, a roll only 3 5/8 inches wide was required for a twenty-note instrument. While the rolls were smaller and thus less expensive, the instrument itself was more complex than its paper-as-a-valve competitor, and sold for about $25 for the smallest model. Gally's valve system and many other details are similar to those later used in player organs and pianos. Gally at first referred to his instruments as "Autophones" but later used the term "Orchestrone," probably to avoid conflict with the organettes made by The Autophone Company of Ithaca, NY. Some of the larger Orchestrones had automatic stops and expression, all controlled from the roll, and as well could be operated by hand to achieve greater expression. The Bijou Orchestrone was a finely-crafted organette of twenty notes, with four feeders and a reservoir to give it ample and steady air. Another Gally

Figure 176, above: primary valves of the Gally Orchestrone. Figure 177, below: secondary valves.

Figure 175: Gally Bijou Orchestrone. This is the early model, made by Gally. Later models made by licensees had the rolls running from left to right.

organette was the slightly smaller Jubal Orchestrone. The large Models 26A and B and the 44A and B were roll-operated foot-pumped reed organs without keyboards. Gally also produced a pushup piano player (vorsetzer) using the same system. He sold the rolls at prices of 75 cents to a dollar, and claimed to have over 1200 selections. Gally later licensed the Munroe Organ Reed Co. to produce the Orchestrone.

In addition to the paper-as-a-valve and pneumatic valve organette mechanisms, the so-called key frame was also widely used. This system was an adaptation of the method used by Jacquard to control his automatic loom. The key frame organettes used a perforated cardboard or metal tune sheet. As

154

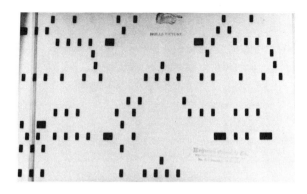

Figure 178

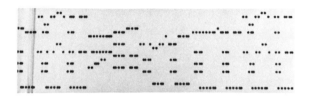

Figure 179: Comparison of the 14-note paper-as-a-valve roll used on the McTammany and similar organettes with the 20-note Gally roll.

Figure 180: The Orgophon, made by Jul. Heinr. Zimmermann of Leipzig, Germany, 1907. This key-frame organette had 26 harmonium reeds and played a perforated metal disk.

the tune sheet passed by, delicate levers would drop through the holes. The levers were mechanically connected to pallet valves which controlled the air to the reeds.[35]

Organettes and music boxes with reeds were built in huge quantities and varieties in Europe. Some of the makers were: B. A. Bremond; Constrution d'Automates et d'Instruments de Musique Mecaniques, France; Joseph Mark Draper, London; du Commun-Girod, Geneva; English Seraphone Co.; Euphonika Musikwerke, Leipzig; Carl E. Fiedler, Germany; Bruno Geissler, Leipzig; Vittorio Giuliano, Naples; J. H. Heller, Berne; Heinrich Hermann, Germany; Kimmerling, Geneva; Langdorf et Fils, Geneva; Armin Liebmann, Gera, Germany; Nicole Freres,

Geneva; Phönix Musikwerke, Leipzig; Schmidt & Co; Giulio Tagliabue, Milan; J. A. Teste, France; Jerome Thibouville-Lamy; Victoria Orchestrionette, Germany; Paul Ehrlich, Germany.

Henry B. Horton of Akron, Ohio, who had previously built a melodeon called the Melo-pean under his own name and in partnership as Horton & Rose and Blodget & Horton, sold his Akron interests in 1879 and moved to Ithaca, New York. There he formed the Autophone Company with F. M. Finch and H. F. Hibbard to mass produce organettes. The first Autophone organettes were of the paper-as-a-valve type, and by 1882 annual production had reached 18,000 organettes. Horton sold out in 1883 to devote himself to his other interest, the Ithaca Calendar Clock Company. Autophone soon developed a simpler and more rugged instrument which used a pinned wooden cylinder as the music storage device. This instrument was produced in great quantities and sold under the names of Gem Roller Organ, Concert Roller Organ, and Chautauqua Roller Organ. They were

155

carried in the mail order catalog by Sears, Roebuck & Co., which at one point contracted for the entire output of the Autophone factory. Sears sold the Gem model for $3.25 and the rollers for 18 cents. Each wooden roller, nowadays referred to as "cobs," contained from 2,500 to 4,000 individual pins. Autophone developed and patented machinery to place the pins automatically, permitting very high volume production. Collectors have identified about 1,000 different song titles. Autophone also produced a larger model called the Grand Roller Organ with a 32-note scale, using cylinders 15 inches long. Sears sold this model for $14.95 and the rollers for 65 cents.

The Massachusetts Organ Company had its offices in Boston and its factory at Chelsea, Mass. It was a large and aggressive maker of organettes, known particularly for the Gem Organetta, the Organina and the Mignonette Organina. It was affiliated with the American Automatic Organ Co., later the Automatic Organ Co., which acted as a lower-priced competitor, selling the Gem Organina for as little as $1.65.

Other American organette makers were Wilcox and White, E. P. Needham, Tourna-

Figure 182: From the Sears Roebuck & Co. catalog of 1905.

Figure 183: Roller organ mechanism showing the pinned roller in place.

phone, A. D. Black, Bates, Gately, Ithaca Organ Co. and Carl Foerster, Milwaukee. Most of them produced models for sale by others using a wide variety of names and stencils. One unique approach was the Musical Sewing Machine Cover made by Garvie & Wood. This instrument was driven by the sewing machine treadle. George Woods produced at least two barrel-operated reed organs.

Numerous roll-operated toy instruments have appeared over the years, for example the Trumpetto, Rolmonica, Play-a-Sax, Clarola and PlaRola Organ were all small paper-as-a-valve free reed devices.

The player reed organs with keyboards produced by McTammany about 1876 led the way for others who saw great potential in this type of instrument. The Style 44-E

Figure 181: Gem Roller Organ.

Figure 184: The Style 44-B Orchestrone used a Gally player mechanism mounted in a full-sized organ case.

Figure 185. Aeolian Orchestrelle Style M, 1907.

Orchestrone, made by the Munroe Organ Reed Co., used a player mechanism licensed by McTammany, as did Taylor & Farley and Taber. The Mechanical Orguinette Company, which sold the McTammany organette under license, developed a number of full-sized instruments under the Aeolian name. The Style 1050 Aeolian organ was made for them by Munroe, and was similar to the Style 44-E Orchestrone. Mechanical Orguinette soon changed its name to The Aeolian Organ and Music Company. The Aeolian Style 1500 used a 46-note roll and was housed in a case similar to that of an upright piano. The Aeolian Grand, introduced in the mid-1890s, was similar in appearance but used the 58-note roll.

In 1896 Aeolian acquired the Vocalion Company, located in Worcester, Massachusetts, from Mason & Risch. Vocalion, under the leadership of Morris S. Wright, produced

an excellent reed organ using qualifying tubes and a pneumatic action. Combining the 58-note roll from the Aeolian Grand with the Vocalion organ, Wright produced the Aeolian Orchestrelle. This instrument became the player reed organ of choice for the wealthy who did not wish to install a player pipe organ. The first Orchestrelles were made in the late 1890s, and production continued at least through 1914. The Orchestrelle became popular enough in Europe to warrant the establishment of The Orchestrelle Co. Ltd., with headquarters and sales rooms at Aeolian Hall, 135-6-7 New Bond Street, London and a factory at Hayes, Middlesex, England. This company also produced the Gregorian organ. Another subsidiary, the Choralion Co. was located in Germany. The ultimate development of this line was the Solo Orchestrelle, playing a 116-note roll. Some models could play both the 58-note and 116-note rolls. The Solo Orchestrelle was also produced in a two-manual and pedal version. Most of the Orchestrelles were pressure-operated instruments, although a few, such as the Style M, were suction machines.

Orchestrelles have become highly prized by collectors, but the type of music found on the original rolls has little appeal to the modern ear. Kevin McElhone, of Kettering, England, has produced a monumental listing of all known Orchestrelle rolls, and has had a number of the more appealing numbers recut.

Wilcox and White produced a high-quality organette, some under license from McTammany, and in 1888 expanded the concept into a full-sized reed organ with a keyboard and an internal player system: the Symphony. This instrument used a 58-note roll, slightly different in size from the Aeolian Grand roll, but which could be played on the Aeolian machines with a slight adjustment of the roll mechanism. Story & Clark's Orpheus used a 58-note roll and had a clockwork roll mechanism and pneumatic action. Many other reed organ makers produced player organs:

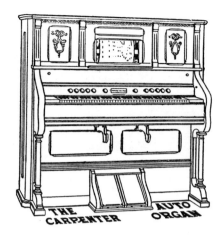

Figure 187

Figure 188: Kimball Self-Playing organ, Case No. 700.

Farrand's Olympia, Carpenter's Auto Organ, Estey, Kimball and others.

The mechanisms perfected for player organs were adapted to the "push-up" piano players, or "vorsetzers." These devices used 65-note rolls and contained mechanical fingers, one for each of the 65 notes, which operated the piano keys. They appeared in the 1890s and remained popular for only a few years until the

Figure 186: Wilcox & White Symphony player organ.

158

player piano, with its internal player mechanism, crowded the push-up players out of the market. Many of the push-up players contained one or more sets of reeds and could be played alone as a player reed organ or, when attached to a piano, play the piano alone or accompany the piano with reeds. Many brands appeared, but Aeolian's Pianola and Farrand's Cecilian were perhaps the most popular. The later push-ups played the 88-note rolls which were becoming the standard for player pianos.

A great variety of mechanically played reed instruments were produced in Europe. Harmonium player attachments were made by Ernst Erich Liebmann of Gera with the Liebmanista, the Transponier-Harmonista by Emil Muller, and another by the Maestro Co. Limonair Freres of Paris, a fair organ builder, made some reed-operated models. Mustel, Leon Mayer-Marix and Gavioli of Paris and Peter Varetto of England made barrel harmoniums. Mustel later built the Concertal, a paper roll instrument. Ludwig Hupfeld of Germany made player reed organs. J. P.

Figure 190: Shiko-kin, a 14-note organette made in Japan by Kindo Toda, patterned after an instrument belonging to the Rev. Christopher Carrothers, a Christian missionary in Tokyo.

Figure 191: The magnificent two-manual Scheola, made by J. & P. Schiedmayer, Stuttgart, Germany.

Nystrom of Karlstad, Sweden made the Reform-Organ, a self-playing instrument with suction bellows which played music recorded on a cardboard disk. Other active builders were Mojon, Manger & Co., London; Poirot Fréres of Mirecourt, Vosges, France; Popper & Co. and Andreas Wider of Germany and Anton Wiest of Vienna, Austria.

Figure 189: Wilcox & White Angelus push-up piano player with reeds, 1902.

159

Fig. 192: The Cotswald Organette, currently being produced by Peter K. Watts, Chipping Norton, England.

Figure 193

Figure 194: This novel organette plays a disk placed vertically on the back.

Figure 195: The Mustel Concertal player organ.

Figure 196: An early organ player attachment.

160

Restoration

Figure 197: Frances Hartmann, Fred Pelton and Gary Besteman work on a Clough & Warren organ at the Hanover-Horton Historical Society, Hanover, Michigan.

The typical reed organ found today was made between 1850 and 1920, with the peak of production occurring about 1890. The makers of those organs were proud of the long life of the instruments but certainly never expected them to be in use one hun-

dred years later. It is a tribute to their workmanship that some organs do survive in good condition. But even in an instrument that has been kept dry, free of dust and under relatively stable temperatures it is only reasonable to expect deterioration of

161

leather, felt and rubberized cloth as well as wear and tear on mechanical components. Inevitably, many organs have been stored in basements, garages or barns where humidity, temperature extremes, insects, animals, dirt and rough treatment have accelerated the deterioration. Other plagues have been visited on some instruments: loss of some of the parts, poorly executed repairs and "modernization."[36]

Bringing a silent, deteriorated ancient instrument back to its original glorious sound and pristine appearance can be a rewarding experience. As the reed organ is a relatively simple device, the techniques involved in its restoration are easily within the capabilities of the average careful worker. The information which follows has been selected from the recommendations of some of the most experienced reed organ restorers, and is intended to help the beginner through a first project.

Before going further, it is useful to consider some of the terms used. While there is no general agreement as to the specific words and their meaning, the following definitions should help bring out some of the issues involved:

MAINTENANCE—Cleaning, polishing and adjustment. Within this category would be the removal of dust particles causing a reed to be silent (an occasional occurrence) or tightening screws which have worked loose. If you find an organ which can be brought to usable condition with this level of attention you have found a gem.

REPAIR—If it's broke, fix it. While it is impossible to specify all the ills needing repair, some of the common ones are stripped screw holes, loosened glue joints and broken components. Replacing the pedal straps or the outside flap valves—which deteriorate much faster than the interior valves—are other examples. Cleaning the reeds probably belongs here rather than in maintenance, as it requires a bit more effort. If the reeds have serious dirt deposits, cleaning may bring most of them back close to the proper pitch.

REBUILD—Major repairs such as repairing a cracked reed pan, recovering the bellows, making replacements for missing components or refinishing the case all require a level of effort beyond mere repair.

TUNING—Reed tuning is within the capabilities of the careful craftsman and could be included under rebuilding, but since it usually requires a specialized tuning instrument and the techniques are different from those usually learned in the workshop, it is considered a separate category.

RESTORATION—Restoration includes some or all of the categories mentioned above, but more importantly it implies preservation, faithfulness to the original in appearance, materials and workmanship, reversibility of repairs and documentation of work done. An organ which has been restored is as close to the original as is practical, without being upgraded or "improved."

RENOVATION—Similar to restoration, but with improvements added to make the instrument more suitable for present-day use. For example: adding an electric blower or suction unit, removing linkage on celeste stops so that each rank can be selected separately, or significant pitch changes to permit ensemble playing.

162

VALUE

When setting out on a reed organ project it is a good idea to make a realistic estimate of the problem. What will the value be of the organ when the project is completed? Reed organs have not been attractive to antique buffs and collectors to the extent that antique music boxes or automobiles have, and so the values have not escalated as dramatically. Maybe they will eventually; maybe not. The good news is that unrestored organs have not escalated in value either, so that they can be acquired relatively cheaply. Does the organ have sentimental value? The melodeon that great-grandmother brought west in a covered wagon would have a certain value to her descendants that it would not have to others. What about historic value? An organ played at Gettysburg after Lincoln made his celebrated address would have undisputable cachet. Musical value? Some organs were made for serious musical performances—in a church or concert hall—containing four, five or more complete ranks of reeds, two or more manuals and pedal bass. Harmoniums made by Mustel are considered by many to be at the top of the list, both for their musical qualities as well as workmanship. The quality of the casework certainly is a consideration, as is original finish in good condition.

On the other hand, a single manual, two rank parlor organ with eleven stop knobs, a veneered case with a checked finish, missing the original decorative top and of unknown history is unlikely ever to have much commercial value regardless of the care and expense involved in its restoration. Restoring such an organ could be an excellent learning experience, giving a great sense of accomplishment. In the process the instrument would acquire sentimental value to the owner. In restoring an organ of this kind it would be unreasonable to go to extremes to preserve authenticity.

Is the organ repairable at all? If the reed pan has several large cracks, or if the reed cells have come unglued from the reed pan, many experts consider the instrument unrepairable, although some have successfully repaired such organs. Hairline cracks are fairly easily remedied. One large crack will require some extra effort. Fortunately, cases where the reed cells have come unglued are rare.

ELECTRIFICATION

Should the organ be electrified? From the preservation point of view, if it was not originally electrically blown, the answer would be "no," but there is plenty of room for discussion. Some large organs, particularly those with bass pedals, which precluded the organist from pumping the bellows, originally had manual, electric or hydraulic pumps. The most common were the manual pumps, consisting of a lever connected through some linkage to the exhausters so that by moving the lever the bellows could be pumped. A second type consisted of an electric motor connected by a chain drive to a crankshaft inside the organ case which in turn was linked to the exhausters. Another type used a hydraulic motor to operate the hand pumping mechanism. These pumps were all very quiet when properly adjusted. A fourth type is more familiar, consisting of an electrically driven rotary vacuum pump. These pumps all make perceptible noise, although if carefully designed and constructed with adequate baffling, they can be tolerable. The pumps available today for conversion of reed organs from foot-pumping to electrically-driven are of this latter type.

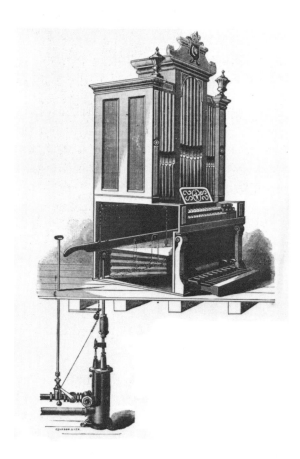

Figure 198

Figure 200: The Estey Studio Organ, 1920, shown with the rotary blow handle. This is similar to the Hinners & Albertsen system, but uses four exhausters mounted at the front of the organ.

Figure 199: The Hinners & Albertsen blowing apparatus for pedal organs. The three feeders are connected to a crankshaft which is fitted with a large flywheel and handle. According to their catalog, a small boy can easily produce an abundant supply of air.

Figure 201: The Rimmer blowing machine connected to the same Estey organ. AC or DC motors were available. Shown with the cover removed.

Measurements:

Figure 202: A rotary electric suction unit made by The Rockingham Engineering Co. of Thornton Heath, England, supplied by R. F. Stevens Ltd.

Figure 204: This Estey Style 39 from 1874 has a conventional blow lever on the side. Just above the lever is a wind indicator.

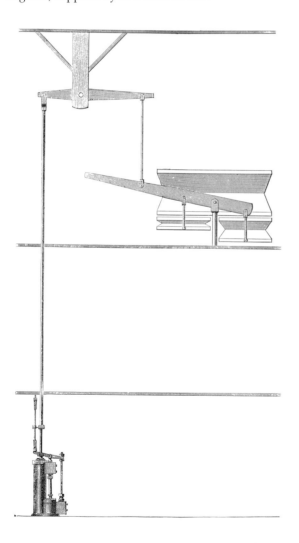

Figure 203

If the bellows is missing from the organ or if the bellows is in a seriously deteriorated condition—not just worn out bellows cloth, and if it is not considered essential to restore the instrument to its original condition, then converting to electric operation is a possibility. This is a matter of personal taste. When installing the electric suction unit, the bellows is removed and the suction unit installed where the bellows used to be. A desirable feature is an adjustable volume control, which can be mounted out of sight but accessible to the organist. It should be kept in mind that by installing an electric unit in this way the organist loses whatever control of expression that was available by varying the amount of pumping. In my own case I have found that pumping the organ becomes automatic and is a part of the mystique of the instrument, and I prefer to restore the bellows or even replace it if necessary when restoring the instrument.

As an alternative to replacing it with a suction unit, the bellows can be retained and an external suction unit added. The suction unit could be located in some

165

remote location so that its sound would not be noticeable. By placing a check valve in the tubing between the suction unit and the organ the suction unit can be turned off and the foot pedals used. With this arrangement, if the suction unit is not providing enough vacuum, the pedals can be used to help.

Figure 205: A Wilcox & White organ with the optional children's blow pedals attached.

RESOURCES

The resources available should also be considered before starting the project. In view of the amount and kind of work that needs to be done, do you have the skills to do the work, or can you reasonably expect to acquire them in carrying out the project? Do you have the necessary tools and the space to work in? Do you have the time and patience to do the job? If you are doing everything yourself, the cost should not be a big item providing you have a reasonably

equipped shop, as the materials are relatively inexpensive. If these considerations deter you there are professionals who can do the work for you. If the cost is within your budget this may be an acceptable solution.

MATERIALS

Using the proper materials will go a long way toward assuring that the repairs are long-lasting and that the value of the instrument is retained. In almost all cases the bellows will have to be re-covered. Attempts to patch a leaky bellows with tape or glue will usually prove futile. Most organs originally used rubberized cloth, although some of the older ones used leather. It is important not to improvise with plastics, artificial leather or upholstery materials, as they will not stand up to prolonged use, and the job will have to be done over. Proper bellows cloth can be obtained from piano supply houses and can be ordered through almost any music store. There are also suppliers who specialize in selling directly to hobbyists. The required material is usually referred to as reed organ bellows cloth, .020 inches thick or so. The same material can be used for both the reservoir and the exhausters. The flap valves are made of heavy, stiff leather, lacquered on one side and with a uniform, fine valve surface on the other. Pedal webbing is used to connect the foot pedals with the exhausters and is also useful for replacing the hinges on both the reservoir and the exhausters. Frequently the bellows on older melodeons used thin wooden stiffeners with strips of leather between them. Alum-tanned New Zealand lamb skin is the material of choice here. Local hobby leather stores are not likely to stock these specialized types, and it would be well worth your while to find a supplier of organ leathers.

Advertisements are frequently found in the *Reed Organ Society Bulletin* for these and other specialized materials.

At the time reed organs were being built, the best glue available was hot hide glue, made mainly from animal skins. Once you get used to its characteristics, hide glue is easy to work with, sets up fairly fast and hardens overnight. When it is completely hardened the glue is fairly brittle. Glue joints on old pieces are sometimes broken by hard blows, then the humidity further loosens them, requiring that they be reglued. Generally speaking, hide glue is preferred for reed organ work, especially when working with leather, bellows cloth or joints which may have to be reopened at some later time. Some modern glues, such as white glue or carpenter's glue, are easier to work with in that they don't have to be heated. They are more permanent, and properly applied become stronger than the surrounding wood. Strict preservation principles would require that hide glue be used exclusively when working on reed organs, but there are probably legitimate places for the modern materials which do not unnecessarily compromise the authenticity of the piece. In my own work I use carpenters' glue to repair cracked or broken pieces and to reglue loose joints which will never have to be opened. The joints have to be cleaned of old glue, since a mixture of white or carpenter's glue and hide glue leaves a weak joint. Epoxies should not be used except in rare circumstances, such as in hardening wood which has been softened by rot or insects. Some workers use contact cement for gluing bellows cloth and leather. It leaves a residue which future restorers will have difficulty removing, so I don't recommend it.

Probably the best gasket material is leather, which was originally used in many reed organs. The leather should be fairly soft to permit it to seal up the joint better—split suede calf skin being the preferred material. Some organs will be found with blotter paper for gaskets, and this is probably one of the few places where upgrading of the original material is justified as the blotter paper tends to decompose and leak. Two modern materials are widely used but of course are not historically correct: rubber-filled cork and closed-cell sponge neoprene. The cork sold in hardware stores is too porous and is not recommended. The rubber-filled kind makes a good gasket but usually comes with preapplied contact cement which leaves an undesirable residue on the wood. Closed-cell sponge neoprene is probably the best at conforming to an irregular surface. It takes a set and thus must be repositioned very carefully if the joint is later opened, and also usually comes with the preapplied contact cement. Do not use materials not intended for use on organs or pianos, such as weather stripping or automotive gasket material.

Felt is used extensively in reed organs. Frequently the old felt will be moth-eaten, badly discolored or otherwise deteriorated and will have to be replaced. The original material was quite dense, and the replacement should be as close as possible in thickness, density and color. The felt sold in fabric stores is too loose for organ work, and piano and organ supply houses are the best sources. When ordering felt, supply a sample of the original so that they can match it as closely as possible.

Fabrics used to cover openings in the case will also usually have to be replaced. Often the material has already been replaced one or more times so it is difficult to determine what was used originally. Many of the instruments used a medium weight unfigured silk, often in some shade of red, although other colors are seen. Modern fabrics should be acceptable unless absolute authenticity is a must.

The pedals were usually covered with carpet, although in later years rubber matting was sometimes used. Again, the material may already have been replaced, so what you find on the organ may not be original. Careful examination of the pedal when removing the old carpet may reveal whether it has been replaced. One good suggestion for replacement material is to look for old, used carpet. The material should have a very short nap with cut loops. If it has a figure, try to match or harmonize the pattern on the two pedals.

PLAN THE PROJECT

Before you start working on your organ restoration project, it's a good idea to think through the whole process and plan your approach. Although some people may find it too regimented, I actually prepare a list of tasks to be accomplished, as detailed as possible. I seem to get a lot of satisfaction out of crossing out the items as they are completed. The following points illustrate a typical sequence of work:

Figure 206: Coleman Kimbrell used matching pieces from an old carpet to re-cover these pedals.

168

1. CLEAN. Vacuum out loose dust and dirt, keeping an eye open for small pieces of wood or stop labels which may have fallen off, and for evidence of termites or other wood-boring insects. If there are active wood-borers, the entire piece should be pressure-treated by an exterminator. Remove surface dirt and wax, keeping water away from joints. Mineral spirits can be used here.

2. INSPECT. Check the condition of the finish; look for damage to the case; check stop board lettering, stop knobs and faces, ivories, sharps; identify missing pieces; remove action and check condition of straps, valves, bellows cloth and hinges. Check reeds to see that none are missing or broken.

3. PLAN. Make the basic decisions: restore the existing finish or refinish? Recover the bellows or electrify? Replace the stop board lettering? Make or buy new stop faces? Repair or replace broken or missing pieces? If you are a list maker, prepare a list of tasks to be accomplished.

4. BUY. Order the materials you will need to restore the instrument.

5. REFINISH. While you are waiting for the materials to arrive you can start on the case. Repair any damage and replace missing parts. If it is to be refinished, strip off the old finish, apply the new finish, apply decorative cloth and re-cover the pedals. The completed case can then be set aside in a dust-free environment or covered until you are ready to install the bellows, action, keyframe and stop board.

6. BELLOWS. Repair any damage, then re-cover the bellows, replace the flap valves and gaskets, test for leaks. Install the bellows in the case and install new pedal straps. Test for strange noises when pumping and eliminate them at this time.

7. ACTION. Clean throughly and repair any damage, recover pallet valves and mutes if necessary, replace weak springs and broken hinges. Clean reeds. Replace gaskets. Check for proper operation of all mechanical parts. Install action in organ case. Test and eliminate leaks. Make sure each reed sounds properly. Test and regulate tremolo.

8. KEYBOARD. Clean thoroughly, repair keys, replace felts if necessary. Install keyboard on action, align and level keys, regulate octave couplers.

9. STOP BOARD. Clean and repair the stop action. Refinish and reletter if necessary, then check for proper mechanical operation. Install on action, connect and regulate linkage.

10. TUNE. If the reeds are to be tuned, this is the last step. The reeds should be tuned in their own cells. Tuning will be covered in the next chapter.

TOOLS

The only specialized tool required for general reed organ work is a reed puller. The most common type has a hook on one end and a screwdriver blade on the other. The hook is formed so that it fits into the slot in the end of the reeds. When the restoration is completed, the reed hook should be left with the instrument, as it will be needed occasionally when removing dirt particles from reeds.

A few other tools will be needed if you intend to tune the reeds. They are described in the chapter on tuning. If extensive keyboard repairs are needed there are a number of handy tools, available from piano supply houses, which make this work much easier.

Figure 207: Reed organ action dolly.

A glue pot is almost indispensable if you are planning to use hot hide glue. Some models have a fixed automatic temperature control and others have adjustable controls. The organ action and bellows often will have to be tested together. While it can be done in the case, I have found it much more convenient using a dolly which I built from scrap wood and a set of casters. It can be easily pushed into a corner and covered while you are working on other components. The uprights are spaced far enough apart and are high enough to permit operating the bellows by hand. The shelf on the bottom has built-up sides and serves as temporary storage for tools and small parts. Sometimes I also use it while tuning, especially when the case is too confining to permit easy access.

169

DISASSEMBLY

Disassembly of the organ is usually fairly straightforward. Always look for a simple and logical method of removing the components, as they were almost all made to come apart. It would be helpful to take photographs or make a video tape as you go along to assist in reassembly. Also take notes as to what materials will be needed for repair and keep an eye open for serial numbers and dates.

First remove the decorative top, if any, then the upper casework—that is, the wooden pieces above the stop board which can be easily removed by taking out a few screws. Replace the screws in the holes they were taken out of or in some other way identify them so that when you are reassembling they will be easily located. I put them in plastic bags together with a slip of paper identifying where they came from. This at least limits the amount of trial and error in putting them back.

Figure 209: On many organs the entire action, including the bellows, can be removed as a single unit.

Figure 208: The stop board is mounted above the key frame, which in turn is mounted on the reed board. The octave coupler can be seen below the key frame.

The stop assembly comes out next. It is helpful to label both ends of the stop linkage where it is to be disconnected to aid in reassembly. The stop linkage should then be disconnected—there are usually two screws on each end of the stop assembly to be removed and sometimes there are hooks to

be opened. The stop assembly should then lift out in one piece.

The key frame can then be taken out after removing a few screws and loosening the center support brackets, if any. Sometimes a few keys will have to be moved aside to reveal the screws. If you prefer the key frame can usually be left on the action and removed later.

On some organs the action and bellows can all be removed together by removing two or three large screws from each side of the chest. This makes a heavy and unwieldy piece to handle, so it may be easier to remove all the screws holding the action to the bellows assembly and lifting the action out first. The stickers (or pitmans) should be removed from the action, numbered and put aside before they fall out and are lost. If they are mixed up they will make the process of leveling the keys even more laborious than usual. Be sure that you have found all the screws holding the action in place, since in addition to numerous screws around the edge, sometimes there are one or more in the middle of the reed pan.

Before removing the bellows, the exhauster springs should be carefully removed, and if they are mounted outside the reservoir it is a good idea to remove the reservoir springs too. The pedal straps will have to be released before removing the bellows. Sometimes they can be reached by removing a panel from the front of the organ below the keyboard. If this is not possible, the organ can be laid on its back and the straps disconnected from the pedals.

Figure 210: Bellows removed from the action. The outer flap valve has been removed from one exhauster to show the wind openings.

Figure 211

Lap organs often had brass pins which held the case together, similar to those used on accordions. These pins have to be pushed in, then the case opens. Melodeons were usually held together very simply with a few screws.

Figure 212: The typical harmonium can be easily opened up, as each section is hinged.

Most harmoniums are built with articulated sections for easy access. After folding the top back on its hinges and releasing a pair of latches, the stop board hinges back, giving access to the bottom of the stop board and the top of the keyboard. Then, returning the stop board to its normal position and releasing two more latches, the keyboard can also be hinged back, giving access to the bottom of the keys and some of the stop mechanism. After returning the keyboard to its normal position and releasing two large latches at the back, the entire harmonium action will hinge forward, giving access to the reeds and the stop valves. Each section can be removed by releasing the hinge pins or removing the hinges.

Figure 213

171

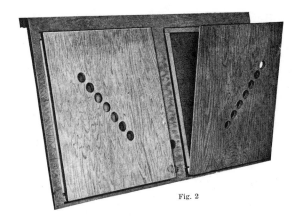

Fig. 2

Figure 214: Harmonium key frame, reeds and stop valves are accessible by opening hinged sections.

Figure 215: Exhausters with the bellows cloth and valves stripped off.

If the case is repaired and refinished first, it will then be available as a place to store the various assemblies as they are completed. Do any case repairs before stripping it for refinishing—the existing finish will protect the wood from stains and minor damage during the repairs. Of course if the original finish is in good enough condition to be preserved, do so. Generally, antiques are said to be more valuable if the original finish is retained. However, in my experience, most owners of old musical instruments prefer to have them restored to original condition, including the finish, particularly if they are to be played, and this does not seem to detract from their value. There are plenty of good texts available on furniture refinishing, which should be consulted if you are in doubt as to how to proceed.

BELLOWS

The next component to be restored should be the bellows, so that when it is finished it can immediately be replaced in the already completed case. Usually the bellows proper is attached by a number of screws to the foundation board, the large flat board which forms the bottom of the

action. Usually a gasket permits separating them, but sometimes they were glued together. If that is the case the glued joint will have to be broken open. After removing the screws, a few blows with a hammer on a chisel placed strategically at the joint will break it apart. Any damage to the wood will have to be repaired before it can be reassembled.

Before stripping off the old cloth, measure the distance across the widest part of the reservoir when it is fully open. I have found it most useful to take the inside distance. Be sure to write this measurement down where it won't be misplaced, since after recovering, if the reservoir opens too far it will hit against the rear of the organ case, and if it is too narrow you risk having insufficient wind. The length of the new cloth is measured along three edges of the reservoir. Allow an extra two inches or so at each end for overlap. The width will be the inside width already measured plus enough for gluing—an inch and a half on each side is usually plenty. It is better to cut the new piece wider than needed, then it can be trimmed exactly to size after it is glued on the reservoir and the glue has begun to set. By looking at the original

172

bellows cloth you can determine exactly what the pattern should be and how the cloth folds as the bellows closes. Take particular note of the cuts made in the cloth to permit turning the corners. Also note where carpet tacks, if any, were placed.

By running an old steam iron set to a low temperature along the glued cloth it is sometimes possible to loosen the glue enough to permit easy removal. Often the cloth can be pulled off fairly easily, but sometimes it has to be removed bit by bit. If the springs are mounted inside the reservoir, make a slit in the cloth and carefully remove them before the cloth is completely stripped off.

Measure the length of cloth needed for the exhausters in the same way as for the reservoir, being sure to leave an extra two inches at each end for overlap and a generous excess in the width. It would be useful to remove the old cloth from the exhausters in one piece to use them as patterns. If the old cloth can't be removed easily in one piece, cut it off carefully at the edge of the glued portion so that it can be used as a pattern. It will also allow you to see the size and location of the stiffeners. If the stiffeners are omitted from the exhausters or if they are not wide enough, the exhausters will make an annoying pop when you pump the pedals. A little space has to be left between the stiffeners and the wood so that they don't rub, which also makes annoying noises.

The old cloth and glue remaining on the edges can be removed by using a belt sander, an orbital sander, or it can be carefully steamed off using an old steam iron. Any tacks used in gluing should be removed first.

The leaf springs should be tested before being replaced. Press one of the leaves against a scale, holding the other leaf in the hand. The exhauster springs should read about six pounds when fully closed, and the reservoir springs about eighteen pounds for a typical parlor organ. If they measure much less they should be replaced. Any rust should be removed from the springs before proceeding. Replace the felt bumper pads if necessary. Any damage to the wood should be repaired, giving special attention to potential leaks.

Figure 216: A block of wood is used to prop the exhauster or reservoir open to the correct width.

Recover the reservoir first since it is easier, and you can learn in the process. The illustrations show an exhauster being recovered, but the procedure is the same. Cut a piece of cloth long enough to go across the

173

open end and the two sides, plus about two inches at each end for overlap. The width should as described above. Do not taper the sides at this time, as that can be done more accurately after the cloth is glued on. Close the reservoir and draw a pencil line outlining the movable part on the back board. This will serve as a guide when gluing the cloth. Prop the reservoir open to the correct width by placing a piece of wood inside the reservoir. The springs should be left off at this point, and the large screw used to operate the relief valve can be removed. Hold the cloth up to the opening, center it and mark it so that you can locate it the same way when the glue is in place. Place a heavy coating of glue on the open end of the movable side of the reservoir, but not so heavy that it drips down. Put the cloth in place and rub it so that the glue penetrates. Be careful that no excess glue remains where the cloth folds against the wood. A few small carpet tacks strategically placed will prevent the cloth from slipping while the glue is setting up. Put them only where they were placed originally—don't put them every few inches. Also use the small flat-headed tacks, not the large ones with the rounded heads. You can speed up the procedure by using wooden strips about $1/8$ inch thick lightly tacked over the glued cloth. This will assure good contact between the cloth and the wood and also permit you to move on to the next step faster.

When the glue has set up enough to permit you to continue, glue the opposite side in the same way, using the pencil line as a guide. A tack strip will be especially useful for this step. The strip could also be clamped instead of tacked. Keep the reservoir propped open until the glue is well set. If the springs go inside the reservoir, allow the glue to harden overnight, then place the springs inside and continue gluing the

Figure 217

sides. Make sure that the springs are placed in the original holes, then close the bellows to check that they are placed correctly.

Make a cut in the cloth at each corner to permit it to bend around the sides, as was done on the old cloth. Then pull the cloth straight along the side so that there are no wrinkles. There should be about two inches of extra length, which will be wrapped around the end later. Glue the cloth, making sure there are no gaps. Again, tack strips will be helpful. Before gluing the second side, remove the wood prop from inside the reservoir if it is still there. If the springs go on the outside, the reservoir can be temporarily propped open by inserting a stick through the relief valve hole at an angle.

174

Figure 218

Figure 219: Exhauster with new hinge and inside flap valves.

Mark the locations of any screw holes which will be covered by the cloth so that you can later locate them easily when mounting the outside springs. If the springs go inside the reservoir they must be in place before you glue the second side.

When both sides are glued and the glue has set up, the tack strips can be carefully removed, and the excess cloth trimmed along the edges. It will be easier to trim if this is done before the glue completely hardens. Then allow the glue to harden overnight and glue down and trim the overlaps. Two tacks on each will hold them in place while the glue is hardening. Cut out a piece of bellows cloth to cover the hinged end of the reservoir plus about three quarters of an inch of the back board, and glue it in place. Close the bellows and make creases in the cloth so that it folds neatly. A potential source of leaks is the corner where the cut was made. To be safe, cut out two circular pieces of lamb skin about one inch in diameter, and glue them to these corners, shaping them to completely enclose the corner.

When recovering the exhausters, both the inner and outer flap valves should be replaced. If the hinges are loose or damaged they should also be replaced at this time. Carefully observe how the old hinges were made.

Pedal strapping makes good hinge material. The pedal straps put a lot of strain on the exhauster and frequently the screw holes are badly enlarged. Sometimes there are numerous holes where the straps have been attached in different places. If the hinges are being replaced, you can exchange the exhausters left to right which will put the attachment point of the pedal strap in an unused area.

Replacing the cloth on the exhausters follows the same technique as for the reservoir, except that the stiffeners must be glued to the cloth before it is glued in place. If you were able to remove the old cloth more or less intact, use it as a pattern. Draw a center

Figure 220: Bellows cloth with stiffeners attached, ready to be glued to the exhauster.

175

line down the long dimension of the cloth and mark the location of the corners and the edges, so that the stiffeners can be located exactly. The old stiffeners are rarely reusable, so new ones can be made of cardboard or preferably $1/32''$ plywood available from hobby stores. Glue the stiffeners to the cloth.

Place some flat pieces of wood with weights on them over the stiffeners as the glue hardens so that they will not curl. Then glue the cloth in place as was done with the reservoir. Glue down the overlaps and glue a strip of bellows cloth over the hinged ends. Glue the leather circles to the corners which were cut. Close the exhausters and form the folds. Work the exhausters to make sure that they do not bind.

Close the reservoir and replace the relief valve screw. Then attach the releathered valve. Make sure the screw is adjusted so that the valve opens before the reservoir is fully closed. When all the finishing touches are done and all the glue has hardened well, replace the springs on the reservoir if they are mounted on the outside. Then close the wind ways at the top of the bellows with masking tape and work the exhausters to see if the reservoir holds vacuum. It should take a minute or more to open if there are no significant leaks. Leaks can be detected by listening with a stethoscope, or by blowing smoke at the glued joints and valves. Leaks can usually be easily repaired by adding a little glue to the offending opening.

The bellows attaches to the bottom of the foundation board, to which the action will eventually be reattached. If any of the screw holes are enlarged so that the screw won't seat tightly they should be repaired, as described below. Sometimes the board is a solid piece but more often it is built up, with gaps intentionally left for expansion

and contraction of the wood. These gaps are covered with bellows cloth, which should be replaced. If the bellows was originally glued to this board, It would be a good idea to use a gasket instead of glue, as the joint may have to be reopened in the future. When the bellows is reattached to the bottom board and any braces reinstalled, it should again be tested for leaks. It's much easier to deal with them before the bellows is mounted in the cabinet. When you are satisfied that everything is airtight, mount the entire assembly back in the case, install the exhauster springs and connect the pedal straps.

At this point it is perhaps worthwhile to mention the proper way to repair loose screw holes. Do not put a match stick or a toothpick in the hole, do not use liquid joint tightener or the little aluminum inserts, and do not substitute larger screws. None of these methods will prove adequate in the long run. The proper method is to drill out the hole and glue in a wood plug cut from a piece of wood of the same type and thickness. The plug should be set in place with the same grain orientation as the surrounding wood. Resist the temptation to put in a piece of wooden dowel, as the screw would go into the end grain which is not strong enough to hold properly.

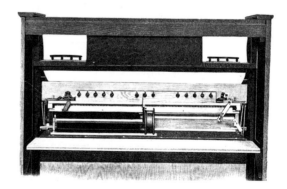

Figure 221: Back of action showing tremolo.

176

ACTION

Before starting any repairs to the action, remove the reeds, keeping each set separate and labeled so that it eventually gets back in the right place. Frequently the reeds will be very difficult to remove, but must be taken out very carefully, so as not to break the edges of the cells. Remove the tremolo and the octave coupler, if any.

If the pallet valves can be removed, number and remove them. If they are fastened by a leather hinge, leave them in place for the present. Check for cracks in the reed pan or sounding board. This is the large wooden base that the reed cells are attached to. It is usually made of $3/8''$ spruce, similar to the sound board on a piano. As previously mentioned, if there are

several large cracks or if the reed cells have come unglued from the reed pan, many experts would not bother with repairing the instrument. If a crack is present it very often extends to the slots below the reeds. Small cracks can be remedied by forcing glue into the crack, letting it dry, then applying more. This process is repeated until the crack is sealed up. If the crack extends under the pallet valve, the surface will have to be smoothed off so that the valve will be air tight. Large cracks can be repaired by gluing a wedge-shaped thin strip of spruce into the crack, trimming off the excess, then filling the remaining interstices with repeated applications of glue as previously described. Many restorers would not object to using white glue, carpenters' glue or epoxy to fill large cracks.

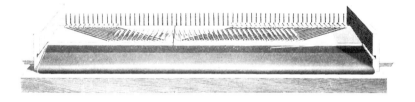

Figure 222: Octave couplers

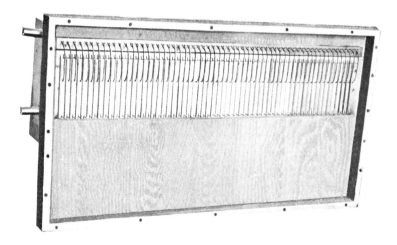

Figure 223: The reed pan or sounding board, showing the pallet valves and springs.

177

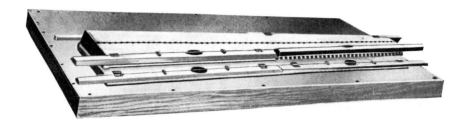

Figure 224: Reed cell board showing mutes.

Sometimes the edges of some of the reed cells will be broken. If the pieces are found they can be glued in place, but if not, the surface will have to be built up so that the cell will be sealed air tight when the mute closes. If there are small vent holes connecting to the highest reeds, make sure that they are open.

If the mutes do not seat properly, one or more of the reeds will cipher, or sound, when they shouldn't. Warped mutes can cause this problem, but I have found that to be a rare occurrence. If the leather is deteriorated it will have to be replaced. Lambskin or split calfskin can be used. If the new leather is not of exactly the same thickness as the old, the mutes will not seat properly unless the mute hinges are reset, a delicate task.

The pallet valves usually are faced with a piece of felt covered with a thin strip of leather. If the felt and leather are in good condition and the valves do not leak, they should probably be left alone. Very often the felts have been eaten by insects and must be replaced. Use leather and felt as near to the original as possible. In removing the old material, notice that the felts are usually attached only by a thin line of glue in the center, and the leather by a few small dots of glue. This permits the material to seal better by adapting itself to the valve opening. If you are not bothered by using modern materials, 1/8" closed-cell sponge neoprene works just fine as the neoprene makes a very good seal. This material can be attached with a uniform coat of the proper plastic glue, and sometimes it is available with self-sticking glue. If any springs are broken or weakened they should be replaced. New springs are available commercially, and experienced organ repairmen usually have a boxful in various sizes.

Almost invariably the reeds need to be cleaned. Sometimes they will have verdigris deposits from the mute leather, insects, coal dust and other unidentifiable gunk. Carefully clean off the thick deposits by hand, then soak them in a cleaning solution. There are as many favorite solutions as there are restorers. Almost any cleaning solution which contains ammonia will do the job. Plain household ammonia diluted with water, brass cleaner and even toilet bowl cleaner are regularly used. After soaking for a while rinse them thoroughly in water and let them air dry. Do each set of reeds separately so that they are not mixed up. Inspect each reed, particularly looking for small particles stuck between the movable reed and the brass frame. By holding it up to a light, space should be visible around three sides of the reed. Then replace them in the reed cells.

178

The tremolo, being a moving part, is very often in need of attention. The most common type is the fan tremolo, which has a small impeller inside a wooden housing coupled to a long two-bladed fan made of cardboard. When the tremolo stop knob is pulled, a valve opens allowing air to flow into the impeller and out to the chest. Very often there is a mechanical arrangement which imparts an initial spin to the fan when the stop knob is pulled. Another type of tremolo sometimes found in American organs and also in harmoniums is the beater tremolo. This device has a weighted spring attached to a small pneumatic and a valve. The pneumatic vibrates open and closed, alternately passing and stopping the air flow to the reeds.

The usual type of octave coupler has a series of levers which are located on the top of the action just below the keys. When the coupler assembly is raised by pulling the appropriate stop knob, one end of each lever comes into contact with a key and the other end with a wooden disk glued to a pitman one octave above or below the key. When the key is pressed, both the pitman below the key and that operated by the lever are simultaneously depressed. Over the years dirt falling through the keys will accumulate in the coupler assembly to the extent that the levers fail to operate. Sometimes a good cleaning will correct the problem, and sometimes the assembly must be taken apart, any rust removed and the felts replaced. The job looks more daunting than it really is.

After making any necessary mechanical repairs, removing rust from metal parts and replacing the gaskets and felt, the action can be reinstalled in the organ. Test each reed in each rank separately to make sure it sounds properly.

KEYFRAME

Before removing the keys from the keyframe they should be individually numbered if they are not already, starting with number 1 at the bass end. Alternatively, a straight diagonal line can be drawn across the key tops in back of the ivory. Then, when the keys are to be replaced on the frame it is a simple matter of making sure the line is straight or that the numbers are in sequence. In order to remove the keys, the keeper must be removed from the rear of the keyboard. Usually the sides of the keys will be badly discolored. A little sanding will bring them back. If the felt bushings are worn, they can be replaced. Bushing cloth and specialized tools for key repair and adjustment are available from piano supply houses. Some reed organs had ivory key tops, especially the older ones. If only a few ivories are missing or badly damaged, it is sometimes possible to find used genuine ivories for replacement. Otherwise, there is a substitute called Ivorine which can be stained to match the originals. Remove a broken ivory by heating carefully with a warm iron, then prying it off with a putty knife. Yellowed ivories can be whitened by polishing with tripoli buffing compound. Ivories can be glued in place using ivory cement, which is hide glue, used warm, with titanium dioxide whitener added so that it will not make a shadow through the ivory. Celluloid tops will melt or catch fire if too much heat is applied, so proceed with caution. Ivorine and celluloid tops require Ivorine cement when replacing.

Felts should be replaced if necessary with material of the same thickness and consistency. After all felts have been replaced, the keys replaced on the frame and the keeper back in place, the keyframe can be mounted on the action and the keys straightened and leveled.

The entire key-frame can be shimmed up if it is too low with repect to the stop board. The keys rest on the pitmans which are about halfway between the hinge point at the back of the key and the key front, so any variation in the height of the pitman is doubled at the key front. Some leveling can be accomplished by moving the pitmans around. Any remaining problems will have to be solved by trimming the top of the offending pitman or gluing a small piece of thin cardboard to it to build it up. When leveling the keys the keeper should be in place or the backs of the keys held down by weights.

When the keys are leveled to your satisfaction, then regulate the octave couplers. This is accomplished by adjusting the small dowels under the keys so that when the coupler is engaged, none of the keys lift up, and when the keys are depressed there is little or no lost motion before the coupler lever is contacted. When the coupler is not engaged, there should be no noticeable key movement an octave higher or lower when a key is depressed.[37]

Figure 225: Skilled craftsmen install the stop action at the Estey factory.

STOP ACTION

The stop action usually accumulates dust and dirt, so a good cleaning will be required. Watch to see that small broken parts are not inadvertently thrown away. Very often the stop board will have to be completely disassembled, the felts replaced, rust removed, and then reassembled. The felts lining the holes for the stop rods are made from a single straight piece of felt with the opening at the bottom. A little cut-and-try will show you the exact length to cut the felt so that it fits without a gap.

Piano supply houses often stock replacement stop knobs and rods. Very often the rods can be made from stock dowels. If the exact size of knobs cannot be located, they can be turned on a lathe, provided they are the straight variety. The beveled knobs would require specialized machinery to duplicate, but fortunately they are available commercially. A wide variety of stop faces are also available commercially. They can also be made by photocopying another one with the correct name or by using transfer letters available from an artists' supply store. If you have access to a computer they can be typeset using the appropriate font, usually an Old English face. The result can be printed out oversized on a dot-matrix printer and then reduced on a copy machine to smooth out the rough edges. A cleaner job can be obtained by printing with a laser printer, in which case it can be printed at the actual size. Finally it can be copied on a glossy glue-backed paper. Many of the popular stop names are reproduced in an Old English type face in Appendix A. The page can be copied on a copy machine, adjusting the size as necessary, and the names cut out as needed.

I try to keep the original finish on the stop board even when the case is being refinished. They can often be touched up so that they look quite presentable. If not, then the next preference is to retain any lettering on the board by masking it off, carefully stripping the old finish around it, and refinishing. If the lettering cannot be salvaged, there are several alternatives. First, if you can get a good sharp photograph of the identical lettering on another organ, you could have a decal made up. The cost would be quite high, however. There are a few piano fallboard decals available which would be usable, such as Aeolian, A. B. Chase, Melville Clark, Estey, Gulbransen, Hamilton, Kimball, Lakeside, Mason & Hamlin, Packard, M. Schulz & Co., Shoninger, Story & Clark, and Weaver. Trade magazines such as Piano Technician's Journal often list specialty outlets for these, and while the style and size is not likely to be the same as the original, they may be better than nothing. Another alternative is to use transfer letters. They are available in a wide variety of styles and sizes in black and in

gold and are quite attractive if carefully applied.

When the stop board is completed, mount it on the action, and connect and regulate the linkage. The stop knobs should pull easily and smoothly, remain open, and close easily when pushed. The mutes should close completely so that only the selected sets of reeds will sound. The tremolo should start with a spin and continue running as long as the knob is out. The octave couplers should engage and disengage easily.

The organ is now ready to be tuned. Refer to the next chapter for detailed information on tuning. If tuning is not contemplated, then reassemble any remaining components, and the job is done.

IDENTIFYING AND DATING REED ORGANS

Often owners of reed organs would like to establish the date of manufacture of the organ. Sometimes a careful examination of the inside of the organ will reveal a date, usually handwritten. Frequently a date is found on one of the keys. Remove the stop action and look at the part of the key tops

Figure 226

Figure 227: Above: original stop board lettering on an Aeolian Orchestrelle. Below: lettering applied with transfer letters.

Figure 228: Organ labels.

181

which have been covered by the stop action. Occasionally a label will be found with a legible date written or stamped on it. Some makers carefully stamped each instrument with a serial number. In some cases these numbers have been preserved and are collected in *Gellerman's International Reed Organ Atlas*. Serial number lists are available for the following makers: Allmendinger, W. Bell & Co., E. P. Carpenter, Estey, Farrand & Votey, Fort Wayne Organ Co. (Packard), Hamilton, Hoffberg, Hoffman & Czerny, John Holt, M. Hörügel, Isachsen & Renbjør, Ernst Kaps, Kawai, Kimball, Kinnard Dreher, Lindholm, Mannborg, Mason & Hamlin, Aeolian Orchestrelle, Petrof, Prince, Sauter, Schiedmayer, Smith American, Spang, Waters, Weaver, Wurlitzer, Yamaha, and Zimmerman.

In most cases the numbers were assigned in chronological order, so that dating within a year or so is possible. Mason & Hamlin assigned numbers according to some yet undeciphered system, so that dating from those numbers is haphazard. A further complication results from the practice of some makers of using different numbers for the action and for the case.

Some manufacturers made organs with other names on the stop boards, the so-called "stencil" organs. Kimball, for example, made organs under the names of Goggin, Thiery, Pacific Queen, and Great Western. The numbers of organs with those names should all fit within the Kimball serial number list.

The business names and addresses of many of the makers changed over the years, and it is possible to get a clue as to the age of the instrument by comparing the name or address on the organ with that shown in the Atlas. For example, Abraham Prescott changed the name of his business in the following years:

A. Prescott, 1836
Abraham Prescott & Son, 1845
A. Prescott & Sons, ca 1849
Prescott and Brothers, 1850
Prescott Brothers, 1853
Prescott Organ Co., 1871
Prescott Piano & Organ Co., 1887
Prescott Piano Co., 1891

Alexandre-François Debain was at the following addresses in the years shown below:

Boulv. St. Denis, Paris, 1839
76-78 rue de Bondy, Paris, 1843
rue Vivienne 53 & 15, Paris, 1845
Place de LaFayette 24-28, Paris, 1856
116-118 Place de LaFayette, Paris, 1865
15 rue de Chaligny, Paris, 1888

An approximate date can often be inferred from the case style. In the 1840s and 50s, melodian makers copied shamelessly from each other, so that each new style change was soon reflected in those of other makers. Wherever possible in this book, illustrations of organs are dated to help as a guide.

Figure 229: Prescott's Patent Reed Instruments, Patented April 17, 1849.

number 9912 must be from about 1851.

The melodeon with contoured octagonal legs, shown in Figure 232 below, was made by Prescott & Brothers. That name was used from 1850 to 1853, and consequently the instrument dates to that period.

Figure 230: D. M. Dearborn, Concord, New Hampshire. Working under this name 1847-1853.

As an example of estimating the date, the square piano-style melodian shown in Figure 229 on the previous page contains a label stating, "Prescott's Patent Reed Instruments. Patented April 17, 1849." Therefore it had to be made after that date. Note the square corners and the rounded peg legs.

The instrument in Figure 230, above, was made by D. M. Dearborn of Concord, New Hampshire. He worked under this name from 1847 to 1853. The style differences from Figure 229 are minor: the squared-off music stand, the pedal bracket is inverted and the peg legs are turned with different contours at the top. The Dearborn shop was close to Prescott's, his instruments were sold in the Prescott shop, and they must have worked closely together. It is likely that both instruments were made in the period 1850-53.

The instrument depicted in Figure 231 was made by George A. Prince & Co. and bears the serial number 9912. Note that the peg legs are octagonal rather than rounded. The Reed Organ Atlas lists serial number 8000 in 1850 and number 11200 in 1852. The

Figure 231: Geo. A. Prince & Co., serial number 9912, circa 1851.

Figure 232: Prescott & Brothers, 1850-53.

183

Figure 233: Mason & Hamlin five octave piano-style melodeon, 1856.

Figure 235: Melodeon made by Liscom, Dearborn & Co. between 1856 and 1859.

The melodeon shown in Figure 233, above, is from Mason & Hamlin's 1856 catalog. The corners of the case are well rounded, but the legs are of the octagonal peg style. Since the legs screwed into the case, it was easy to change the style. This is probably a rather late date for that type of leg, but it is likely that it was used to differentiate the appearance of the five-octave from the six-octave melodeon shown in Figure 234, below.

The instrument shown in Figure 235, above, bears the name Liscom, Dearborn &

Co., a name used during the period 1856-59. Note the matching stool. The handsome melodeon with the rounded corners, serpentine molding and cabriole legs in Figure 236, below, was made by A. MacNutt of Philadelphia and is dated 1865. In 1867 the piano-style melodeon made its last appearance in an Estey catalog (see figure 237, shown on the following page). Note the elaborately shaped octagonal legs, the serpentine molding and the fretwork on the key slip.

Figure 234: Mason & Hamlin six octave piano-style melodeon, 1856.

Figure 236: Melodeon made by A. MacNutt, 1865.

Figure 237: 1867 Estey square piano-style melodeon, styles 6, 7, 8, 10, 11, 12, and 13.

Some members of the *Reed Organ Society* are able to help in identifying and dating organs. When requesting assistance, it is necessary to provide clear photographs of the instrument with the keyboard cover closed and open, the full name and address of the maker as shown on the stop board or elsewhere on the instrument, and the model number, serial number and name, if shown. Mason & Hamlin frequently stenciled the style number on the back of the case. The number of stops and their names are sometimes of use. The Estey Style S was produced for about thirty years with only minor changes in appearance, but the names of the stops changed more frequently. Patent numbers are usually not of much help, except for the obvious indication that the instrument must have been made after that date.

The lettering placed on the stop board by the maker in most cases is done in an elaborate style, Old English being the favorite. When the lettering is in good condition and the maker is well known, it can be deciphered without too much trouble, although even the Estey name has been misread as Estep.

When the letters are faded it can require some detective work to identify an obscure name. Don Clark of Moravia, Iowa sent me a photograph of an organ, presumably English, with a name previously unknown to me. I read the name at first as John Carr.

𝕵. 𝕰stey & 𝕮o.
𝕵. 𝕰step & 𝕮o.

Figure 239

Some time later I ran across the picture again and read it as John Barr. On its third appearance, this time with the aid of a computer and a laser printer I was able to identify it positively as John Hare, as shown below.

Figures 240, above, and 241, below

John Hare

Figure 238

185

Figure 242

In another case, an organ in the Conklin Museum in Hanover, Michigan has a name in which only the two initials "H.D.," the first letter of the last name, "B," and another letter, "e," were reasonably legible. A search through the *Atlas* and other sources yielded two possibilities: Butzen and Bowen, both names associated with organ building in Chicago. However, either name is too short for the space on the stop board.

This name remained a mystery for several years until another careful reading, aided by laser-printed examples, suggested that the last letter could be "y." Still another search of the *Atlas* revealed H.D. Bentley of Freeport, Illinois, a maker of organ and piano stools, and B.D. Bentley of Chicago, a reed organ maker.

H. D. Bentley
B. D. Bentley

Figure 243

The initials on the Museums's instrument were clearly "H.D." and the city was Chicago, but H.D. Bentley made organ benches in Freeport, Illinois. Since the Old English letters for B and H are similar, the possibility existed that only one name was involved, B.D. Bentley, and that after making organs in Chicago he relocated to

186

Figure 244: An H.D. Bentley organ.

Freeport and concentrated on organ benches and piano stools. A telephone call to the owner of a "B.D." Bentley organ confirmed that it was indeed H.D. Bentley. As a result, the Museum's instrument has been identified, the B.D. Bentley organ corrected to read H.D., and the *Atlas* entries for the two names corrected and combined.

While not all Old English typefaces are identical, and the style has been simplified over the years, comparison with a modern version can be of real help in identifying illegible names. The following alphabets are included here for that purpose.

ABCDEFGHI
JKLMNOPQ
RSTUVWXYZ
abcdefghijklmn
opqrstuvwxyz

Figure 245

Chapter Eight

Tuning

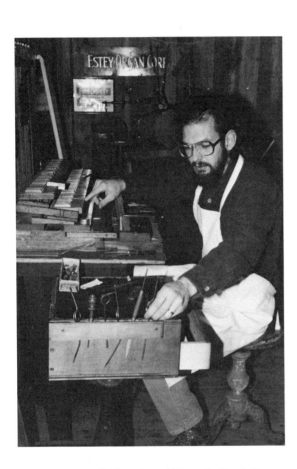

Figure 246: Ned Phoenix, of Phoenix Reed Organ Resurrection, working at an original Estey voicing jack.

The effort expended on tuning while rebuilding an organ will pay off in the quality of the music produced and in the satisfaction of knowing that the restoration is done right. Reed organs were originally popular before air conditioning and central humidified heat were in use, and as a result they were subject to extremes of dryness, humidity, temperature and dust rarely

found these days. In spite of these difficult conditions, reed organs stayed reasonably in tune over many years. The main enemy was and still is dust and dirt getting into the reeds. These days the use of filters on furnaces and air conditioners and using vacuum cleaners instead of feather dusters have drastically cut down the amount of dust in the home. As a result of fairly constant temperatures, controlled humidity and dust control in modern homes, once a reed organ is tuned it should stay acceptably in tune for years.

Tuning does not require a knowledge of music, an ability to play the instrument or an exceptional ear—you need to be able to find the various notes on the keyboard, have adequate hearing, good concentration and lots of patience.

As compared to tuning a piano, the process of tuning a reed organ is really quite simple, for three reasons: first, the notes can be sustained continuously, so the beginner can take as much time necessary to identify the beats; second, it is easy to determine whether a reed is sharp or flat by slowly raising the key and listening to the change in beats; and third, the octaves are tuned perfect and not "stretched" as in the piano. Anyone who has attempted, successfully or unsuccessfully, to tune a piano will find the reed organ child's play by comparison. For those interested in learning to tune a piano, beginning with a reed organ would be good training. The practice in identifying and counting beats is the same, without the need to do it quickly as in tuning a piano. While reed tuning is easy, it is tedious, usually requiring five to ten attempts per reed. Thus, in a simple instrument with two rows of reeds, the same process of removing, scraping, inserting, and testing could easily be repeated a total of a thousand times.

In order to tune a reed organ or a piano by ear you must be able to hear the "beats." Technically, beats are the difference frequencies produced by the combination of two tones in a nonlinear medium. In this case the tones are either the fundamental musical notes or their harmonics, and the medium is the tuner's ear. The beat is produced when the frequencies of the two notes are almost, but not quite, identical. When that happens, the sound produced by one reed alternately enhances and diminishes the intensity of the other. The combined sound increases and decreases in intensity. These variations are the beats.

To illustrate, pull out the proper stops so that each key sounds only one reed. These are usually the Diapason and Melodia stops, although the names may vary. Hold down the A key above middle C and the A below middle C. If these two reeds are exactly in tune with each other, the two notes will be heard without any wavering or change of intensities. If they are not in tune a faint warble or beat will be heard. The slower the beat, the closer the reeds are to being in tune. Slowly let up on the lower A key. This slightly lowers the pitch of the corresponding reed. The number of beats per second should change, or if there were no beats at all, you should now hear them. If the beats become faster as the key is let up, that reed is flat with respect to the higher reed. If the beats become slower as the key is let up, the reed is sharp. Compare other notes an octave apart and determine which reeds are flat, which are sharp and which ones are in tune. Repeat this procedure until you can instantly pick out the beats and quickly determine which reeds are out of tune. You have now identified one of the easiest musical intervals to tune—the octave, and you are now ready to graduate to a slightly more difficult one—the musical fifth.

Figure 247: A reedmaker at the Estey factory checks the fit of a reed in its brass frame.

Figure 248: Careful filing sets the pitch of the reed at the factory.

188

The musical interval called the fifth consists of two different notes such that the frequency of the higher note is one and one-half times the frequency of the lower note. Conversely, the frequency of the lower note is two-thirds of that of the upper note. It is not necessary to understand this relationship in order to tune the interval, but it helps. Take, for example, the fifth formed by A below middle C and E above middle C. The frequencies are 220 Hz and 330 Hz, approximately, in the currently accepted international pitch, or,

$$220 \text{ Hz} \times 1.5 = 330 \text{ Hz}$$

The second harmonic of 330 Hz is 660 Hz, and the third harmonic of 220 Hz is also 660 Hz. If we were tuning reeds which had exactly these frequencies, we would hear perfect harmony—there would be no beats. Letting up slowly on the E key would flat the E slightly, lowering its frequency, and beats would be heard. Since we are now listening to beats between two harmonics, they are fainter than the beats resulting from the octave. Try several pairs of notes forming fifth intervals, such as: E-B, F#-C#, G#-D# and G-D and listen for the beats. Determine which is flat and which is sharp. In tuning the modern equal-tempered scale, this interval is never tuned perfect, that is, we always tune for a certain number of beats, for reasons which are explained later.

Another interval which is useful in tuning is the fourth. The fourth is made up of a pair of notes such that the frequency of the lower note is three-quarters of the frequency of the higher. As a result, the third harmonic of the higher note and the fourth harmonic of the lower note have the same frequency. Take the interval formed by A below middle C and the E below it:

$$^3/_4 \times 220 \text{ Hz} = 165 \text{ Hz}$$

Figure 249: Sets of reeds are assembled in trays at the factory.

The third harmonic of A220 is 660 Hz, and the fourth harmonic of E165 is 660 Hz. Try listening to some fourths such as A-E, B-F#, C#-G#, D#-A#, A#-F#, C-G and D-A, to see if you can hear the beats. They are usually even fainter than those produced by the fifths. Again, when you hear the beats, determine which note is sharp and which is flat. Hearing the beats requires normal hearing, quiet surroundings, concentration and practice. If after giving it a really good try you cannot hear the beats produced by fourths, don't despair; you can tune by ear perfectly well using fifths, octaves and unisons.

The last interval that you need to recognize in tuning a reed organ is the unison. Unison means having the same pitch. The sound is very much like that of the octave.

In tuning there are two critical phases which must be done with precision—setting the pitch, and tuning all twelve notes of one complete octave to the equal-tempered scale, called "laying the bearings." Once these steps have been done properly, tuning the other notes becomes easy. Setting the

189

pitch is important especially if the instrument is to be played together with other instruments.

In the past there was considerable variation in standard pitches. Middle A has varied from 374.2 Hz to 567.3 Hz over the years. The most widely-accepted standard pitch today is to tune A above middle C to 440 Hz. Some reed organs will be found tuned to A440, but more to A435, A452 and other pitches. A check of three manufacturers in Boston in 1880 revealed three different standards in use in the same city: 450.9 Hz, 452.4 Hz and 452.6 Hz, all different from today's 440 Hz. After 1891, thanks in large part to the efforts of Levi K. Fuller of the Estey Organ Company, the musical instrument manufacturers in the United States standardized on A435. After 1917 the international standard pitch of A440 was adopted by all musical instrument makers in the United States.

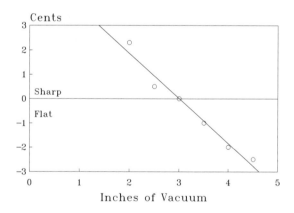

Figure 250: Reed pitch versus vacuum. Note that as the vacuum is increased the reed goes flat.

It is a good idea to use an electric suction unit to provide the vacuum when tuning a reed organ, so that the vacuum can be maintained at a constant level. The suction unit can be temporarily attached by removing the tremolo unit and attaching a hose

there, or by attaching a hose under the relief valve. The level of vacuum affects the pitch of the reeds, as shown in the graph at left. Notice that increasing the vacuum decreases the pitch since the reed is traveling farther and thus takes longer to complete a cycle. The reed will maintain its vibration down to about two inches of vacuum. At the higher levels, say four inches or more, the quality of the sound begins to deteriorate because the reed is being driven into its nonlinear region. Sometimes the reeds can be driven hard enough so that the tip physically touches the reed cell or the pallet valve, causing an undesirable buzzing sound. The reeds can be damaged by overdriving, so keep the vacuum at a reasonable level. The level to be used while tuning should be checked all across the keyboard for all stops, to make sure that the reeds will sound, and that none is overdriven. About 2.5 to 3 inches of vacuum is typical. A little experimentation will show the right level. It is possible to tune the reeds by foot-pumping the bellows, but harder to maintain the vacuum at a constant level. In both cases it is a good idea to use a manometer to check the level of vacuum. When an organ is played the vacuum varies somewhat, but all reeds are affected at the same time, so discords are kept to a minimum. The reservoir helps to smooth out the vacuum at the desired level.

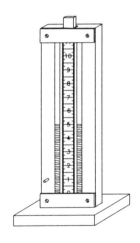

Figure 251: A Manometer, used to measure air pressure or vacuum.

190

Because the vacuum (or pressure) used to operate a reed organ is so slight it is difficult to measure with a conventional pressure or vacuum gauge, so a manometer is used. A manometer is easy to make, and is useful for both reed and pipe organ tuning. It consists of a U-shaped tube made of glass or clear plastic, half filled with water. One end of the U is left open, and the other is connected to the reed chest. When vacuum is present in the reed chest, the water falls on one side of the U and rises on the other side. The difference in water levels, measured in inches or centimeters, is the amount of vacuum or pressure. A drop of red food coloring added to the water makes it more visible. The manometer can be of any reasonable length—twelve inches will permit measuring up to about ten inches of pressure in a pipe organ. The manometer shown in the illustrations uses $3/8$ " plastic tubing, (smaller tubing will not be as sensitive because of capillary action.) The tubing is brought down the back of the manometer and terminated in a $1/8$" nipple to permit easy connection and disconnection. The wooden base serves only to hold the manometer in a vertical position. The base could be dispensed with and the manometer mounted on a wall. Drawings for making a manometer are included as Appendix B.

It should be pointed out that it is possible to tune an organ without learning to tune intervals by ear, other than the octave and unison, by using an electronic tuning device. The simplest of these generates a continuous tone which can be set to each note of the musical scale and can be offset sharp or flat by precise amounts. The reeds are then tuned by ear to that tone. The other kind of tuning machines are measuring instruments; they are somewhat easier to use and will give a direct visual indication on a meter or dial of the sharpness or flat-

ness of a tone. While a reed organ can be tuned strictly by ear, and for some this is the "real" way, the practical problem of determining the original pitch of the instrument and then tuning to that somewhat arbitrary pitch is much more conveniently done with an electronic tuner.

Instrument Estey No. 131322					Pitch A440	
Owner Cal Rosenberg					Date 22 April 1989	
Stop ►	Melodia	Viola	Diapason	Celeste	Celeste2	
F	+21	+15				
F#	13	17				
G	23	21				
G#	18	19				
A	16	20				
A#	16	22				
B	8	18				
C	7	16	+13	+8	+26	
C#	7	16	17	17	25	
D	14	13	8	8	24	
D#	8	10	13	11	23	
E	17	16	15	13	23	
F	9	19	17	11	22	
F#	14	12	11	11	21	
G	18	18	15	10	20	
G#	18	19	16	11	19	
A	21	17	21	17	19	
A#	18	20	14	10	18	
B	14	18	17	13	17	
C	14	18	24	13	17	
C#	17	20	17	18	16	
D	13	11	14	14	15	
D#	12	15	16	11	15	
E	16	18	20	19	14	
F	16	17	17	12	14	
F#	11	10	9	17	13	
G	11	18	23	20	13	
G#	17	18	21	22	12	
A	12	14	23	22	12	
A#	10	21	28	19	11	
B	14	10	25	16	11	
C			31	23	10	
C#			26	23	10	
D			24	18	9	
D#			22	13	9	
E			25	21	8	
F			25	16	8	
Average	14.3	16.6	18.9	15.2		
Std Dev						

Figure 252: A reed organ tuning chart used to determine the pitch of the organ. A blank form, which is included in Appendix B, may be photocopied.

Unless the organ is to be used with other instruments, it is best to leave it tuned to its original pitch or as close to original as possible so as to avoid weakening the reeds by excessive scraping. To determine the original pitch, measure and record the deviation in cents[38] from A440 of each reed in each stop and compute the average deviation in each stop. A tuning chart like the one shown above is a convenient place to record the data. If one or two reeds in a stop are drastically out of line with the others you may want to eliminate them from the computation of the average. If you have access to a calculator or computer with statistical functions, the stop with the lowest standard deviation is probably nearest to the original pitch. Lacking such a calculator, look for the stop which has the least variation in pitch. To determine the frequency corresponding to the average pitch use the nomograph shown below. For example, 20 cents flat is the equivalent of A435; 40 cents sharp would be A450. In the example shown in the tuning chart, all four stops are close to A440 so it was decided to tune to that pitch. The method of tuning the celeste reeds will be described later.

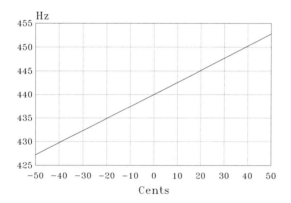

Figure 253: Nomograph for determining the pitch of A.

The tuning instructions in this chapter are based on A440, the current international standard pitch. Alternate instructions are given for tuning to A435 and A452. Using an electronic tuner the pitch can be set to any value. The following tables show the theoretical frequencies of equal temperament for the two octaves below "violin A," accurate to plus or minus one one-thousandth Hertz, for the three standards mentioned above. For convenience in reference, the notes are referred to in the following discussion by the letter designating the note, followed by the frequency to the nearest whole number. For example, middle C in international pitch is referred to as C262, the nearest whole number to the theoretical frequency of 261.625 Hz. In the same way, C259 refers to middle C in the old standard based on A435. If the organ was originally tuned to some other pitch than A440 and you must tune it to international pitch, each reed will have to be changed quite a bit in pitch. Some tuners claim to accomplish this by physically moving all reeds one space to the left in the reed cells if they were originally tuned to A435, and one space to the right if they were tuned higher than A440. From the table it is obvious that this approach will not improve matters. I recommend keeping the reeds in their proper positions and changing the pitch by scraping or filing. If the pitch must be moved as much as a half-tone the filing can become tedious, but you will end up with the reeds tuned to the same pitch stamped on the base of the reed. As previously mentioned, this will weaken the reeds somewhat and may shorten their life. Moving the reeds to the left or right will lead to confusion, since the stamp on the reed will not correspond to its pitch. Moving the reeds has another disadvantage in that you must obtain a new reed for the highest or lowest note, depending on whether the shift was to the left or to the right.

192

FREQUENCIES OF
THREE STANDARD PITCHES

A	435.000	440.000	452.402
G#	410.585	415.305	427.011
G	387.541	391.995	403.045
F#	365.790	369.994	380.423
F	345.260	349.228	359.072
E	325.882	329.628	338.919
D#	307.591	311.127	319.897
D	290.328	293.665	301.942
C#	274.033	277.183	284.996
C	258.653	261.626	269.000
B	244.135	246.942	253.902
A#	230.433	233.082	239.652
A	217.500	220.000	226.201
G#	205.293	207.652	213.505
G	193.770	195.998	201.522
F#	182.895	184.997	190.212
F	172.630	174.614	179.536
E	162.941	164.814	169.459
D#	153.796	155.563	159.948
D	145.164	146.832	150.917
C#	137.016	138.591	142.498
C	129.326	130.813	134.500
B	122.068	123.471	126.951
A#	115.217	116.541	119.826
A	108.750	110.000	113.101

If the pitch is being raised or lowered more than a few cents, it is a good idea to do it in several steps, as it is easy to overshoot. Change the pitch, but leave it a few cents sharp of the desired pitch, then let it rest overnight. The next day you will probably find that the pitch has changed slightly and may need to be touched up. Get it as close as you can—it will never be perfect.

The standard pitch of 440 Hz for A above middle C can be set by using a tuning fork. Tuning forks can be obtained from any tuners' supply house and also from many retail music stores. These forks are good enough for most purposes, but are not perfect. The purist can check the frequency of the tuning fork against the National Bureau of Standards radio station WWV, which broadcasts a standard 440 Hz tone on a regular schedule. If the fork is low or high, its frequency can be shifted by filing in a similar way to filing reeds. WWV broadcasts continuously on 2.5, 5, 10, 15, 20 and 25 MHz, and can usually be heard throughout the United States on any short wave receiver on at least one of these frequencies at any time. The accuracy of the A440 as broadcast by WWV is, for musical purposes, perfect. Standard tones are also broadcast in several other countries. A tuning fork can also be checked against a stroboscopic tuner. The tuning fork is simple, inexpensive, portable, durable and accurate enough, so it is the most popular of the tuning aids. A set of 12 forks tuned to the notes of one octave are also available and make laying the bearings much easier than doing it by counting beats. The drawback of using tuning forks is that you can only tune the pitch to which the fork has been set.

The electronic tuner is a tuning aid used by some professional tuners, and would be ideal for the amateur were it not for its cost. It permits tuning musical instruments easily and with great accuracy to any pitch by visual means instead of by ear. In the stroboscopic tuner the sound of the note being tuned is picked up by a microphone, amplified and used to turn a neon light on and off at the same rate as the frequency of the note, much like an automobile timing light. The light shines on a rotating stroboscopic disc, similar to those used for checking the speed of a phonograph turntable. A twelve-position switch on the front of the instrument changes the speed of rotation of the disc in accordance with the note being tuned.

When the note is exactly in tune, the dots on the stroboscopic disc appear to stand still. If the note is flat, the dots appear to move to the left, and if the note is sharp the dots move to the right. Its operation is quite simple, and excellent results can be obtained with very little practice. The stroboscopic tuner permits tuning the twelve notes of one octave to their theoretical equal-tempered frequencies by direct measurement. The accuracy of some stroboscopes depends on the accuracy of the frequency of the AC power line, which in most places is very good indeed. Other instruments have built-in standards. Stroboscopic tuners are available through most music dealers. Other types of electronic tuners are available and will give comparable results.

Often all that is needed to bring an old decrepit reed organ into reasonably good tune is to clean the reeds, and a good cleaning is a must before tuning. Cleaning a reed will raise its pitch, the amount depending on how much dirt has accumulated, but an increase of ten cents is typical. Suggestions on reed cleaning will be found in Chapter 7.

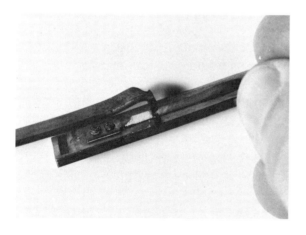

Figure 254: Using a reed scraper to lower the pitch of the reed.

The reeds are tuned by filing or scraping away some of the material. A reed scraper such as that shown above is the traditional tool, although a small file or a piece of fine sandpaper can also be used. To lower the pitch the reed is filed or scraped near the base. To raise the pitch, file near the tip. If the pitch must be lowered considerably, on the order of a semitone, file diagonally across the base. When the pitch needs to be lowered a small amount, scrape lengthwise along the reed at the base with the scraper, as shown above. It is a good idea to slide a reed slip between the reed and the frame when filing or scraping. Reed slips can be purchased from some musical suppliers or they can be improvised by using a razor blade or a thin piece of cardboard. The treble reeds are made thinner at the tip than at the base. Be very careful filing the tips of the high-pitched reeds, as they are extremely thin. The finest sandpaper available is preferable to a file for these reeds, and the sanding motion should be away from the base toward the tip. The bass reeds are made thicker at the tip than at the base. These reeds are usually very rugged, but they can break at the base due to metal fatigue or excessive filing.

In general, go slowly, be sure you are changing the pitch in the right direction, and check your progress frequently. It will usually take from five to ten attempts to get each reed to the right pitch. The reed will ordinarily have to be removed from the reed cell to scrape or file it, and should be replaced in its own cell to check the pitch since the immediate surroundings of the reed affect its pitch. This "confinement" effect is the same effect which is used in determining whether a particular reed is sharp or flat by gradually raising the key. The key is linked to the pallet valve, and as the key is raised the valve gradually comes

194

closer to the reed, causing the pitch to decrease. In some harmoniums the reeds can be left in place as they are tuned, but the case has to be closed each time a reed must be tested, a process which is guaranteed to teach patience and persistence.

The sequence of chords used to lay the bearings is known as a tuning chain. There are a number of different tuning chains, some better than others for specific purposes. One of the disadvantages of tuning chains is that errors made in each step are cumulative. Beginners will often find that they don't come out right at the end. On a piano, making mistakes in the chain only means that the process has to be repeated. The only loss is time, and possibly a little patience. In the case of reed organs, the reeds are adjusted by scraping or filing away material from the reed. Each tuning takes away a little more material, and eventually the reed will be weakened.

For the beginning reed organ tuner who has difficulty in hearing the beats, the author has developed a special tuning chain using only fifths and octaves. It also cuts the chance for error in half, thus reducing wear and tear on the reeds. This procedure consists of the twenty steps shown in the following table. Take your time and work slowly. If you begin to make mistakes, take a break and then try again. With proper care you can achieve professional results with this tuning chain, as it has an extremely good theoretical accuracy. The same tuning chain can be used for organs tuned to A435 or A452. The procedures are summarized in the tables which follow.

Finally, a word of caution: in some of the older books on reed organ and pipe organ tuning, a tuning chain is described which requires flatting by two beats. The result will sound very sour indeed if you follow the instructions, so forget that one!

REED ORGAN
TUNING CHAIN FOR A440

STEP   PROCEDURE

1. Tune A440 in unison (no beats), with an A440 tuning fork.
2. Tune A220 a perfect octave below A440.
3. Sound A220 and E330 above it simultaneously. Tune E330 flat seven beats in ten seconds.
4. Tune E165 a perfect octave below E330.
5. Sound E165 and B247 together. Tune B247 flat six beats in ten seconds.
6. Tune B123 a perfect octave below B247.
7. Sound B123 and F#185. Tune F#185 four beats flat in ten seconds.
8. Sound F#185 and C#277. Tune C#277 flat ten beats in ten seconds.
9. Tune C#139 a perfect octave below C#277.
10. Sound C#139 and G#208. Tune G#208 flat eight beats in ten seconds.
11. Sound A440 and D294. Tune D294 SHARP ten beats in ten seconds.
12. Sound D294 and G196. Tune G196 sharp seven beats in ten seconds.
13. Tune G392 a perfect octave above G196.
14. Sound G392 and C262. Tune C262 sharp eight beats in ten seconds.
15. Sound C262 and F175. Tune F175 sharp six beats in ten seconds.
16. Tune F349 a perfect octave above F175.
17. Sound F349 and A#233. Tune A#233 sharp eight beats in ten seconds.
18. Sound A#233 and D#156. Tune D#156 sharp five beats in ten seconds.
19. Tune D#311 a perfect octave above D#156.
20. Sound D#311 and G#208. MAKE NO ADJUSTMENTS! G#208 should be sharp seven beats in ten seconds. If not, recheck steps one through 19 and make small adjustments if necessary.

REED ORGAN
TUNING CHAIN FOR A435

STEP   PROCEDURE

1. Tune A435 in unison (no beats), with an A435 tuning fork.
2. Tune A218 a perfect octave below A435.
3. Sound A218 and E326 above it simultaneously. Tune E326 flat seven beats in ten seconds.
4. Tune E163 a perfect octave below E326.
5. Sound E163 and B244 together. Tune B244 flat six beats in ten seconds.
6. Tune B122 a perfect octave below B244.
7. Sound B122 and F#183. Tune F# four beats flat in ten seconds.
8. Sound F#183 and C#274. Tune C#274 flat ten beats in ten seconds.
9. Tune C#137 a perfect octave below C#274.
10. Sound C#137 and G#205. Tune G#205 flat eight beats in ten seconds.
11. Sound A435 and D290. Tune D290 SHARP ten beats in ten seconds.
12. Sound D290 and G194. Tune G194 sharp seven beats in ten seconds.
13. Tune G388 a perfect octave above G194.
14. Sound G388 and C259. Tune C262 sharp eight beats in ten seconds.
15. Sound C259 and F173. Tune F173 sharp six beats in ten seconds.
16. Tune F345 a perfect octave above F173.
17. Sound F345 and A#230. Tune A#230 sharp eight beats in ten seconds.
18. Sound A#230 and D#154. Tune D#154 sharp five beats in ten seconds.
19. Tune D#308 a perfect octave above D#154.
20. Sound D#308 and G#205. MAKE NO ADJUSTMENTS!. G#205 should be sharp seven beats in ten seconds. If not, recheck steps one through 19 and make small adjustments if necessary.

REED ORGAN
TUNING CHAIN FOR A452

STEP　　　　　　PROCEDURE

1. Tune A452 in unison (no beats), with an A452 tuning fork.
2. Tune A226 a perfect octave below A452.
3. Sound A226 and E339 above it simultaneously. Tune E339 flat eight beats in ten seconds.
4. Tune E169 a perfect octave below E339.
5. Sound E169 and B254 together. Tune B254 flat five beats in ten seconds.
6. Tune B127 a perfect octave below B254.
7. Sound B127 and F#190. Tune F#190 five beats flat in ten seconds.
8. Sound B127 and C#285. Tune C#285 flat six beats in ten seconds.
9. Tune C#142 a perfect octave below C#285.
10. Sound C#142 and G#214. Tune G#214 flat five beats in ten seconds.
11. Sound A452 and D302. Tune D302 SHARP ten beats in ten seconds.
12. Sound D302 and G202. Tune G202 sharp seven beats in ten seconds.
13. Tune G403 a perfect octave above G202.
14. Sound G403 and C269. Tune C269 sharp nine beats in ten seconds.
15. Sound C269 and F180. Tune F180 sharp six beats in ten seconds.
16. Tune F359 a perfect octave above F180.
17. Sound F359 and A#240. Tune A#240 sharp eight beats in ten seconds.
18. Sound A#240 and D#160. Tune D#160 sharp six beats in ten seconds.
19. Tune D#320 a perfect octave above D#160.
20. Sound D#320 and G#214. MAKE NO ADJUSTMENTS!. G#214 should be sharp seven beats in ten seconds. If not, recheck steps 1 through 19 and make small adjustments if necessary.

After you have finished laying the bearings, the remaining reeds are tuned perfect octaves up and down the keyboard until all remaining reeds in the ranks being tuned have been completed. The other ranks of reeds are usually special voices, and are discussed in Chapter Four. The reeds used in a Sub-Bass stop extend the range of the Diapason stop, and are tuned perfect octaves down from it. The Melodia stop is also tuned in unison with the Diapason. Stops which extend the range above the high end of the Melodia stop are also tuned perfect octaves above it.

Anyone who has tuned a piano knows about "stretching the octaves." Piano strings vibrate in the fundamental mode—the pitch to which they are tuned—as well as in higher modes, or overtones. The first overtone is slightly sharp of a perfect octave higher than the fundamental. For example, if the A440 string is tuned to exactly 440 Hz, its first overtone will be a few cents sharp of 880 Hz. In order to avoid dissonance, the A one octave higher is "stretched," or tuned in unison with the first overtone of the A440 string, rather than to an exact 880 Hz. This process is repeated successively up to the upper octave of the piano, where the C string is tuned about thirty cents sharp of its theoretical pitch. This phenomenon does not apply to reed organs, and consequently the octaves are tuned perfect.

If you plan to do a lot of reed tuning a tuning jack will be a great help. A tuning jack can be made from the action of a reed organ, to which is added an electric suction unit with adjustable speed, a small reservoir and a manometer. One complete rank of reeds should be tuned very carefully to the pitch which you consider to be the most usual, and left permanently in the rear of the action to be used as the reference set. The front set is removed, and the reeds to be

Figure 255: An Estey Tuning or Voicing Jack.

tuned are inserted there. Each one is tuned in unison with the corresponding reed of the reference set.

TUNING CELESTES

The celeste makes use of two sets of reeds, one slightly out of tune with the other, to produce the characteristic undulating tone. Since we are listening to the beats between the fundamental notes themselves, they are quite strong and easy to hear. There are three basic stop arrangements of celestes: fully derived, semi-derived and independent.[39.] The fully derived celeste uses two separate stops, one tuned in unison and one tuned slightly sharp or flat; each stop able to be used separately. The semi-derived celeste uses one unison stop, which can be used alone, plus an out-of-tune set of reeds used only for the celeste effect in conjunction with the unison set. The third type is somewhat rare in reed organs, found in the more complex and expensive models, and uses two sets of reeds which always operate together and only as a celeste. This type often has one set of reeds tuned slightly flat and one slightly sharp, straddling the unison pitch and sounding in tune when played together. The celeste stop is usually an eight foot stop found only in the treble, although occasionally it is found in four-foot or two-foot stops in the bass. An eight-foot celeste in the bass requires an extremely wide pitch separation of the two reed sets and is very difficult to tune.

When tuning the independent and semi-derived celestes, the stop mechanism which couples the two reed sets together should be disconnected so that each set can be operated separately. In old organs, even though the unison stops may be in relatively good tune, the celestes are usually out of tune, as can be seen by referring to the celeste and diapason stops shown in the Reed Organ Tuning Chart, Figure252.. In an old instrument such as this one it is difficult to determine the original width of the celeste. The difference for each note is typically about eight cents at the highest F, gradually increasing in a uniform way for each lower note down to 33 cents for the lowest C in that stop. In this particular case it appears that originally the celeste set was tuned flat of the diapason, since the average pitch of the celeste stop was slightly lower than that of the diapason. However, since it was decided to lower the pitch of the organ to A440, it appeared desirable to tune the celeste sharp, as that would require less change of pitch of these reeds.

In the absence of any other clues as to the original width of the celeste, the beginning tuner may wish to use a method which I have usually found to be satisfactory. The celeste reeds are tuned sharp (preferably) or flat with respect to the diapason reeds by the amounts in cents shown in the celeste tuning table to the right. The effect of the celeste depends upon very small differences in pitch and therefore the tuning must be extremely accurate. However it is impractical to tune reeds closer than within one cent.

The width of the celeste, that is the beat rate, is very much a matter of taste, and the tuning mentioned above may not be acceptable to everyone. Those wishing to experiment should tune just the four F reeds first. Start with the top F and tune it sharp until the sound is a pleasing but somewhat fast beat. Then tune the lowest F until it has a pleasing slow beat. Each intermediate F is then tuned so that each successively higher F has a faster beat rate. When these notes are tuned satisfactorily then tune the Bs. Each B should have a beat rate between that of the immediately lower and higher F. Then the remaining notes can be tuned so that each successively higher note across the stop has a slightly higher beat rate.

CELESTE TUNING TABLE

	OCTAVE		
	LOW	MID	TOP
F	33		
F#	32	21	13
G	31	20	13
G#	30	19	12
A	29	19	12
A#	28	18	11
B	27	17	11
C	26	17	10
C#	25	16	10
D	24	15	9
D#	23	15	9
E	23	14	8
F	22	14	8

199

A MUSEUM OF VICTORIAN REED ORGANS AND HARMONIUMS

the Collection of

Phil and Pam Fluke

Victoria Hall·Saltaire Village Shipley·W Yorks

The Museum is open daily, 11 a.m. - 4 p.m. (except Tuesdays)
Closed for 2 weeks at Christmas and New Year

For further information ring Bradford (0274) 585601
after 5 p.m.

200

Chapter Nine

Collecting and Collections

Figure 257: The Pease Collection of Historical Instruments, located in Palmer, Massachusetts, is very likely the world's largest collection of reed organs. Also included are early pianos, pipe organs, music boxes and other early mechanical and manually played instruments. Nelson and Beverly Pease, owners.

The reed organ reached the peak of its popularity in the 1890s and by the time of World War II production was down to a trickle. There was a brief resurgence of demand after the war, but that soon died as electronic organs, the phonograph and radio satisfied the public's demand for music. Large numbers of the instruments still survive, mostly in the hands of individuals who value them for their unique sound and as an authentic piece of nineteenth century history. A number of collections have been assembled, some of them quite large.

The Pease Collection of Historical Instruments in Palmer, Massachusetts is probably the largest existing collection of reed organs. Nelson and Beverly Pease admit to owning 500 organs, but a good look at his collection leaves one to believe that this is just a guess and that they haven't all been counted one by one. Most of them are unrestored and kept in warehouses, but some of the choice pieces are displayed in the "retail showrooms," a combination store and museum located at 351 Main Street in Palmer. In addition to reed organs there are also pianos, pipe organs, music boxes and other early mechanical and manually played instruments. Some are for sale and some are just on display.

There are a number of museums dedicated exclusively or mostly to the reed organ. Most of these have started as the private collection of an individual and grown into a full-scale museum. Probably the best of these is the Fluke collection in Victoria Hall, Saltaire Village, Shipley, West Yorkshire, England. Phil Fluke spends full time as curator and restorer, and Pam Fluke is an educator who is a fine organist as well as a reed organ researcher, and has held several positions in the Reed Organ Society. The Flukes have sponsored several well-attended reed organ conventions at the Saltaire Museum, and were instrumental in publicizing the reed organ through concerts on BBC television. The collection contains over fifty beautifully restored instruments in a wide variety of styles as well as catalogs, posters, wood-block engravings used for advertising and other items.

The Neville Blakey Collection, Burnley Road, Brierfield, Lancashire, England contains several fine instruments by Debain as well as the Mustel owned by Francis Duckworth, upon which he composed *Rimington*. This melody set to music the words by Isaac Watts, "Jesus Shall Reign Where'er the Sun." Many other instruments

Conklin Antique Organ Museum

Hanover, Michigan 49241

78 Reed Organs & Melodeons

1st & 3rd Sunday, April thru October

(517) 563-2311

Figure 259

are on display, including fine examples by John Holt, J.W. Sawyer, Rushworth & Dreaper, an Aeolian Orchestrelle and an Everett Orgatron.

The British Piano Museum at 368 High Street, Brentford, Middlesex, England is dedicated mostly to pianos, of course, but also includes what is probably the most complete collection ever of Aeolian Orchestrelles.

The Hanover-Horton Historical Society in Hanover, Michigan contains a collection of about ninety organs started by the late Lee Conklin and augmented by numerous acquisitions. By means of organ restoration clinics sponsored by the Society, many local collectors have been able to restore reed organs for their own use and for display in the museum.

Figure 258: The Musical Museum, Deansboro, New York contains a wide variety of musical instruments, from roll-playing orchestrions to reed organs.

202

Figure 260: A part of the collection at the Miles Mountain Musical Museum in Eureka Springs, Arkansas.

The Miles Mountain Musical Museum, P.O. Box 488, Eureka Springs, Arkansas contains the collection begun in 1955 by Floyd and Martha Miles and now operated by their two daughters, Joan and Marlene. The museum opened in 1960 and presently contains over 12,000 square feet (1,200 square meters) of floor space. Instruments on display include organettes, orchestrions, band organs and calliopes, a Belgian dance organ and numerous reed organs. Other collections incorporated into the museum are the Paul Jarvis collection of stringed instruments, the Charley Stehm collection of onyx and wood carvings, the Yates collection of orientalia and the Burns-Worth miniature animated mechanical circus.

The Shannon Collection, Upper Black Eddy, Pennsylvania, put together by Carl and Cris Shannon contains some eighty instruments, all in playing condition. One interesting piece is the "New American," possibly made by F.N. Dexter of West Winfield, New York. This instrument contains seventeen full sets of reeds on the single manual and three more sets on the pedals. The pedal reed chest is placed under the pedals so that the organist's seat is a dizzying four feet off the floor.

Other reed organ museums are:

•The Enstone Museum, owned by Ian Thompson, 27 Binsey Lane, Oxford, England. The museum, containing over 100 organs, is in an old church in the nearby village of Enstone.
•The Heiss Haus, 8301 Lawrence Road, Nashville, Michigan. This antique organ

Figure 261: Part of the extensive organette collection of Mike Perry, Marion, Ohio.

Figure 262: Carl and Chris Shannon on the New American Organ.

203

museum has over sixty instruments on display.

•Dieter Stalder's Harmonium Museum in Liestal, Switzerland.

•Gregory Filardo's Kalvelage Schloss, at 2432 W. Kilbourn Ave., Milwaukee, Wisconsin is an exquisite restoration of a Victorian mansion filled with period antiques and musical instruments, including an extensive collection of roll-operated reed organs and organettes.

In addition, the directory of the Reed Organ Society lists over thirty private collections of more than twenty reed organs each. Most of these can be visited by appointment.

THE REED ORGAN SOCIETY

In 1981 a small group of aficionados began discussing the formation of an organization devoted to the reed organ. Early in 1982 the organization was founded with Georgia and Dale Williams, Arthur Sanders, Ed Peterson, John Ogasapian, Lynn Ware and James H. Richards as charter members. At first the new group was called the Reed Organ Society of America but by the time it was incorporated later that same year the name was shortened to The Reed Organ Society, reflecting its expected international membership. One of the first and still the most visible of its activities is the publication of *The Reed Organ Society Bulletin.* This periodical prints articles on a wide variety of aspects of the reed organ, including scholarly research, information on music for the instrument, restoration projects, restoration techniques, news about members and classified advertisements. Another important activity is the registration of reed organs. Members and others are encouraged to submit relevant information on

their instruments which is recorded by the Society and made available for study. The Society provides a label with a serial number to be placed on the instruments showing that it has been registered with the Society. Membership has grown to over 600 members in fourteen countries.

Another ongoing activity of the Society is gathering a list of reed organs in public places. Many museums and historic sites have one or more reed organs on display. Eventually the list will serve as a guide for reed organ enthusiasts.

EPHEMERA

While most reed organ fanciers are content to have one treasured instrument, others have extended the hobby to collection of other items related to the organ. Among the areas of interest are collections

Figure 263: A reed organ music box.

of method books and music books as mentioned in Chapter 4, recorded music of the reed organ, manufacturers' catalogs, trade cards, posters, post cards, scale models, toys and numerous other items. The reed organ has been featured or at least mentioned in popular books and is occasionally seen in movies or on television.

Newspaper comic strip stories and cartoons occasionally revolve around the reed organ, as did the following sequence in Dick Moores' *Gasoline Alley®*, which appeared from January 15 through February 14, 1981. Here, historical facts and the laws of physics are ignored where they conflict with the story line.

Figure 264: Even a doll house can have a reed organ.

Figure 265, below: The McDonald Wild West band-chariot, featuring a reed organ.

GASOLINE ALLEY®
by Dick Moores

210

Figure 267

Trade cards are valued collectable items—the cost is reasonable and they take up much less space than the organs themselves. The front was usually an attractive picture printed in full color by the latest process, as in these examples by Estey, Mason & Hamlin and the Ithaca Organ Company. The back of the card usually had more detailed information and was sometimes more interesting than the front, as in the Shoninger card below.

Figure 269

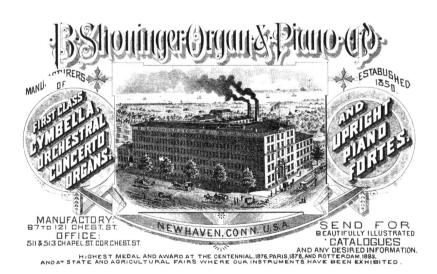

Figure 268

Figure 270

213

Also highly collectable but much harder to find than trade cards are postcards picturing reed organs.

Figure 272

Figure 271

Figure 273

Figure 274

Figure 275

Figure 276

Figure 278

Figure 277

For several years reed organ music collector Chris Sheldon sent a series of attractive Christmas cards with reed organ themes painted by Pauline Jackson, some of which are shown on this and the previous page. Below, the ultimate Victorian reed organ is depicted in a Christmas card sent by Pam and Phil Fluke.

215

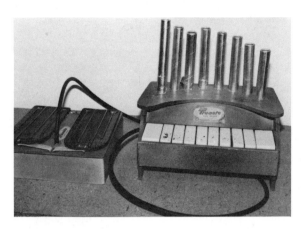

Figure 281: The Tru-note Pipe Organ, a toy reed organ with separate foot-operated feeders.

Figure 279: A two-octave toy organ.

Figure 280 (above): A one-seventh scale model made by Keith Jarrett is pictured above. The original, restored by Jarrett, a two-manual Mustel model 4, serial number 3206/1461, made in August of 1926, is shown in Figure 282, at right.

"AND WOULD YOU BELIEVE I NEVER HAD A LESSON IN MY LIFE!"

And finally, reed organs have been used in calendar art, as in this great example, originally in color, found by Al D. Robinson (figure 283, above).

217

Figure 284: A lyre-legged melodeon made by A. Worcester, New York, on display at the Lightner Museum in St. Augustine, FL.

Chapter Ten

A Reed Organ Gallery

Figure 285: Mason & Hamlin, Boston, Massachusetts.

Figure 286: Baker & Randall, Providence, Rhode Island.

MELODEONS

The five-octave lyre-legged melodeon appeared about 1850 as an improvement on its four-octave predecessor with the straight folding legs, pictured in Chapter 5. The instruments were mechanically similar with a single exhauster and a foot operated swell pedal. On the lyre-legged version the swell pedal was moved to the center, alongside the single bellows pedal.

A larger melodeon made to look like a square grand piano was introduced a few years after the lyre legged instrument. Both instruments usually had a single set of reeds, but occasional examples are found of organs with two or more ranks. Both were illustrated in the Estey catalogs at least through 1867, but were absent from the 1871 and later issues.

Figure 287: Mervin T. Landfear, Manchester, Connecticut.

Figure 289: Pruden & Cordley, Adrian, Michigan.

Figure 288: S.D. & H.W. Smith, Boston, Massachusetts.

Figure 290: Carhart & Needham, New York.

220

Figure 291: Xavier Spang, Syracuse, New York, six octave keyboard.

Figure 292: Melo-Pean Company, Akron, Ohio.

Figure 293: E.M. Bishop, Painesville, Ohio.

Figure 294: Estey & Green, Brattleboro, Vermont.

Figure 295: Hintermeister United Organ Co., Buffalo, New York.

THE FLAT-TOPPED ORGAN

The organ to which we now refer as the flat-top, introduced by the then newly-formed firm of Mason & Hamlin in 1855, revolutionized the American reed organ industry. The configuration of the various components—stop action, keyboard, organ action, reservoir, two exhausters and two blow pedals—had a simple logic that was not to be improved upon during the remaining life of the instrument. The style was soon accepted by all major builders.

Figure 298: George Woods & Co., Boston, Massachusetts.

Figure 296: Mason & Hamlin, Boston, Massachusetts, 1870.

Figure 297: J. Estey & Co., Brattleboro, Vermont, 1869.

Figure 299: S.D. & H.W. Smith, Boston, Massachusetts.

222

Figure 300: Ling & Chandler, Detroit, Michigan.

Figure 301: William Case & Co.

Figure 302: The Mason & Hamlin Metropolitan, 1868.

223

Figure 303: Mason & Hamlin Style No. 1, 1874.

Figure 304: Treat & Davis, New Haven, Connecticut.

THE HIGH-TOPPED ORGAN

In 1866 when the boxy flat-topped organ was the dominant style and melodeons were still in production, Estey introduced a new style of case, their No. 33, called the "Boudoir" organ. This new design was thirteen inches taller than the flat top, but the mechanism was unchanged. Estey referred to the additional space as "sounding chambers." The Boudoir organ was also available with a false pipe top, Case No. 40, reaching a height of seven feet, six inches. While false pipe tops had been available for several years for church organs, this marks the first time that Estey offered a high-topped organ

for home use. By 1871 both the melodeons and the flat-tops had disappeared from the Estey catalog. All cases were taller, some by only a few inches. The pipe-topped Boudoir organ was the only one offered with a high top. The Case 33 was restyled with more carvings, although the pipe top model remained the same. In 1874 the Boudoir organ was again redesigned as Case 34 in an ornately carved style which became the new fashion. This model had a genuine high top as shown in Figure 307. The optional pipe-top version was denominated Case No. 41.

224

Figure 305: The Estey Boudoir Organ, Case No. 33, 1866.

Figure 307: The Estey Boudoir Organ, Case No. 34, 1874.

Figure 306: The Estey Pipe Top Boudoir Organ, Case No. 40.

225

Figure 308: The Estey Pipe Top Boudoir Organ, Case No. 41, 1874.

Figure 309: Mason & Hamlin Case No. 25.

Figure 310: Mason & Hamlin Case No. 25 with the extended top.

Figure 313: J. Estey & Co., Brattleboro, Vermont.

Figure 311: Smith American Organ Co., Boston, Massachusetts, 1875.

Figure 312: C.A. Gardner, Grand Rapids, Michigan.

Figure 314: Smith American Organ Co., Boston, Massachusetts.

The new taller case quickly became the standard and high tops followed. Mason & Hamlin offered their new instruments either with or without an extended top, as shown in Figures 309 and 310. They also made extended tops available to owners who wished to bring their instruments up to the latest style as shown on the next page.

227

Extended Top. No. 6. Price $12.50. (For style 218.)

Extended Top. No. 25. Price $18.75. (For styles 226, 316, 317, 307, 42 and 421.)

Extended Top. No. 17. Price $25. (For styles 301 and 400.)

Extended Top. No. 28. Price $25. (For styles 228, 319 and 320.)

Extended Top. No. 21. Price $12.50. (For style 302.)

Extended Top. No. 31. Price $18.75. (For styles 315, 417 and 419.)

Extended Top. No. 22. Price $12.50. (For Styles 303, 318 and 422.)

Extended Top. No. 47. Price $12.50. (For styles 225, 314, 414 and 416

Extended Top. No. 23. Price $12.50. (For styles 232, 304, 406 and 413.)

Extended Top. No. 62. Price $18.75. (For styles 233 and 325.)

MASON & HAMLIN ORGAN COMPANY,

Figure 315

228

Figure 316: D.W. Karn Co., Ltd., Woodstock, Ontario, Canada.

Figure 318: The Ohio Beauty, made about 1875 by A.J. Tschantz, now the Schantz Organ Co., Orrville, Ohio.

Figure 317: Waters Centennial Concerto organ, 1876. Probably made by Shoninger

Figure 319: Eureka clock organ, probably made by Shoninger.

Figure 320: Smith American Organ Co., Boston, Massachusetts.

Figure 322: Beethoven Organ Co., Washington, New Jersey.

Figure 321: Smith American Organ Co., Boston, Massachusetts.

Figure 323: Bell Organ & Piano Co., Guelph, Ontario, Canada.

230

Figure 324: Wilcox & White Organ Co., Meriden Connecticut, 1891.

Figure 326: Fort Wayne Organ Co., Fort Wayne, Indiana. Packard organ.

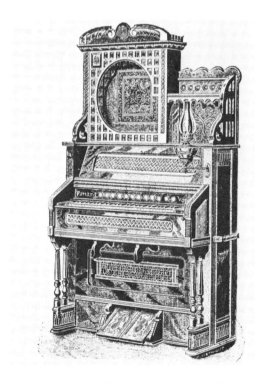

Figure 325: Farrand & Votey, Detroit, Michigan. Case No. 50.

Figure 327: Clough & Warren Co., Detroit, Michigan.

Figure 328: Putnam Organ Co., Staunton, Virginia.

Figure 330: Cornish & Co., Washington, New Jersey.

Figure 329: Beethoven Organ Co., Washington, New Jersey.

Figure 331: Cornish & Co., Washington, New Jersey. 1879.

PEDAL ORGANS

Pedal organs almost always represented the manufacturer's honest attempt to get the best performance possible from a reed organ. These organs were often used in small churches where the purchase of a pipe organ was beyond the budget. False pipe tops were sometimes added to give a more imposing appearance.

Figure 333: A.B. Chase, Norwalk, Ohio. Style No. 309.

Figure 332: This Vocalion, made by William Hill & Son, London, is in St. James' Church, Mile End, South Australia.

Figure 334: W. Bell & Co., Guelph, Ontario, Canada.

233

Most pedal organs had a blow lever at the back, operated by a helper, but many single manual and even some two manual examples also had foot pedals for blowing, as shown in the Kelly organ above left and the Prince below.

Figure 335, left: This elaborately carved case contains an organ made by Charles Kelly & Co., London, "makers of harmoniums to H.M. the Imperial family of France." This instrument is now in the collection of Phil and Pam Fluke. A close-up view of one of the gargoyles is shown at bottom left.

Figure 336: A close-up view of the carving on a Kelly harmonium.

Figure 337: The George A. Prince pedal organ sold for $260 in 1874.

234

Figure 338: A Bell organ from the Fluke collection.

Figure 340: R.F. Stevens, Ltd., London. Unit C organ made to R.C.O. specifications, in a theater organ case.

Figure 339: A Smith American organ, 1877.

Figure 341: Stevens Unit C organ in a traditional case.

235

Figure 342: Stevens Abbey organ, model 77.

Figure 344: A Hinners organ.

Figure 343: Jacot organ, made by Michel Jacot, Birmingham, England.

Figure 345: Model 95a made by Theodor Mannborg, Leipzig-Lindenau, Germany.

Figure 346: Model B, made by Olaf Lindholm Harmiumfabrik, Borna, Germany.

Figure 348: Köhler Model 25.

Figure 347: Model 21, made by Harmoniumfabrik Köhler, Pretsch, Germany.

Figure 349: Mason & Hamlin two manual and pedal Liszt organ, Style 41.

237

THE CHAPEL ORGAN

The chapel organ is a single manual organ without a high top intended for use in small churches. As the organ was often placed with the back to the congregation, the back of the organ was usually finished in the same style as the front.

Figure 351

Figure 350 above: A chapel organ in rural Alabama, 1936. Jesse French Piano & Organ Co., Nashville, Tennessee.

Figure 352: Chicago Cottage Organ Co. chapel organ. The typical finished back is shown at right.

238

Figure 353: The Vocalion Organ Co., New York, 1901.

Figure 355: John Malcolm & Co., London.

Figure 354: Mason & Hamlin Liszt organ, 1888.

Figure 356: Farrand Organ Co., Detroit, Michigan.

Figure 357 above: Smith American Organ Co., Boston, Massachusetts.

Figure 358 above: Newman Brothers Organ Co., Chicago, Illinois.

Figure 359 left: W. Doherty & Co., Clinton, Ontario, Canada.

240

Figure 361 right: Farrand Organ Co. Style R, 1902.

Figure 360: Marchal & Smith, New York, 1892.

Figure 362: Isachsen & Renbjør Harmoniumfab-rikk, Levanger, Norway, 1884. Johann Cornelius Isachsen, left; Petter K. Renbjør, right.

THE HARMONIUM

The classical harmonium is best represented by these examples by Victor Mustel, Paris. Note the similarity in the 1881 and 1901 models.

Figure 364: Mustel No. 1100/832, made in 1901.

Figure 363: A two-manual Mustel.

Figure 365: Mustel No. 345, made in 1881.

Figure 368: Venables & Co., London, 1869.

Figure 366: J.-B. Napoléon Fourneaux, Paris, about 1850.

Figure 367: N.L. van Gruisen, Paris. Made for the Exposition Universelle, 1855.

Figure 369: J. Jacobsen, Hadersleben, Denmark.

243

Figure 370: Alexandre et Fils, Paris, about 1855. The Alexandre harmonium was made under license from Debain.

Figure 371: Phillip J. Trayser & Co., Stuttgart, Germany. Trayser was trained at the Alexandre factory.

Figure 372: Couty & Richard, Paris. Couty also was trained at the Alexandre factory.

244

Figure 373 above: A small Alexandre harmonium.

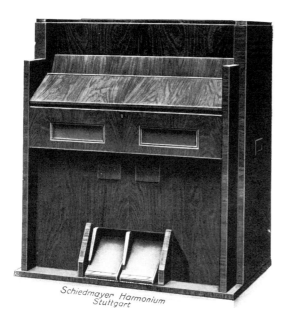

Figure 374: J. & P. Schiedmayer, Stuttgart, Germany. Harmonium in a "modern" case, 1950.

Specially Constructed for Tropical Climates

Figure 375: R.F. Stevens, Ltd., London. Abbey Model 90 harmonium, tropicalized.

245

Figure 376: J. & P. Schiedmayer, Stuttgart, Germany—harmonium.

Figure 377: The Crown piano cased organ made by Geo. P. Bent, Chicago.

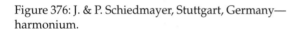

THE UPRIGHT PIANO-CASED ORGAN

About 1890 the traditional parlor reed organ, with its ornate high-backed case, shelves and mirrors, had reached the height of its popularity. While it was still the king of home music, its share of that market had begun to decline. Most of the old-line organ makers had already introduced pianos into their line of products, and many of them had changed their corporate names to include the word "piano." A certain segment of the instrument buying public really wanted an organ but hated the old fashioned look, and for these people the piano-cased organ was offered. The idea of making an organ to look like a piano was not new. The square melodeons produced from about 1850 to 1865 were consciously designed to look like a square grand piano, but the expression "piano-cased" usually now refers to an organ built into a case like that of an upright piano.

H. Lehr & Co. of Easton, Pennsylvania advertised that it was the first manufacturer to make a piano-cased reed organ. The Lehr firm was established in 1890 and George P. Bent produced his first piano-cased organ in 1893, so if Lehr was correct the style dates from about 1890. The Karn Style C Organ was designated by the manufacturer as a piano-cased organ, but it had traditional reed organ pedals, stop knobs, candle holders, a small mirror and a six octave F-scale keyboard, so it probably fooled no one. Karn's Style I could more properly be called a piano-cased organ, since it had a seven-octave C-scale keyboard, piano style pedals, no visible stop knobs, candle holders, mirrors or knee levers and was in all respects identical in outward appearance to an upright piano.

246

ALWAYS HAVE ONE OF OUR PREMIUM CERTIFICATES ON HAND.

A New Instrument

No Bellows Straps to Break
A Child can Operate Bellows
No Carpets to Wear Out
All Piano Music Written can be Played

SWEET AND POWERFUL

Reeds • •
We use 15½ full octaves of the
Celebrated Golden Toned Reeds
distributed as follows:
15½ Octaves, 188 Reeds in all,
thus making one of the most powerful of Reed Organs. It has two
nickel stops and three patent nickel
Piano Pedals.

ANOTHER
GRAND IMPROVEMENT IN
REED ORGANS

For full description see opposite page

Dimensions • •
55¼ inches high.
25½ inches deep.
53 inches long.

Weight, about 450 lbs., boxed.

Figure 378: The Beethoven Organ Co., Washington, New Jersey.

The usual piano-cased organ had two sets of reeds. One set was "open," that is it was not controlled by a stop knob and played all the time. The other set was controlled by a stop knob or lever next to the keyboard, or by the Grand Organ knee lever. Estey's Style W-75 had a 7 octave keyboard, two sets of reeds and octave couplers, all neatly housed in what had become the classic upright piano case. The octave couplers were controlled by the center foot pedal. The organ action in this type of organ was located below and to the rear of the keyboard, with the bellows and pumping mechanism in the lower part of the case. The upper portion of the case was empty.

Piano-cased organs have not been particularly attractive to collectors, probably because of the large, plain cases and few stops. It's safe to say that a much smaller percentage of these organs has survived than have the conventional reed organs with ornate cases.

247

An Absolute Necessity in Every Home. **Cornish American Pianos and Organs.** The People's Popular Educators

Positively One of the Most Beautiful Instruments in the World.

THE 1898 MODEL,
Cornish American
Upright Cabinet Grand,
— STYLE NO. 42,000. —

Dimensions: 56 INCHES HIGH, 62 INCHES LONG, 28 INCHES DEEP; WEIGHT, BOXED, ABOUT 600 LBS.

THE PIANOSYMIL

Regular Retail Price

$200

Elegant Piano Stool, Silk Scarf and the Cornish Practical Instructor.

Full Piano Size Keyboard—7 Octaves. In Polished American Black Walnut, Natural Cherry or Antique Oak Case.

THIS instrument differs from all our other styles, both in construction and appearance. The case is exactly like that of our Upright Grand Pianos. It is piano finished with a very high and permanent piano polish and cannot be distinguished from one of our finest pianos. The case can be had in either solid walnut, cherry or oak, and is beautifully embellished with the most exquisite natural wood carvings and ornaments. The fall board has a continuous nickel hinge, the blow pedals are electroplated in silver, and action and case are mouse and climate proof.

THE TONE is remarkably beautiful, and the **orchestral reeds used in this patent action are so tuned and voiced that the most** brilliant allegretto or staccato music can be played the same as on a piano.

THE ACTION contains **six sets of reeds**, divided as follows: Three octaves of Diapason, four octaves of Melodia, three octaves of Principal, four octaves of Vox Celeste, three and a half octaves of Saxophone. It has double octave couplers. **Compass, seven octaves, C to C. No stops are used;** the action is entirely controlled by two knee swells which operate as follows: **The right knee lever opens the Vox Celeste and Principal Reeds, and swells the Diapason and Melodia sets. The left knee lever opens the Saxophone Reeds and the Octave Couplers. The Diapason and Melodia reeds are always open and ready for use.**

The two swells, when kept **wide open,** put on the **whole power of the organ** (two stop holders render the full combination permanent when desired). **The whole action is thus easily operated, and the most beautiful graduations of tone can be secured at the will of the performer.**

This extraordinarily fine instrument has been specially designed and constructed by us to meet the thousands of requests made for a piano organ that should possess in **form** and **appearance** the **exact similitude of a piano**—hence the name, **Pianosymil.** The case represents exactly an elegant upright grand piano and is fashioned after our famous "Columbian Gem" model. The most elaborate music for piano or organ can easily be performed with full pipe organ and orchestral effects, and we feel confident that this excellent instrument will be warmly appreciated by all lovers of music. As a valuable piece of furniture, it is handsome enough to adorn a palace, while as a first-class high-grade musical instrument, it ranks far in front of anything yet placed before the public in the same line.

NOTE.—For Special Offers and Factory Price See Next Page.

Cornish & Co. Established 36 Years, Makers of American Pianos and Organs, **Washington,** New Jersey, U. S. A.

You Get Full Value Can't Get It from Us—You Elsewhere.
We only add a Very Small Personal Profit.
The Actual Value of a Cost to Build.
Piano or Organ is its

Note: We are the Only Firm of Actual Manufacturers Who Sell Exclusively Direct to the General Public at First Cost. Don't be Misled by Imitators of our Method. Remember it is Cornish Only.

Figure 379: Cornish & Company advertisement, 1898.

Figure 380: Cornish Style 42,000 "Pianosymil" organ.

Figure 381: The Estey Case XL, 7 octaves, 1911.

Figure 382: Estey Style J-74, seven octaves.

Figure 383: Estey Style XX, 1907.

Figure 385: The Karn Style C was available in a half-traditional, half-piano-style case with a mirror top, or also without the mirror top. F scale, 11, 12 or 13 stops.

Figure 384: Estey Case W, 7 octaves, 1907.

Figure 386: Karn Style I, 7 octaves, C scale, with piano pedals and no knee levers.

Figure 387, left: Kimball Case 710, six octaves, 11, 12 or 13 stops; 1912.

Figure 388, right: Kimball Case 660, seven octaves.

Figure 391: The Lehr organ, Style A, 1895.

Figure 389, above, and 390, below: the Kimball Case 680 organ came with both piano and organ style pedals, 1912.

Figure 392: The Marchal & Smith 6 octave organ, $140.

Figure 393, right: The Miller styles 440 and 442 organ, 7 octaves.

SPECIALIZED ORGANS

Some musicians find the compromises built into the equally-tempered scale annoying. Over the years a number of special organs, often referred to as enharmonic organs, have been built in an attempt to eliminate or at least minimize these compromises. One such instrument was designed by R. H. M. Bosanquet, a Professor of Acoustics at Oxford, and built by T. A. Jennings of London.

Figure 395: The Lindholm Scalaphone, an enharmonic harmonium which features plug-in reed boards.

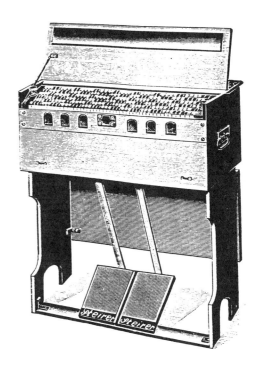

Figure 394: The Bosanquet Enharmonic Harmonium. The horrendous keyboard covers four and a half octaves with 53 equally spaced notes per octave. This is an adaptation of the keyboard invented by Paul von Jankó, a student of Helmholz.

Figure 396: The Steirer Model 41 harmonium with the Jankó keyboard.

253

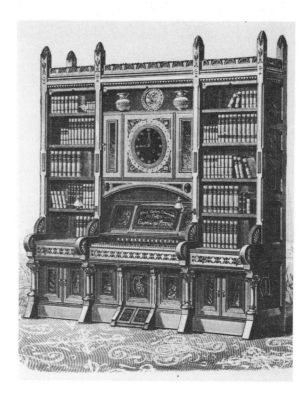

Figure 397: The Mustel Model 6 Celeste-Organ. One manual plays a rank of tuned metal bars or orchestra bells; the other two manuals constitute a two-manual harmonium.

Figure 399: The Carpenter Library Organ, No. 184. This instrument cum bookshelf was nine feet six inches high and nine feet long.

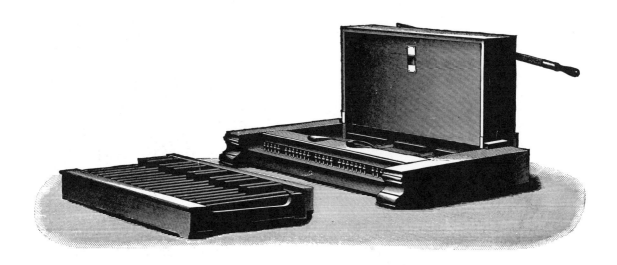

Figure 398: The Packard pedal bass attachment. Packard advertised that it could be used with any reed organ by connecting a wind-way from the organ reservoir to the pedal bass pumper.

254

Figure 400: The Desk Organ made by A. MacNutt, Philadelphia, Pennsylvania. The keyboard cover served as a writing surface.

Figure 402, right: A reed-pipe organ made by the Cabinet Pipe Organ Co., Syracuse, N.Y., 1874. The upper manual controlled a rank of reeds equipped with brass resonators or qualifying tubes.

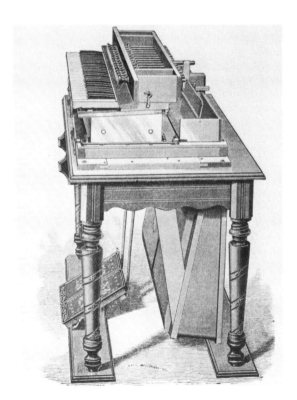

Figure 401: The School Organ, Model 124, made by E. P. Carpenter, Brattleboro, Vermont, used for demonstrating the mechanism of the reed organ.

COMBINED PIANO AND ORGAN.

Figure 403: The R. F. Stevens Combined Piano and Organ.

255

Figure 404: The Estey Style A bench.

Organ Bench No. 1.
Length, 21 in.   Width, 12 in.   Height, 24 in.

Figure 405: Mason & Hamlin's equivalent was their Organ Bench No. 1, shown in the 1874 catalog.

THE CORRECT BENCH

Many reed organs were sold without benches (presumably a chair could always be found when the organist was ready to play) and a good many were sold with piano-style swivel stools, but the serious reed organists insisted on a proper bench with a sloping seat. Possibly the best example of the classic reed organ bench is Estey's Style A, described in many of their catalogs as follows:

> To play the Organ properly it is necessary to sit correctly, and to achieve this, it is absolutely essential to have a Correct Bench, as illustrated.
> These Benches are sloped, just at the right angle, so that the performer has complete control over the instrument, and can manipulate the blow pedals with ease.

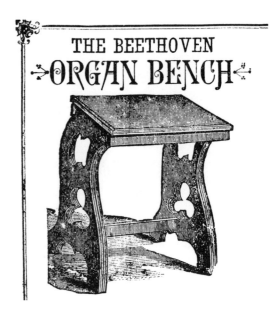

Figure 406: The Beatty Style No. 23 organ bench.

256

Figure 407: The Estey Gothic organ and matching bench. This instrument included an electric blower.

Figure 408: The Estey Old Dutch organ, Style D 56 with matching bench.

Daniel F. Beatty's observations on the organ bench:

For some time I have been sending ORGAN BENCHES with my best Organs, instead of the ordinary Piano Stools, as benches are much superior to stools, for Organ playing. The Bench herewith illustrated is made of walnut, handsomely finished, with carved and beaded edges. It is put together with screws, and is carefully packed in the box with the Organ.

I have concluded, notwithstanding the fact that benches cost more than stools, to send them with all my Organs hereafter, as a proper seat for the organ is of much importance, facilitating the use of the instrument with comfort and accuracy. This bench is perfectly adapt-ed to the purpose, being firm and unyielding, having its top slightly inclined towards the instrument, and so giving the best position for playing and especially for blowing with ease. For practical use it is better without a cushion top, and will be found much superior to a piano stool of any description.

Although reed organ benches were formerly quite common, they are fairly rare today. Occasionally reproduction benches are offered for sale, and for those wishing to make their own, plans for three popular models are included in Appendix 3.

In later years it became the fashion to provide benches which matched the organ case design. Estey was perhaps the leader, as shown in these examples.

Figure 409: Bench for the Beckwith (Sears) Choir Gem Organ.

Figure 410: Bench for the Beckwith (Sears) Cathedral Chapel Organ.

Figure 411: Kawai offered a special folding chair to go with its PD-29 school organ.

Figure 412: The Estey Children's Organ, also called the Miniature Organ, came with its matching child-sized bench.

Figure 413: The bench with this Alexandre harmonium may have been made later to match the organ.

Figure 414: The Yamaha No. 3A Organ, with bench.

Figure 415: Clough & Warren Organ, with bench.

The bench shown with the Clough and Warren organ at top right has an integral pedal clavier and contains two ranks of reeds built into the seat. It is winded by a tube from the main organ. The keys are concave and can be arranged in a radiating or straight configuration. The seat can be adjusted in height and backward or forward.

Folding organs were usually provided without benches in order to keep the weight down, but Bilhorn Bros. actually made a folding bench to match. A. L. White, Bilhorn's competition, offered folding chairs or stools made of steel and canvas, which doubled as camp chairs.

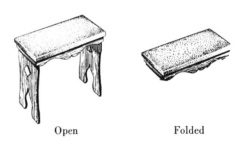

Open   Folded

Figure 416: The Bilhorn Folding Bench.

Figure 417, left: The Bilhorn DeLuxe Model D Folding Organ, shown with the folding bench.

CHAIR OPEN

(OPEN)

CHAIR FOLDED

[CLOSED]

Figure 418: The Colonial Folding Chair (left) and the Liberty Folding Camp Stool (right), made by A. L. White Mfg. Co. for use with its folding organs.

Figure 419

Figure 420

Figure 421: Joshua Briggs made the Crown Piano
Chair with a tilting back and a seat that could be
adjusted in both tilt and height.

The Crown Piano Chair,
FOR
PIANO, ORGAN, SEWING-MACHINE, DINING-ROOM, PARLOR, &c.

MADE BY Joshua Briggs,
MANUFACTURER OF THE CELEBRATED
Briggs Patent Piano Stools and Ottomans.

FACTORY AND OFFICE:
Peterboro', Hillsboro Co., N.H., U.S.A.

ESTABLISHED 1861.

Figure 422

261

Figure 423: Because just any old chair could not be used with a pedal organ, special benches were customarily provided. This example of an Estey Style 46 flat top two manual and pedal organ from 1873 has the original bench.

Appendix A: Stop Faces

To make a replacement stop face, make a photocopy of the page with the desired name, adjusting the size as necessary. Center the copy of the name in a circle of the appropriate size and cut. The paper can be tinted to match the color of the existing stop faces.

Æolian	Aeoline	Æoline	Aulodia	Baritone	Barytone	Bass Coupler

Bass Forte	Bassett	Bassoon	Bourdon	Bourdon Base	Bourdon Pedals

Bourdon Treble	Bourdon 16 ft.	Bourdon Dolce 16 ft.	Campanella	Celeste	Celeste 8 ft.

Celestina	Celestina 8 ft.	Cello	Cello 16 ft.	Choir to Great	Choral	Clarabella

Clarinet	Clarinet 8 ft.	Clarinet 16 ft.	Clarinette	Clarionet	Clarionet 8 ft.	Clarionet 16 ft.

Contra Basso 16 ft.	Cor Anglais	Cornet	Cornet Echo	Cornettino	Corno	Corno 16 ft.

Corno d' Bassetto	Corno Inglese	Corno 16 ft.	Coupler	Coupler Harmonique	Cremona	Delicante

Delicato 8 ft.	Diapason	Diapason Bass	Diapason Dolce	Diapason Dolce 8 ft.	Diapason Forte

Diapason Treble	Diapason 8 ft.	Dolcan	Dolce Tremulant ft.	Double Bass	Dulcet	Dulcet Bass 8 ft.

Dulcet	Dulcet Bass 8 ft.	Dulciana	Diapason Treble	Dolce	Dulcet	Dulcet 8 ft.

Dulcet Treble 8 fr.	Dulciana	Echo	Echo Horn	English Horn 8 ft.	Eolian Harp 2 ft.	Euphone Echo

Expression	Fagotte	Fagotti	Flute	Flute 4 ft.	Flute d' Amour

Flute Dolce 4 ft.	Flute Forte	Flutina	Flutina 4 ft.	Forte	Forte I	Forte II

1 Forte	2 Forte	I Forte	II Forte	Forte to Choir	Forte to Great	French Horn

264

French Horn Solo	Full Organ	Gamba	Gamba 8 ft.	Grand Expressione	Grand Organ	Grand Swell
Great to Pedals	Harmonic Attachment	Harmonique Coupler	Harp Aeolienne	Harp Æolienne	Harp Aeoline	
Harp Æoline	Harp Angelica 2 ft.	Hautboy	Hautboy 8 ft.	Horn	Kalophon	Keraulophon 8 ft.
Lower	Manual Coupler	Manual Sub-Bass	Melodia	Melodia 8 ft.	Melodia Dolce 8 ft.	Melodia Forte
Motor	Musette 16 ft.	Muted Strings	Oboe	Octave Coupler	Orchestral Forte	Pedal Bass
Pedal Bourdon	Pedal Coupler	Pedal Dulciana	Pedal Point	Pedals	Piano	Piccola
Piccolo	Piccolo 4 ft.	Picolo	Pipe Diapason 8 ft.	Pneumatic to Manual	Principal	
Principal 4 ft.	Principal Bass	Principal Forte	Principal Treble	Regal	Re-Roll	Roman Pipe
Royal Jubilante	Sackbut	Salicional	Salicional 8 ft.	Saxaphone	Saxaphone 8 ft.	

Saxophone   Seraphone 8 ft.   Sub Bass   Sub-Base 16 ft.   Sub-Bass 16 ft.   Sub-Bass Dolce 16 ft.

Sub-Bourdon   Sub-Bourdon 32 ft.   Swell   Swell to Great   Swell to Pedals   Treble Coupler   Treble Forte

Treble Coupler   Treble Forte   Tremolo   Tremulant   Trombone   Trumpet   Upper Forte

Viol d' Amore   Viol di Gamba   Viola   Viola Dolce   Viola Dolce 4 ft.   Viola 4 ft.   Violetta   Violetta 4 ft.

Violette   Violin   Violina   Violina 4 ft.   Violoncello 8 ft.   Violoncello Pedals   Voix Celeste

Voix Celeste 8 ft.   Voix Celeste 16 ft.   Vox Argentina   Vox Celeste   Vox Cœlestis   Vox Humana   Vox Jubilante

Wald Flute   Wald Flute 4 ft.   Wald Flute Forte   Wald Horn

Appendix B: Tuning Devices

A manometer is useful, almost indispensable, when tuning a reed organ. They are simple to make, and a scale drawing is included here for that purpose. The essential part is a U-shaped clear tube, which could be made of glass or plastic. Plastic tubing is available at any hardware store and is easily bent into the desired shape. About four feet will be required. Use at least ³/₈ inch tubing, as a smaller diameter will give erratic readings due to surface tension. In this model, the tube is pressed into the ³/₈ inch channel starting at the upper right, bent smoothly and without kinks around the dowel at the bottom, and back up the ³/₈ inch channel at the left, where it is cut off. A U-shaped brass nipple is used to join the U-tube with another piece of plastic tubing inserted in the back channel. Cut a notch between the left front and rear inch channels to make space for the nipple. The bottom of the piece of tubing in the rear is brought out to the front by means of a ninety degree nipple made of the same brass tubing.

The brass nipples can be made of tubing of the proper diameter to fit snugly inside the plastic tubing. Small diameter brass tubing can usually be found in hobby stores. One way to bend the tubing without kinking it is to crimp one end, fill the tube with sand, then crimp the other end. Then carefully bend to the desired shape, cut to size and de-burr the ends.

The top right end of the plastic U-tube is left open to the air.

Add water to the tube until it is about half full as shown below, left. A drop of food coloring will make the water more visible. When measuring vacuum, the left column of water will rise and the right side will drop. Slide the ruler up until the zero is even with the lower column of water as shown below, right, and measure the difference in water levels. That is the vacuum as measured in inches of water. To measure the vacuum in centimeters, use a ruler marked off in centimeters. When measuring air pressure, the left column of water will drop and the right side will rise.

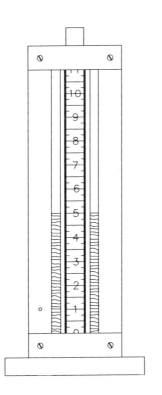

Figure 425: Manometer showing atmospheric pressure.

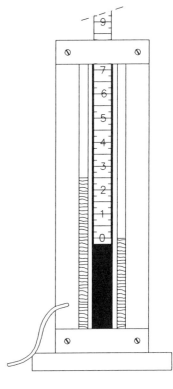

Figure 426: Manometer showing 2.5 inches of vacuum.

267

MANOMETER

NOTES:

1. The center channel is lined with lightweight felt, and the inside surface of the retainers are lined with the same material.

2. The U-tube is made from a 26" length of clear plastic tubing, 3/8" in diameter. The return tube is made of the same material.

3. The markings on the ruler can be made with a wood-burning tool. The back of the ruler can be marked in centimeters if desired.

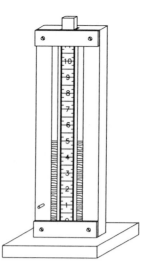

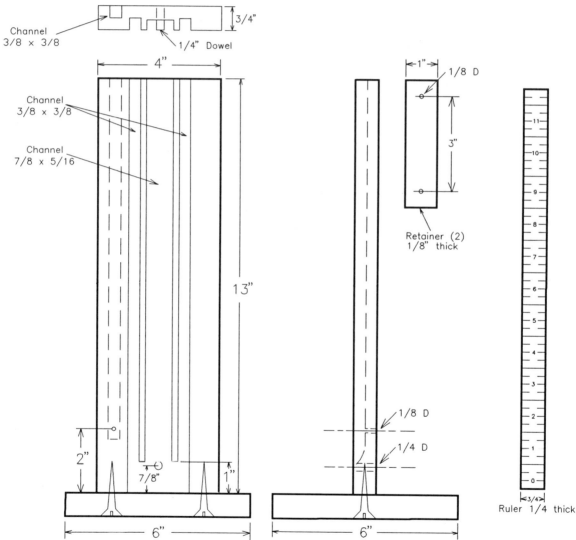

Figure 427

Stop ►							
Instrument					Pitch		
Owner					Date		
F							
F#							
G							
G#							
A							
A#							
B							
C							
C#							
D							
D#							
E							
F							
F#							
G							
G#							
A							
A#							
B							
C							
C#							
D							
D#							
E							
F							
F#							
G							
G#							
A							
A#							
B							
C							
C#							
D							
D#							
E							
F							
Average							
Std Dev							

Figure 428: Tuning chart for F-scale organs

Instrument						Pitch		
Owner						Date		
Stop ►								
C								
C#								
D								
D#								
E								
F								
F#								
G								
G#								
A								
A#								
B								
C								
C#								
D								
D#								
E								
F								
F#								
G								
G#								
A								
A#								
B								
C								
C#								
D								
D#								
E								
F								
F#								
G								
G#								
A								
A#								
B								
C								
Average								
Std Dev								

Figure 429: Tuning chart for C-scale organs.

Appendix C: Bench Plans

The bench plans included here are scale drawings of the original benches. They were made of walnut, oak or mahogany. These drawings may be photocopied for personal use.

ESTEY STYLE A BENCH

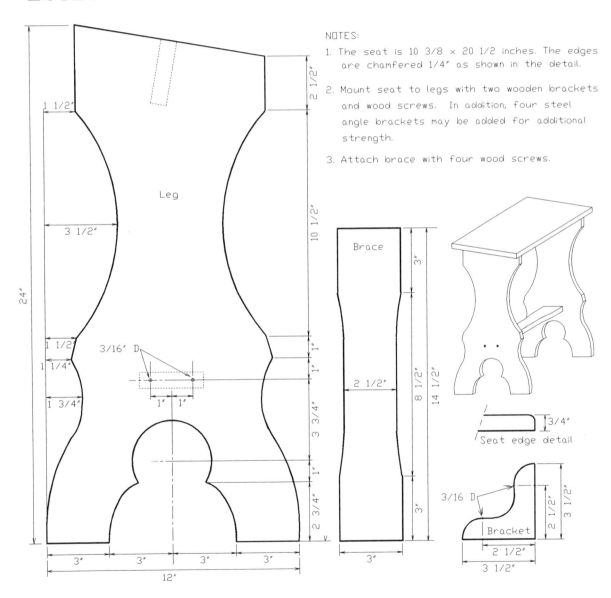

NOTES:

1. The seat is 10 3/8 x 20 1/2 inches. The edges are chamfered 1/4" as shown in the detail.

2. Mount seat to legs with two wooden brackets and wood screws. In addition, four steel angle brackets may be added for additional strength.

3. Attach brace with four wood screws.

Figure 430

MASON & HAMLIN STYLE 3 BENCH

NOTES:

1. The seat is 12 x 21 inches. The edges are rounded as shown in detail.

2. The brackets (2) are made from a solid block 2 inches wide. The legs and top are attached to it with wood screws. The front and back trim strips are mounted below the seat and and attached to the bracket with wood screws.

3. The brace has the top rounded as shown. It is attached to the legs with wood screws.

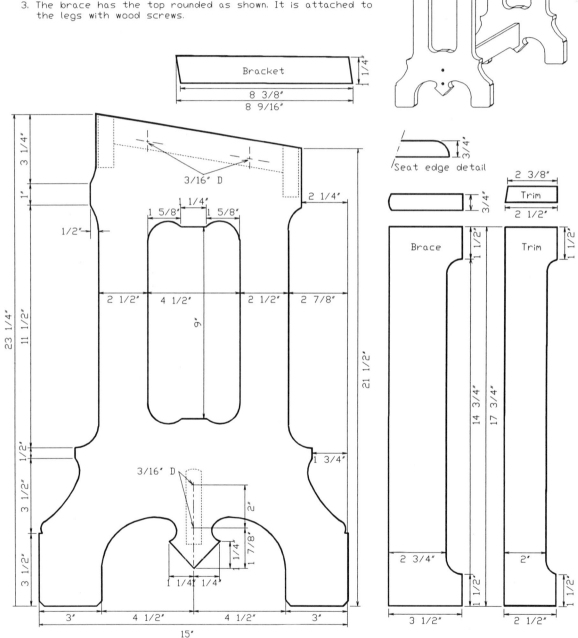

272   Figure 431

TREFOIL BENCH

NOTES:

1. The seat is 10.5 x 19 inches with the edges routed as shown in the detail. Fasten to legs with steel angle brackets.

2. Leg edges and inside cutouts are routed as shown in detail.

3. Brace is attached with wood screws below the trefoil pattern in the legs.

4. Trim strips 1 5/8 x 17 3/4 x 3/16 are mounted below seat, front and back. Chamfer lower edge.

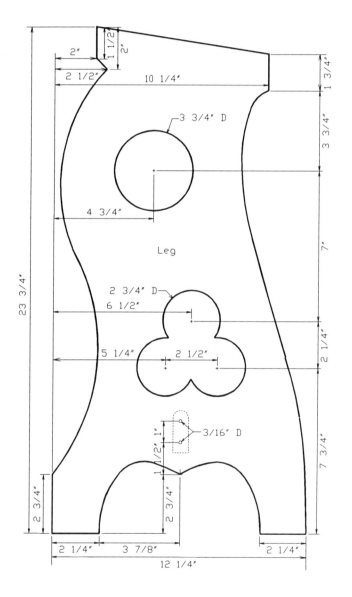

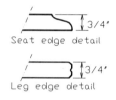

Seat edge detail

Leg edge detail

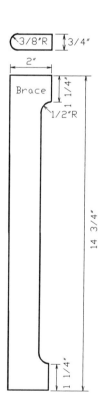

Figure 432

Figure 433

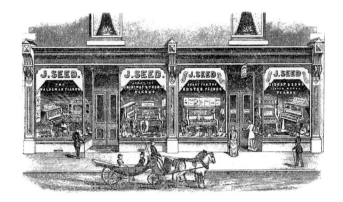

SEED'S MUSIC WAREHOUSE,
107 & 108, CHURCH STREET, PRESTON.

Figure 435

Always Best CHASE

ORGANS,

MANUFACTURED AT

NORWALK, = OHIO.

POINTS OF SUPERIORITY.

1. Choicest Material and Workmanship.
2. Tone, Smooth, Rich and Pure.
3. Action Light, and Touch Even and Elastic.
4. Music Rest Large, and at the right angle.
5. Book Receptacle under the Music Desk.
6. Bevel-faced French Mirror in Ornamental Top.
7. Perfect Sliding Lockboard.
8. Mouse Proof. Mice cannot get into them.
9. Red Cedar Tracker Pins keep out Moths.
10. Solid Substantial Handles on the ends.
11. Acclimatized Lumber used throughout.
12. Varnished Inside as well as Outside.
13. Substantial Lamp-stands.
14. Warranted for FIVE Years.
15. Just the Organ you want every way.

We take great pleasure in showing the merits of these superior instruments and recommending them to our friends.

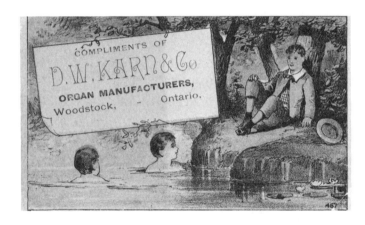

Figure 436

Figure 434

274

Figure 437

End Notes

1. For a more detailed discussion of beating reeds, see George Ashdown Audsley, *The Organ of the Twentieth Century.*

2. Henry A. Goodrich, "Church Organs—Some Early Builders in New England," in *Choir and Choral Magazine,* V6 No. 5, p. 5.

3. Quoted in Nugues, Pouget and Martin, *Practical Manual for the Piano and Harmonium Tuner,* Léon Pinet, Paris, 1913, p. 27.

4. The patent examiners might have done well to question the Prescotts, who used serial number 541 in 1845, or George A. Prince who used number 3870 in 1846.

5. Alfred E. Dolge, *Pianos and Their Makers,* The Covina Publishing Co., Covina, California, 1911, p. 343.

6. David H. Fox, *A Guide to North American Organ Builders,* The Organ Historical Society, Richmond, VA, 1991, p. 127.

7. Some of these names may refer to instruments other than reed organs.

8. Pam and Phil Fluke, "John Holt Reed Organs," *Reed Organ Society Bulletin,* Nov. 1990, p. 11.

9. Pam and Phil Fluke, "Sawyer of Leeds," *Reed Organ Society Bulletin,* Feb. 1990, p. 7.

10. Frederick Leland Rhodes, *Beginnings of Telephony,* Harper & Brothers, New York, 1929, pp. 28-30.

11. *Michel's Organ Atlas* says he began about 1868; Pierce's Piano Atlas gives 1870 as his starting date.

12. Beatty catalog, 1883.

13. Beatty catalog, 1883.

14. *The Vermont Phoenix,* Aug. 19, 1892.

15. William H. Barnes, *The Contemporary American Organ,* Sixth edition, J. Fischer & Bro., New York, 1956, p. 36.

16. Some authorities feel that the word "stop" should only be used in reference to a speaking stop. Most American reed organs makers, however, used the term in its broadest sense.

17. Nugues, Pouget & Martin, *Practical Manual for the Piano and Harmonium Tuner,* Léon Pinet, Paris, 1913, p. 27.

18. *The Music Trade Review,* New York, 3 Sept. 1877, "Who was the original inventor of the art of voicing reeds?" quoted by Howard A. Jewell in "Alfred Little and the Lap Organ," *Reed Organ Society Bulletin, Spring* 1993, p. 5.

19. Air pressure or vacuum in pipe and reed organs is usually measured in inches or millimeters of water. One inch of water equals 0.03613 pounds per square inch or 2.54 grams per square centimeter. Ten millimeters of water equals one gram per square centimeter or 0.0142 pounds per square inch.

20. Hermann Helmholz, *Sensations of Tone as a Physiological Basis for the Theory of Music*, Appendix 8, 1863.

21. J.C. Grieve, "The Harmonium and American Organ," in *The Musical Educator*, Caxton, London, V. 4, p. 58-59.

22. Ian C.L. Thompson, "Celestes," in the *Reed Organ Society Bulletin*, Aug. 1984, p. 18.

23. Also called the valve tremolo or clapper tremolo.

24. L.B. Green, "The Fan Tremolo," *Reed Organ Society Bulletin*, Nov. 1985, p. 22.

25. Additional information on tremolos can be found in Vernon Neufeld's "Reed Organ Tremolos," *Reed Organ Society Bulletin*, May 1984, p. 22 and in Paul Searfoss' "Rebuilding the Vox Humana," *Reed Organ Society Bulletin*, May 1985, p. 23.

26. For a full discussion of octave couplers see Ian C.L. Thompson, "Octave Couplers," *Reed Organ Society Bulletin*, Nov. 1984, p. 11.

27. J.C. Grieve, quoted by W.V. Henderson in the Reed Organ Society Bulletin.

28. Prof. E. Lee Chaney, "When Reed Organs Went to War," in the *Reed Organ Society Bulletin*, Nov. 1990.

29. The S.S. Biancamano as a troop carrier is mentioned in John D. MacDonald's book *The Executioners*.

30. Henry George Farmer, *The Organ of the Ancients*, 1931, p. 85.

31. Ibid., p. 165.

32. See Arthur W.J.G. Ord-Hume, *Collecting Musical Boxes and How to Repair Them*, Crown, New York, 1967, and *Player Piano*, A.S. Barnes, New York, 1970 for details on the development of modern musical player mechanisms.

33. John McTammany, *The Technical History of the Player*, The Musical Courier Co., New York, 1915.

34. Q. David Bowers, *Encyclopedia of Automatic Musical Instruments*, The Vestal Press, Vestal, NY, 1972, p. 740.

35. For more detailed information on automatic organette mechanisms, see Arthur W.J.G. Ord-Hume, *Player Piano*, A.S. Barnes & Co., 1970.

36. Readers requiring a more detailed treatment of restoration should refer to Arthur Reblitz' *Player Piano Servicing and Rebuilding*, much of which is directly applicable to reed organs, and to *Restoring & Rebuilding Antique Reed Organs*, by Horton Presley. Both are published by the Vestal Press. Also many articles have appeared in the *Reed Organ Society Bulletin* on particular aspects of restoration.

37. More information on keyboard repair and adjustment can be found in Arthur A. Reblitz, *Piano Servicing, Tuning & Rebuilding*, The Vestal Press, Vestal, NY, 1976, 1993.

38. One cent is one-hundredth of a semitone.

39. Ian C.L. Thompson, "Celestes," in the *Reed Organ Society Bulletin*, Aug. 1984, p. 18.

Bibliography

Audsley, George Ashdown, *The Organ of the Twentieth Century,* (New York, Dover reprint 1970.).

Barnes, William H., *The Contemporary American Organ,* (New York, Fischer, 1956, 6th ed.).

Barry, H.A. et al, *Before Our Time,* (Brattleboro VT, Greene, 1974).

Bent, George P., *Four Score and More,* (Los Angeles, Bent, 1929).

Bowers, Q. David, *Encyclopedia of Automatic Musical Instruments,* (Vestal, NY, The Vestal Press, 1972.

Bradley, Van Allen, *Music for the Millions,* (Chicago, Henry Regnery Co., 1957).

Charuhas, Toni, *The Accordion,* (New York, Accordion Music Pub. Co., 1955).

Conrad, Pam, *Prairie Visions,* New York, HarperCollins, 1991).

Dolge, Alfred, *Pianos and Their Makers,* (New York, Dover reprint 1972).

Dolge, Alfred, *Men Who Have Made Piano History,* (Vestal, NY, The Vestal Press reprint).

Dorf, Richard H., *Electronic Musical Instruments,* (Mineola, NY, Radio Magazines, 1954).

Draper, D. Murray, *W.D. — The Story of Doherty & Sherlock-Manning,* (Clinton, Ontario, 1986).

Edgerton, William H., *Silver Anniversary Collection,* (Summit, NJ, Mus. Box Soc. Int'l., 1974).

Fox, David, *A Guide to North American Organbuilders,* (Richmond, VA, The Organ Hist. Soc., 1991).

Gellerman, Robert F., *Gellerman's Int'l. Reed Organ Atlas,* (Vestal, NY, The Vestal Press, 1985).

Gellerman, Robert F., *The American Reed Organ,* (Vestal, NY, The Vestal Press, 1973).

Gernhardt, Klaus, et al, *Orgelinstrumente Harmoniums,* (Wiesbaden, Breitkopf & Härtel, 1984).

Grieve, J.C., "The Harmonium and the American Organ," *The Musical Educator,* (London, Caxton).

Hartog, W., *De Bouw en de Behandling van het Harmonium,* (Utrecht, Joachimsthal Publishers, 1981).

Hutchinson, Thomas, *The American Musical Directory, 1861,* (New York, Da Capo Press reprint, 1980).

Irwin, Stevens, *Dictionary of Pipe Organ Stops,* (New York, G. Schirmer, 1965).

Kemp, R.A., *Directions for Tuning & Regulating the Alexandre Harmonium,* London, Metzler, 1869).

Kjeldsberg, P.A., *Piano i Norge,* (Oslo, Huitfeldt, 1985).

Kolnes, S.J., *Norsk Orgelkultur,* (Oslo, Det Norske Samlaget, 1987).

Laffert, O. & de Wit, Paul, *Internationales Hand- und Addressbuch,* (Leipzig, Paul de Wit, 1883).

Maloney, Tom, *U.S. Camera 1946,* (_____, Duell, Sloan & Pearce, 1945).

McElhone, K.A., *Aeolian 58 Note Organ Rolls,* (Kettering, England, McElhone, 1990).

McTammany, John, *The Technical History of the Player,* (New York, The Musical Courier, 1915).

Michel, N.E., *Michel's Organ Atlas,* (Long Beach, CA, 1969).

Milne, H.F., *The Reed Organ: Its Design and Construction,* (London, Musical Opinion, 1930)

Nugues, Pouget & Martin, *Practical Manual for the Piano and Harmonium Tuner,* (Paris, Pinet, 1913).

Ochse, Orpha, *The History of the Organ in the United States,* (Bloomington, IN, Ind. Univ. Press, 1975).

Olson, Harry F., *Music, Physics and Engineering,* (New York, Dover, 1967).

Ord-Hume, A.W.J.G., *Collecting Musical Boxes and How to Repair Them,* (New York, Crown, 1967).

Ord-Hume, A.W.J.G., *Harmonium,* (London, David & Charles, 1986).

Ord-Hume, A.W.J.G., *Player Piano,* (New York, Barnes, 1970).

Paganelli, Sergio, *Musical Instruments,* (Feltham, England, Hamlyn Publishing Group, 1970).

Pierce, Bob, *Pierce Piano Atlas,* 9th Ed., (Long Beach, CA, Pierce, 1990).

Pierre, Constant, *Les Facteurs d'Instruments de Musique,* (Geneva, Minkoff Reprint, 1971).

Presley, Horton, *Restoring & Collecting Antique Reed Organs,* (Blue Ridge Summit, PA, TAB, 1977).

Reblitz, Arthur, *Piano Servicing, Tuning & Rebuilding,* (Vestal, NY, The Vestal Press, 2nd ed., 1993).

Reblitz, Arthur, *Player Piano Servicing and Rebuilding,* (Vestal, NY, The Vestal Press, 1985).

Rhodes, F.L., *Beginnings of Telephony,* (New York, Harper, 1929).

Rulli, Angelo, *Musical Boxes,* (St. Paul, The Musical Box Society International, 1987).

Ryan, J.C., *Early Loggers in Minnesota,* V. II, (Duluth, Minn. Timmber Prod. Assoc., 1976).

Whiting, Robert B., *Estey Reed Organs on Parade,* (Vestal, NY, The Vestal Press, 1981).

_____, *History of the Yamaha Corporation,* (Hamamatsu, Japan, in Japanese).

_____, *Sheng Method Book,* (China, 1987).

Acknowledgements

Figure 1   Burdett organ: Douglas Eyman
2   George Woods organ: Mrs. Pauline Culp.
3   Sheng: author.
4   Beating reed: author.
5   Sheng: author.
6   Sheng pipe: author.
7   Sheng pipe: author.
8   Sheng reed: author.
9   Regal: Prof. E. Lee Chaney, Jr., in the *ROS Bulletin*, Nov. 1987, p. 4.
10   Orgue Expressif: Alphonse Mustel, *L'Orgue-Expressif ou Harmonium*, 1903, p. 26.
11   Physharmonica: photo by Volkmar Herre, Stralsund, Germany.
12   Seraphine: Wim Olthof.
13   Bazin: Canton Historical Society, Canton, Mass. Photo by David Ciolfi, Studio 525, Canton, Mass.   Courtesy of Howard Alan Jewell and the *ROS Bulletin*, Feb. 1989.
14   Prescott lap organ: author.
15   Factory: Prince catalog, 1876.
16   Organ-Harmonium: Mason & Hamlin catalog, 1856.
17   Estey factory 1855: Brattleboro P.H.O.T.O.S.
18   Estey factory 1846: Estey catalog , 1910.
19   Estey factory 1858: Brattleboro P.H.O.T.O.S.
20   Estey factory 1866: Brattleboro P.H.O.T.O.S.
21   Estey factory, Dickinson farm site: trade card.
22   Estey Manufactory description: trade card.
23   Brattleboro Melodeon Co. factory: Brattleboro P.H.O.T.O.S.
24   E.P. Carpenter factory: Brattleboro P.H.O.T.O.S.
25   W.W. Kimball portrait: Van Allen Bradley, *Music for the Millions*, Regnery, Chicago, 1957; frontispiece.
26   E.S. Conway portrait: *Music for the Millions*, p. 91.
27   Vocalion: L.B. Green collection, photo by author.
28   Modernistic organ: Estey catalog.
29   Miniature organ: Estey catalog.
30   New Melodeon: Estey catalog.
31   Wurlitzer 4601: *Choral & Organ Guide*, April, 1954, p. 6.
32   Ketterman organ: Sylvan K. Ketterman, Littleton Studio photo.
33   Mannborg organ: photo by Volkmar Herre, Stralsund, Germany.
34   Ann Page: ROS Bulletin, Nov. 1988 cover.
35   Debain organ: Pam & Phil Fluke.
36   Factory building: Schiedmayer catalog, 1950.
37   Style 97 organ: Mannborg catalog.
38   Holt organ: Nick Beveridge, "Holt Reed Organs—the New Zealand Connection,"

ROS Bulletin, Nov. 1990, p. 19. Photo courtesy of Muriel Bradshaw.

39   J.W. Sawyer's Beeston Organ Works: Phil Fluke, *ROS Bulletin*, Feb. 1990.

40   Isachsen & Renbjør factory: courtesy of Leif Renbjør.

41   Nishikawa organ: Rey Akai.

42   Prof. Sakao Ito playing Yamaha organ: Rey Akai.

43   Dominion organ: Joop Rodenburg.

44   Factory building: Karn catalog.

45   Campus Martius: J. Bardwell, photographer. Courtesy of the Burton Historical Collection of the Detroit Public Library. Photocopy by Nemo Warr.

46   Hortense, Georgia: courtesy of Jerry Roberson.

47   Crown on top: Geo. P. Bent catalog.

48   Estey wagon: Bailey-Howe Memorial Library, University of Vermont, used with permission.

49   Horse cart: Williams Bros. catalog.

50   Prairie family: Pam Conrad, *Prairie Visions: The Life and Times of Solomon Butcher*, HarperCollins, New York, 1991, frontispiece. Photo by Solomon Butcher. Courtesy of Chris Sheldon.

51   Estey wagon: Bailey-Howe Memorial Library, University of Vermont, used with permission.

52   Story & Clark poem: trade card.

53   Story & Clark trade card.

54   Mason & Hamlin catalog cover, 1856.

55   Estey catalog collage: author.

56   Catalog collage: author.

57   Telegraph code: Kimball catalog, 1915.

58   Centennial Exhibition scene: Burdett trade card, 1876.

59   Burdett organ: Durward Center.

60   Burdett organ detail: Durward Center

61   Page from Mason & Hamlin catalog, 1895.

62   St. Louis World's Fair Display: Beckwith catalog.

63   Story & Clark Centennial display: trade card.

64   Mustel medals: Mustel catalog, 1910.

65   Medals: Estey catalog, 1871.

66   Old Way, New Way: Beckwith catalog.

67   Beatty portrait: Helen P. Leedom, *Washington New Jersey Centennial 1868-1968.*

68   Warranty: Beatty catalog.

69   Map: Beatty catalog.

70   Beatty Music Hall: Beatty catalog.

71   Switchback Railroad: Beatty catalog.

72   Estey letter: Brattleboro P.H.O.T.O.S.

73   Advertisement: Cornish catalog.

74   Cornish factory interior: Helen P. Leedom, *Washington New Jersey Centennial 1868-1968.*

75   Cornish employees: *Washington New Jersey Centennial 1868-1968.*

76   Sterling Organ Co. trade card.

247   Reedmaker: Estey advertisement.
248   Reed filing: Estey advertisement.
249   Reed sorting: Estey advertisement.
250   Reed pitch: author.
251   Manometer: author.
252   Tuning chart: author.
253   Nomograph: author.
254   Reed scraper: author.
255   Tuning jack: Paul Toelken.
256   Museum of Victorian Reed Organs: Fluke collection.
257   N.B. Pease & Co.: Nelson and Beverly Pease.
258   Musical Museum, Deansboro, NY: Art Sanders.
259   Conklin Museum: advertisement in *ROS Bulletin*, Nov. 1987.
260   Miles Museum: Floyd C. Miles.
261   Organettes: Mike Perry.
262   Carl & Chris Shannon: *ROS Bulletin*, Aug. 1987. Photo by Don Boorse, *News Herald*, Perkasie, PA.
263   Reed organ music box
264   Reed organ for dollhouse: author.
265   Bandchariot: Dickinson County Historical Society, Abilene, KS, courtesy of Fred Dahlinger, Jr.
266   Gasoline Alley: Reprinted by permission of Tribune Media Services.
267   Estey Orchestra Club: trade card.
268   Shoninger factory: trade card.
269   Mason & Hamlin Baby Organ: trade card.
270   Ithaca organ: trade card.
271   Postcard, woman at organ: courtesy of Harvey Roehl.
272   Postcard, Camp Northfield: © 1904 by A.R. Levering.
273   Postcard, Petersburg, VA: origin unknown.
274   Postcard, Rev. Wills' Helper: origin unknown.
275   Christmas card: original watercolor by Pauline Jackson, American Artists' Group, New York, used with permission.
276   Christmas card: Pauline Jackson.
277   Christmas card: Pauline Jackson.
278   Cartoon Christmas card: Fluke collection.
279   Toy organ: Harry Hunter, Jr.
280   Tru-note Pipe Organ: author.
281   Mustel harmonium model: Keith Jarrett.
282   Mustel harmonium, full size: Keith Jarrett.
283   Chimp calendar: origin unknown, courtesy of Al D. Robinson.
284   Worcester melodeon: Lightner Museum, St. Augustine, FL. Photo by author.
285   Mason & Hamlin melodeon: Culp collection.
286   Baker & Randall organ: Barry Bierwirth.
287   Landfear melodeon: Grand Rapids, Michigan, Public Museum.
288   S.D. & H.W. Smith melodeon: Mrs. Eldon Addy.

378   Beethoven organ: catalog.
379   Cornish Style 42,000: catalog.
380   Cornish organ: 1898 catalog.
381   Estey Case XL organ: 1911 catalog.
382   Estey Style J-74 organ: catalog.
383   Estey Style XX organ: 1907 catalog.
384   Estay Case W organ: 1907 catalog.
385   Karn Style C organ: catalog;
386   Karn Style I organ: catalog.
387   Kimball Case 710 organ: catalog.
388   Kimball Case 660 organ: catalog.
389   Kimball Case 680 organ: 1912 catalog;
390   Kimball Case 680 organ: 1912 catalog.
391   Lehr organ: catalog;
392   Marchall & Smith organ: catalog;
393   Miller organ: catalog.
394   Bosanquet organ: Phil Fluke, *ROS Bulletin*, May 1987.
395   Lindholm Scalaphone: photo by Volkmar Herre, Straslund, Germany.
396   Steirer Model 41: catalog.
397   Mustel Celeste-Organ: catalog;
398   Packard pedal bass attachment: catalog.
399   Carpenter Library Organ: catalog;
400   MacNutt desk organ: Green collection, photo by author.
401   Carpenter school organ: catalog;
402   Goodman organ: Cabinet Pipe Organ Co. catalog.
403   R.F. Stevens Piano-organ: catalog.
404   Estey Style A bench: catalog;
405   Mason & Hamlin bench No. 1: 1874 catalog;
406   Beatty bench: 1883/4 catalog .
407   Estey Gothic organ and bench: catalog.
408   Estey Old Dutch organ and bench: brochure.
409   Beckwith bench for Choir Gem organ: catalog.
410   Beckwith bench for Cathedral Chapel organ: catalog.
411   Kawai organ: catalog;
412   Estey Children's organ: catalog;
413   Alexandre harmonium: Relics of Times Past, San Antonio, TX.
414   Yamaha No. 3A organ: catalog;
415   Clough & Warren organ: Rey Akai.
416   Bilhorn folding bench: catalog.
417   Bilhorn folding organ and bench: catalog;
418   White folding chairs: catalog.
419   Seated one day: © 1907 by Samforth & Co.
420   Seated one day: © 1907 by Samforth & Co.
421   Briggs Crown Piano Chair: trade card.
422   Briggs trade card, reverse.

288

Index